NOW YOU SEE ME

NOW YOU SEE ME

LESBIAN LIFE STORIES

Edited by Jane Traies

Tollington

First published in 2018 by Tollington Press, Machynlleth, Wales
Reprinted 2018, 2019
www.tollingtonpress.co.uk

A catalogue record for this book is available from the British Library.

ISBN 978-1-909347-10-6

Cover photographs (Hilary and Pauline; Julia) and all other photographs
reproduced with kind permission of individual contributors

Designed and typeset by Helen Sandler

Printed and bound in Wales by Y Lolfa, Talybont, Ceredigion,
on FSC-certified paper

FSC

Dedicated to all those
whose stories were never told

CONTENTS

INTRODUCTION

Let's start with a story.

One day, early in the Second World War, a lorry full of prisoners of war trundled down the main street of a small market town in Middle England on its way to deliver the men to their work on local farms. The county secretary of the Women's Land Army watched it from her office window, and took particular note of the driver. Perched up in the cab of the lorry in shirt and cravat, her beret at a jaunty angle, the only woman driver employed by the War Agricultural Committee was certainly an unusual sight. Aged twenty-two, with a preference for wearing breeches and a passion for motor cars, Joan had left her respectable middle-class family far away and earned her living in a string of non-traditional jobs. She had tried to join the armed forces when war broke out; judged medically unfit, she was now determined to help the war effort in other ways, and driving was what she did best. The secretary of the WLA who watched her so intently that morning was a respected local figure: a forceful unmarried lady of good breeding, she was well known for her powers of persuasion. And she had plans for that young driver.

Which was how Joan, though entirely unqualified for the job in question, was persuaded not only to leave the 'War Ag' and join the Land Army, but to become the warden of the local milkers' hostel. For only six pounds a week, she was to be responsible for recruiting, training, supervising and deploying dozens of young women from all over the country who would be sent to local dairy farms to fill the places left by men called away to fight. It was a challenge, but Joan rose to it with characteristic enthusiasm, teaching the girls to pass their proficiency exams as well as to milk cows and ride motorbikes. One day, she heard of a particularly good milker, equally skilled with hand and machine, working on a nearby farm that was soon to be sold. Joan drove out to see if she could persuade the girl to come into the hostel when her employment ended. Slipping quietly into the milking parlour, she watched from the shadows as a shy, dark-haired teenager expertly milked her cow. The pail was brimful, the milk frothy: the girl was clearly exceptional. Joan recruited her on the spot.

I can tell you that much of the story, because later in her life Joan wrote and spoke very entertainingly about her Land Army days, including that moment in the milking parlour when she first met Peggy. But the story of their lives after that, of the sixty-plus years they were to live and work together, was never told; which is why I have not used their real names in this account, and why the rest of their story is not included in this collection. Like so many women of their generation, 'Joan' and 'Peggy' never publicly acknowledged the nature of their relationship. Both are dead now; their long love story was not recognised at either of their funerals, and is known only to a handful of their friends. This is how we disappear from history.

I was born in 1945, so I'm a generation younger than Joan, but I'm still old enough to remember the time when it was quite usual for lesbian and gay people to live their whole lives in the closet. I have seen how secrecy can become a habit that is impossible to break, even when social attitudes change: many lesbians of my own generation, too, have a history of not telling all, and therefore of being invisible to the outside world. For some of those who appear in this collection, taking part has been an act of real courage, an act of coming out. Others, as you will discover from their stories, have been out for years. Our stories are all different.

Now You See Me has been a long time in the making, and has grown out of another, rather different, project. In 2008, I decided to go back to university, and enrolled on a master's course in gender studies. This introduced me to lots of new ways of thinking about women and sexuality, and about the way society sees and represents us. By the end of the course, I had realised that, if you are an old woman and a lesbian, society doesn't really 'see' you at all; and had decided that I wanted to try and do something about that invisibility. So I applied to do a PhD at the University of Sussex, looking at the lives of older lesbians. As part of my doctoral research, I collected a great deal of information about the lives of (self-identified) lesbians born in the first half of the twentieth century. Some of that information was in the form of statistical data, drawn from a questionnaire survey; almost four hundred women aged between sixty and ninety completed the questionnaire. At the same time, I collected around fifty life histories, mostly through interviews, but sometimes in the form of written autobiographies.

Much of this information, including excerpts from the life stories, was included in my doctoral thesis and in my book *The Lives of Older Lesbians*;[1] but neither of those publications really gave me the opportunity to do two things I very much wanted to do. First, I wanted to produce a book which would be available to the general reader and especially to the hundreds of older lesbians who had contributed to my research; to give something back to the community that had given me so much. Second, I wanted some of those women's stories to be heard, perhaps for the first time, and for their history to be preserved. We live in rapidly changing times, when life for many LGBTQ (lesbian, gay, bisexual, transgender and queer) people – at least in the UK – has improved beyond recognition over a comparatively short period. At such times it is particularly important that we do not lose the memory of what went before, and of the experiences of those who lived in harder times.

Choosing the stories to be included has been difficult. I have collected dozens – enough for several books – and each one is precious and interesting. In selecting just twenty, I have tried to reflect the diversity of the older lesbian community now – our differences of class, race and ethnicity, of education, religion or politics – and something of the variety of what old lesbians have been: cradle dyke or late bloomer; butch, femme or neither; feminist, activist; daughter, sister, mother, aunt. The stories are arranged in groups, which has allowed me to comment on some of the recurring themes I've come across in my research; but each

11

story is quite different from the others, and the groupings might well have been different, too.

Creating *Now You See Me* has been a collaborative effort between myself as editor and the women represented. A few of the stories started out as written autobiographies and have needed comparatively little editing. The majority, however, started as oral history interviews. In most of those cases, I have been able to work with the women concerned to edit and polish the interview transcripts until they read as first-person narratives. Sometimes that was a relatively quick and easy process, but sometimes it took many months and many versions until we were both happy with the outcome. Not all the contributors felt able to use their own names, and the names of some other people in the stories have also been changed to protect their privacy. Sadly, two women have died since I interviewed them; two now have dementia; and I have lost touch with another. All five of these had previously given permission for me to use their stories and I hope they would approve the versions I have made on their behalf.

Finally, I'd like to thank not only the women who appear here, but all those whose stories I have collected over the last ten years, and the many other people who have supported and encouraged this book along its way. Big thanks, too, to Helen Sandler at Tollington Press, for seeing it through the publishing process with kindness and humour. Making this collection has been both a pleasure and a privilege; I hope readers will find these previously hidden histories as interesting and moving as I have done.

Jane Traies, Sussex, April 2018

~

1

NOBODY SAW US

For most of the twentieth century, being known to be a gay woman meant facing severe social stigma, and could also mean rejection by your family, the loss of your job, physical or sexual violence, and losing custody of your children. These experiences, or the fear of them, drove most lesbians into the closet. As a result of that need to hide their sexual identity in years gone by, some are still not out to their friends and neighbours, or even, in some cases, their families. Others, however, are coming out in their old age into the climate of acceptance brought about by social and legal change, including the choice of civil partnership or marriage. What is it that allows some older lesbians to take advantage of this new social climate, while others remain in the closet? The first three stories in this book offer different perspectives on that question.

Monica (born 1922) and Edith (born 1919) are the oldest of my interviewees, and at first sight their stories have much in common. Both were children during the Depression and teenagers when the Second World War began; both married young; both were rejected by the first woman they fell in love with; but in every other way their lives were very different. Monica was middle-class, child-free and comparatively affluent. Living in London, financially independent and moving in the more liberal world of the theatre, she was able, over time, to develop a lesbian identity and find a lesbian and gay social circle. Although she always kept her sexual orientation hidden at work and among her straight friends, she moved in a subculture which affirmed her identity.

Edith's less privileged background, her internalised shame and her dread of family disapproval, together with her sense of duty to her husband and her lack of financial independence, not only kept her in her marriage but ensured that she never felt able to reveal or act on her same-sex attraction while her husband was alive. Her lesbian identity was never seen, never affirmed. Perhaps that is why, after her husband died, Edith took the extraordinary step of coming out at the age of 85. We all need to be seen for who we are.

Leo is a decade younger (she was born in 1932) and her story is different again. Even though, as she says, 'gender wasn't a thing' in her generation, she understood herself well enough to avoid marriage. She and her life-long partner lived a deeply closeted life until changes in social attitudes made them visible to their friends, and civil partnership brought them into the public eye in a way they could never have imagined.

What all these women have had in common is the need to be true to themselves in spite of social pressures, and the courage to achieve that, however long it took.

JT

~

MONICA

In my very early years, I spent more time with my nanny than with Mummy, because for the first five years of my life, my mother was coping with a large family of stepchildren – my father's family from his first wife – as well as her own two sons. So I was surrounded by grownup siblings, who used to come and see me in the nursery, but they were more like uncles and aunts.

I was born in 1922, and I am three-quarters a Jew – or perhaps only a half, since they say you take your Jewishness from your mother, and my maternal grandmother was Irish. However, my father was a hundred percent Jew, in spite of his bright blue eyes and blond hair. The Jewish God always seemed to me so angry and full of wrath, which was not surprising, when one considered what was being done to his people at the time. I didn't understand much about this, but every now and then a German girl would appear and stay with us, and we were told to be kind to her. We knew nothing then of the horror they had been forced to flee.

Being a member of a very conservative middle-class family, whose parents were born in the Edwardian era, I was brought up to expect to be married, at the latest, by my early twenties. But I was drawn to my friends at school. So I was aware of my attraction to girls early in my teens, and was disturbed and frightened by it. There was one particular girl in my form… You were allowed to have a crush on a prefect, or the form mistress, but you weren't meant to have a crush on someone in your own form; that was considered strange. And I thought, 'Why do I fancy her, instead of the boys?' I didn't understand it. I was just attracted to her. I suppose I was about twelve, and you start getting sexual feelings when you're about twelve. I don't know what happened to her.

My best friend at school was extremely attractive to men,

and my fears and perplexities were compounded by her not understanding why I held back from what were, to her, delightful adventures with boys. I did try with the boys, but it never worked and always felt wrong. I couldn't tell her what I feared, and probably hoped it would go away and some special boy would come along to whom I would feel attracted. As it was, my teenage emotions were entirely taken up with distant and total adoration of Laurence Olivier.

Life in wartime

I was seventeen when war broke out. Mother joined the Wrens, and my brothers joined up too, so I was left alone, living at first in digs and later with an aunt. I had wanted to work in the theatre and had planned to take a course in stage management and production, but sooner or later I would have been called up for war work, so I decided to take a secretarial course in London in preparation for that. I remember the air raids and the people sleeping in the tube stations, but also many wonderful nights at the ballet and the theatre. In 1940, through a well-connected fellow pupil, I got a job in MI5. I became a temporary woman clerk grade three, sworn to secrecy, and I left London for Oxford, because MI5 was housed at Blenheim Palace. Our office desks and filing cabinets were placed in the grand rooms, and our canteen was in the stables.

But after a couple of years London called, despite the air raids. So I got a transfer, and shared a flat in Belgravia with a group of other young people. It was considered extremely bohemian, then, for young people of mixed sexes to live together, but our motives were entirely sexually innocent, and wartime practical.

I was twenty-three when I finally fell desperately in love, with a beautiful girl who was having a hectic wartime affair with my brother. She loved me dearly, but was totally straight. I wrote to her constantly, what I now recognise as love letters, but she did not want to see them as such and accepted them as letters from a highly emotional dear friend. I finally told her my real feelings and she was quite shattered. She was lovely about it. She said, 'Oh darling, I do love you, but not like that!' She was very beautiful. She's still my best friend, one of the only friends of mine who's still alive. She's six months younger than me. But then, I was desperate, and sure I was doomed to that sort of rejection always. I only told my doctor, who didn't really understand, and my mother, who thought it was a 'crush' I would get over.

My first real lover

My first job after the war was as assistant to the stage manager of a touring repertory company in the south of England, learning by my mistakes. After that I joined the Combined Services Entertainment Unit, touring Europe with a show which provided light relief to those of our troops who had not yet been released from war service. Rome, Capri, Vienna... It was in these romantic circumstances that I met a chap who shared my absorbing interest in the theatre. He was my stage manager on the tour. He fell in love with me and I imagined myself in love with him, because that was the thing you did: you fell in love with a man. I got pregnant, had an abortion, married him, and we settled in a flat at the heart of London's theatre district. Four years later I met my first real lover.

June worked with my husband in the theatre. She was the daughter of a well-known actress. I'd been fancying her for a long time, but didn't do anything about it. After a year of not daring to tell each other how we felt, one day it all happened. And she said, 'Don't worry, I've done this before.' So I was thirty when I finally found out what sex and passion was all about, because I hadn't actually been to bed with a woman until then. It was wonderful, but had to be kept secret from our families – it was still only the 1950s. I never discussed the situation with my husband: he was not a deep personal communicator. We eventually separated, but not primarily because of my affair. I discovered subsequently that he did know, but I hadn't got the guts to tell him.

June and I had a long affair. It lasted until I rather wickedly broke it up, for a girl I was working with, a portrait photographer called Connie. I had begun to feel the need of some sort of social life with other homosexual women, and foolishly left my lover, to look for the experiences and adventures I should have had when young. And it broke June's heart. She didn't understand it. But she recovered and finally found someone else, was quite happy, and lived with her for the rest of her life. But it was a bit awful, what I did.

I was with Connie for quite a long time. I was still living with Tony and I didn't dare tell him; but in those days, you didn't discuss anything. Later on, after we parted, we were great friends until he died. But at that time our relationship just wasn't right. And he'd started having affairs with other people, which I couldn't blame him for. But then we managed to become friends. He just accepted me and became a very good friend. I met one or two of his girlfriends – I remember, when he was dying, going to the hospital with one of them. We never divorced, though, because he didn't want to. Tony really didn't want to be tied down, so he didn't want to be free to marry anyone else!

A fascinating person

After Constance came Joan. She was a well-known actress, and quite obviously a lesbian. She never hid it: she quite obviously was! And she lived with another famous woman, who'd worked with Ivor Novello. They'd obviously started at some point by having an affair, but I think it had faded into a good old friendship. I'd been having this affair with Connie for a long time, and then came the day when I had to tell her about me and Joan. I still remember it. It was on the phone. I told her, and there was a pause, and then she said, 'The two people I love most in all the world!' Which was me and Joan. I thought it was very big of her. She found another lady at some point; it was all right, we remained friends. But I always remember her saying, 'The two people I love most in all the world...'

Joan had a house in Switzerland, and I used to go out and stay with her. She built that house herself. She bought an old cowshed and did it all herself, with her own hands. Joan was a very positive person, very sure of herself, and always busy doing something. She made a swimming pool at her house; she was always building something or making something work. A fascinating person. You could talk to her about anything.

And then I got sort of grotty about it, because she wouldn't live with me. She lived her own life, she had her house in Kensington and her house in Switzerland, and she never actually wanted to live with anybody. She used to come and see me, and I'd go and stay with her, but I got fed up with that. I suppose that was in the end what finished it. So there were two phases in our relationship: when we were together physically, and when we were together just as friends. I went on remaining friends with her forever. When you've had a lot with somebody, after a certain passage of time you realise the real things about a person, rather than just the sex or whatever it was that got you together. So until she died I was friends with her, and I used to go and see her and stay with her. I knew her about ten years, I suppose.

Memories of the Gateways

When I lived in London, we were a group of gay women, and we used to go to that club in Chelsea that everyone went to – the Gateways. You entered this anonymous-looking doorway, just off the King's Road, and you went down a whole lot of stairs, and at the bottom there was a kind of desk, where there was usually this ghastly woman who ran it, and she'd say, 'Are you a membah?' She had a husband, by the way, *and* she had a girlfriend. She was a terrifying woman, everybody was scared to death of her. 'Are you a membah?' And if you weren't, you jolly well soon paid up, and you were! And there were a whole lot of gay girls there, all dancing and sitting around the bar. There was a sort of back room, where you went if you wanted to have a chat to someone. And there you were, with all the gay girls.

One of my memories of the Gateways is going down those steps, and there was my darling friend Elaine, signing people in. She was one of the great loves of my life. I first met her when she came to visit my flat with the girl she was then with, who was a friend of mine, and who later got killed in a motor accident. I remember that first meeting; then I used to see her at the Gateways and we sort of came together. Really, a great love of my life. She died only recently.

I think it was when that friend was killed in the car crash, and I was terribly upset, that I told my mother why I was so upset. That was how she found out I was gay; she didn't speak to me for six months. I think the shock was too much for her. Then I wrote her a long letter, saying that if she didn't love me because she'd discovered something about me she didn't like, she couldn't have loved me anyway. So she rang me up and said, 'Thank you for your letter.' And then it was all right. It must have been very difficult for her to accept. She was a real Edwardian, born in the 1890s. I don't think she discussed it with the rest of the family, but she was friends with a lot of my friends. People like Elaine used to come down and stay, and Mother knew we slept in the same room and she just accepted it.

Leaving London

In the spring of 1966, when the daffodils were out, my mother died. She had been growing visibly older and more frail, and I had prepared myself, but I hadn't realised how difficult it would be to face a world without her in it. I decided to do something I thought I would never do – leave London. So I bought a converted farmhouse in Somerset. (By now I was working for the BBC, and was offered a job with BBC TV in Bristol.)

I had a little Irish girlfriend, Mary. She said to me one day, 'Oh, you're going away, you're going to live in Somerset!'

I said, 'Yes, do you want to come with me?'

And she said, 'Yes!'

It started off that she was with me, but she wasn't really gay, I don't think, and she met a chap down there and got married.

They moved into a wing of my house. I didn't mind, because it wasn't a desperate thing with her, it was just a friendship, really.

Eventually life in Somerset became a bit isolated, because it became more difficult for people to travel and more expensive to get there. And I had a friend, an old friend whom I'd known for years, who was opening a shop in Brighton, and she said, 'Would you like to come and help me with it?' So that gave me an idea of the area I wanted to be in. The job didn't come off, but that was what brought me to Sussex. By the time I left Somerset and came here, I was with another girl, called Val. She was very young – much too young, but rather fun. She was very pretty.

One September morning in 1978, I saw an advertisement in the *Daily Telegraph*: 'Pleasantly situated, with views of the South Downs, a group of mellow farm buildings on three sides of a yard. Suitable for conversion. About half an acre.' Contemplating these roofless ruins and the rubble-filled yard a few days later, I knew this was what I had been searching for. It had once been a farm, but now belonged to the Dominican Order of nuns, who kept a convent school in the adjoining large house. In March 1979, the building work began. Over two years, with the help of a wonderful builder who lived in a caravan on the site, the buildings were transformed into a unique and personal house that fits so well into its environment that it was difficult to persuade people it was new. At the same time, we turned the field into a garden. The garden is mature now, and is a joy and a blessing. I used to hold big parties there, in the summer.

So long ago

When you get to the age I am, the past all seems so long ago. I'm still in touch with one or two of the gay girls who used to come to the parties here. But none of them live anywhere near, so I don't see them. My gay life has been interesting, but it's difficult now: there's no one left to remember it with.

I have failed to make a great success of my emotional life, though I have had several relationships, some with very wonderful people. But the lasting and deep commitment from another has evaded me. I feel that this could be due to the fact that, at the time of life when you should be learning – from experience – the real and lasting values in emotional and sexual encounters, the social pressures of the 1940s and 50s made it difficult for me to express my sexuality in what was, for me, a normal way.

Most of my friends round here don't know anything about my past. And they don't ask me. They all know that I was once married. So all my gay past is sort of dead, which feels sad. The only one who knows about me and loves me is Christine, who is the one who was having an affair with my brother, who I fell in love with all those years ago. She lives quite near and she's my dearest friend really. She's the same age as me. So she's the only person of my era who's left.

~

Monica died early in 2014, at the age of 91. Her family and friends held one last party in her garden, before her beloved house was put up for sale.

JT

EDITH

I was the fourth of six: four girls and two boys. I was born in December 1919, in Birkenhead, but my family moved to Coventry when I was about two or three years old. My father was a butcher; putting two and two together, I think he was a bit of a gambler. We hadn't got a lot of money, and he also liked a drink. He always worked in a butcher's shop. He had his own shop in Birkenhead, but I think that possibly he was losing business, and my mother's father was also a butcher in Coventry, you see, so he came to Coventry. I lived there nearly all my life.

I went to school when I was five. It was just a council school. I wasn't very clever, but I enjoyed school. I very much enjoyed country dancing and I was in the team. We had competitions with other schools, and there was a big prize at the end. We went over to Leamington Spa for the finals – that wasn't far from Coventry, about nine miles. I loved it. I left school when I was fourteen, and I got a little job helping a lady who'd got a daughter of five, just starting school, and she wanted someone to take her and bring her back; and I helped with light housework.

It was around that time, in 1933, that one of my sisters died. Maria. She was only seventeen. She had peritonitis. Nowadays, I think they could have cured her. She was in the Coventry Hospital, and my father was also in the hospital because he'd cut his finger at work and it had gone bad. It was a terrible mess, and they took him and cut the finger off. The police used to come and fetch people, then, if they were wanted in the hospital: there were no telephones, and if people were needed urgently, the police came round. So they came in the middle of the night to Mum, and said she was wanted at the hospital. Well, she didn't know whether it was for her husband or her daughter. My eldest sister Dorothy went with her, the police took them in the car, and when she got there, of course, it was Maria... and she died while they were there.

It was only about March of the next year that I went off to Brighton for two years. I don't think it occurred to me, then, how hard it must have been for my mother. An aunt of mine, my father's sister, came to visit. She'd been a nurse all her life – I don't know whether she got to matron, she might have done – but she nursed all through the First War, then afterwards she did private nursing. Well, she'd heard that I wanted to be a nurse. Which I had said, at one time. You had to have a secondary school education to be a nurse, though, and I'd only been to the elementary; but my aunt pulled a few strings with the matron at Leicester, who said that if I went to a commercial college for two years, she would accept me. So I went to Brighton, where my aunt lived. I stayed with her and my uncle – they hadn't any children – and I went to Clark's College, down by the Old Steine, for two years, learning shorthand and typing and book-keeping.

Now this aunt was a bit of a tyrant. She didn't have any affection for anybody, I don't think, not even her husband. Whenever he was going out to work, he'd say, 'I'm going now,' and she'd come to the door and just stick her cheek out, for him to give her a peck... And of course, she had twin beds; I don't think the poor man got anything very much! I used to go walking with him: his eyesight wasn't very good. He worked at a wholesale butcher's in Brighton, and he used to go out early in the morning, and in the winter of course there were no trams, they didn't start till about six o'clock and he used to go out about five. So when his eyes got bad and the weather wasn't good, I used to have to walk down to town with him, and I'd catch the first tram back then, at six o'clock. And then I used to have to practise the piano for an hour; my aunt was very strict.

Uncle used to take me out, too, and sometimes he'd go into a pub and have beer. I didn't go in, I sat outside and he'd bring me out a lemonade. And he'd say, 'Don't tell your auntie.'

But one day my auntie said to me, 'You would tell me, Edith, if your uncle is drinking beer? Because I've told him not to.' But I never did tell!

And sometimes when Auntie wasn't there and I was near, he used to put his arm round me and give me a kiss; but that's all, he didn't go any further. It didn't seem wrong to me... but of course I've learnt a lot since then. And if my aunt came in, he'd move out of the way pretty quick. The poor man died while I was there. He had TB. He was in the First War, and of course it was terrible in the trenches. They got soaked, didn't they? Terrible... and he got TB from there, and he died at the beginning of '35.

After all that, I decided I didn't want to be a nurse, I wanted to be a shorthand typist. I came home to Coventry and got a job in an office. I didn't realise at that time what a terrible thing I was doing – I mean, they'd paid for me to go to this college so that I could be a nurse. And it didn't occur to me till years after, what I'd done. But I don't think I could have been a nurse, I'm too tender-hearted. I certainly couldn't give anyone an injection. I'd be all right looking after little ones when they'd been ill, talking to them and playing with them and that sort of thing, but I don't think I could have done nursing. I don't know what I should have done if I hadn't got office work.

I drifted into marriage

I think I was only about sixteen or seventeen when I met my husband. It was just after I started work. And of course, a lot of the girls were going out with boys. Norman was lodging at my girlfriend's house, and I often used to go down there. It was another girl's birthday – the three of us were pals at school, and I was asked to this birthday party – and the other two girls had got boyfriends but I hadn't.

So I went down one day and they said, 'Ooh, Edith, we've got a boyfriend for you!' And of course he came in then, and they introduced him – 'Norman's going to take you to the party!'

'Oh, good.' You know. And it went on from there. He was a tool-maker. He worked at the Standard Motor Company.

I sort of drifted into marriage. After I'd been going out with him for a while, I told him I didn't want to see him any more, I didn't want to go with him. But he wouldn't take no for an answer. I used to go out with my friend and he would follow us on his bicycle and say, 'Do go out with me,' and in the end, I gave in. When he said, 'Marry me,' I said, 'Oh, all right then.' And we got engaged; because that was what you did, then. That was what all the girls did, get married. We didn't know about anything else. I was working in a large office at that time and of course all the girls were coming in flashing their engagement rings. Then the war came, you didn't know whether you were going to be here today and gone tomorrow, and in another two years we were married.

It was 1940, in the December. I was twenty-one. They didn't take Norman into the Army, because he had a skilled job in the factory. He and his mates went down half a dozen times to try and join up, but when they asked them where they worked and what their job was, straight away they said no, they couldn't take them. But Norman joined the Home Guard; he was on the ack-ack guns, he would have to go out at night or at weekends. 1940 was the big blitz, the Coventry Blitz; that was three weeks before we were married. My husband had ordered two suits, to make sure he had one, but they both went up in smoke. My white wedding dress and bridesmaid's dress went up in smoke, too – the shop was in the centre of the town, you see – so we'd got nothing to wear for the wedding, in three weeks. So we borrowed my brother-in-law's car and went over to Leicester, and he bought a suit and I bought a dress and coat and hat.

So that was the big blitz, but we ourselves didn't get bombed out until 1941, in the April. A bomb dropped in front of the house and blew all the front of the house out. We were in the front room, but none of us were injured. Only the bird – the poor little budgie had it. My mother, my sister, my husband, my brother and myself were all there. Mum and Jean were underneath the table: we had a very big old-fashioned dining table, very thick wood, and they were underneath it. I don't know where I was. My husband and my brother were sitting either side of the fireplace: they got covered in soot, but none of us were injured.

The house had to be pulled down and rebuilt. My husband and I went to his mother, who lived on the other side of Coventry; my mother and my sister went to my aunt's, and my brother went down the road to his mate's and stayed there. They did give us a house after a while... and then the old one was rebuilt. I went on working for about eighteen months after I was married, until I was expecting my daughter; Linda was born in November '42.

We were still living with Mum when Linda was born, then we got a furnished house. We rented it, but then after a while the people who owned this house wanted to come back and we had to get out. So we were desperate to find somewhere to live. We did find a couple of rooms with a lady and were all right there for a couple of years. By then my husband had got a second-hand car, and he sold it for two hundred and fifty pounds – and that was the deposit for a house! It was, it's true. The house we bought cost £1,850 and it took us thirty years to pay for it.

She didn't want to know me

When we were kids, there was a man who used to go around, I can't remember who he was, and we used to call him 'fancy man', I think it was, or 'cissy boy'. We used to run after him and laugh – I was a naughty girl, wasn't I? – but I didn't know why. I hadn't a clue. And I never thought that I might have feelings about other women. Until... well, Linda was quite little, only about four or five, I think, and I met somebody. I used to take the children to school when they first started. Yes, it was just after Linda started school, she was five. And this woman was taking *her* little girl to school, and I looked at her, and I just couldn't take my eyes off her. I thought, 'Oh, what a lovely woman! Isn't she beautiful? I should like to know her.' Linda was in the same class as her little girl, and of course next time I went to meet them, she was there. I didn't speak to her for a while, but in time we did get to know one another. And she'd got a little boy as well, and I'd got Paul, and when she wanted to go out with her husband, I used to go down and babysit. And then she'd come up and babysit Linda and Paul for me. After a while, I wrote to her and told her how I felt. I can't quite think how I said it... And she didn't want to know me. I had always known she was what they call straight. I thought, 'Well, I won't do that again.' Eventually she moved away. And I couldn't ever tell anyone. But I knew about myself, then. Oh, yes. All those years ago...

I looked at her and we knew

I used to have a weekly magazine, I think it was called *The Woman's Companion*, and they had a section in there for penfriends. You used to have to send the letter to the magazine – they didn't give you the woman's address – and then they sent it off, and if they wanted to write, they would write back to you. I had thirty-five penfriends at one time, altogether. Mostly in England, but there were quite a few in America, one in Australia, one in New Zealand, I think there was one in Canada, and I had one in Japan. They became real friends; we even met several of them. And then there was Chris. We realised we were both on the phone, so she started ringing me up, and it got a bit more than friendly... She asked us down for the weekend, my husband and I, the Easter weekend, and we went down. She lived at the seaside. When we got there and I got out of the car, she looked at me and I looked at her. And we *knew*.

She'd got three bedrooms, but she'd only got single beds. So she put my husband in one room on his own. He didn't like that. And in the room he was in, there were some books, and some of them were about homosexuality. So I said, 'Oh well, she's just interested.' I tried to deny the fact that she was – you know – but he didn't like it, and he didn't like the woman. But I rather more than liked her! She described herself in her letter as 'about five-eight, with grey curly hair'. So she was tall, and she wore glasses. She was born October 31st, and I was born

December 3rd, so she was only a few weeks older than me.

This was about 1970. Then she came up here to look for work. She wanted to get a job and she said there was nothing where she lived, so she came up to Coventry and stayed with me for three months. My husband didn't like it. It wasn't a nice atmosphere. It was nearly Christmas when he put his foot down and said, 'That's it. She will have to go.' He never really said why; he just didn't care for her.

I never saw her any more

So she asked me to go and live with her, to leave my husband and go and live there. But of course, I couldn't. I said, 'I can't, I've a husband and two children.' She didn't find a job in Coventry, and she went back. So that was that. And I never saw her any more.

I can't think how long it was that we kept writing; and then she rang me up one day. She'd known one or two gay women, and there was somebody in Scotland she knew. She said this woman from Scotland wrote and said that her partner had died, and this partner's parents came up and chucked this woman out. She'd got nowhere to live and didn't know where to go or what to do. So Chris told her to stay where she was, and she went up to Scotland and brought this girl back with her, to live with her in her house. So of course, they then got together. And Chris didn't even want me to write to her any more. I suppose that's understandable, if she'd got somebody else.

I was very upset for quite a while. I didn't know how to find anybody in Coventry to talk to. I rang the Samaritans once and told them. I mean, they didn't know me and I didn't know them, it didn't matter. But the woman, she was sort of laughing, and she said, 'Oh, what do you do when you're with your husband? Do you just lie back and think of England?' And I put the phone down. I thought that was the most... She shouldn't have been in that job. I was so lonely. People just don't realise. I couldn't ever tell anyone. My sisters – well, years ago, in the 1970s I think it was, there was this programme on television about these kind of women. And afterwards I heard my one sister say to the other, 'They're disgusting, aren't they? They all ought to be shot.' So I never dared say anything.

After sixty years of silence

My husband died in 2004. Now I am on my own, I get thinking, you know, and wishing that I knew if there was somebody like me here in the retirement houses. But there's no way of finding out. You can't just go up and ask somebody, can you? You'd probably make an enemy, especially if they weren't. But the supervisor comes round periodically, even if you haven't asked her, to chat. And she asked me if I was all right.

She said, 'It's more than a year now since your husband died, and you seem to be getting more and more upset, not less.' She asked if I had something on my mind that was worrying me.

I said, 'Yes, I have. But I couldn't tell you about it.'

And she took my hand, so kindly, and said, 'Don't forget that a trouble shared is a trouble halved. I'll come back tomorrow.'

I thought, I will tell her. But I was scared. And when she came in the next day, I said, 'I do have something I'd like to tell you about, but I'm afraid you might not want to talk to me afterwards.' But I told her.

She was lovely, not a bit shocked. She said, 'How awful for you to have had to keep that secret all this time!' About a week later, she came back with a magazine, and there was an article about this woman, a therapist, who helps people like me – and wasn't it amazing that she was more or less local? So she rang her up for me. And here we are.

~

The perceptive therapist quickly decided that Edith did not need treatment, just the company of like-minded women. She sought out the local lesbian group and rang them to see if they could help. As it happened, I was answering calls for the group at that point; and that was how Edith and I first met. At 85, Edith was almost completely blind and becoming frail, so could not come to our meetings; but group members visited her, listened with empathy to her story, lent her lesbian/feminist talking books, and supported her through the ordeal of coming out to her children and grandchildren. For some years she was able to enjoy the company of other lesbians and occasionally attended group events. In 2017, at the age of ninety-eight, Edith moved to a nursing home because her memory was failing; but she still recognises the lesbian friend who has continued to visit her.

JT

LEO

I remember, when I was quite little, that our house bordered a golf course, and at the far side of the golf course there was a golf club. There were steps going up to a central door; and it seemed to me that the women went up one set of steps and the men went up the other set. And I had the feeling that if ever I were going in, I'd be going up on the men's side. But then, a lot of girls are tomboys, and that sort of thing.

I was born into a loving family, in a small seaside town on the north-east coast. I was christened Rosemarie. All my life I've disliked the name, but my mother was especially fond of it, so I didn't think there was much I could do. In my published work, I've always been RV Bailey. Most people call me Rosie; but UA always called me Leo, because of my birth sign.

The war broke out when I was seven. My father and brother went away to the war, and my mother and I were left alone. We were surrounded by Air Force people, and it was very near the Tyne, so that it was within the bombing area, and bombs fell, indeed; we had air raid shelters, and so on. But that's how life was, and when you've seven and eight, you think that's just what's normal, and although it was cold and there wasn't much food, those things didn't matter all that much. And it was quite exciting when the bombers came over, especially when once they bombed the school and we had an extended holiday. My mother was a very provident, good sort of cook, so I thought I was quite well fed. I never felt afraid – though once all the windows and doors were blown out by blast.

When I grew up a bit more, I went to the local grammar school, where I was very happy. It was a mixed-sex school, and I did well there. It was expected that I'd be in at least the top three or four; a bit of explaining had to be done at home if I wasn't pretty near the top. But I liked it, I made friends and so on. In particular I became aware of another girl, who I thought was rather wonderful. Boys on the whole were just boys, you know, people you borrowed a Latin prose from, and things like that; but I definitely felt differently about this girl. Not that anything happened, she had a perfectly excellent boyfriend, and so on; I remember feeling a little puzzled, that I didn't seem to be quite like other people. But there were so many other things to be interested in at that time, and gender in those days didn't assume the importance that it does now. We discussed things like Free Love in an abstract, sort of innocent, way, but gender wasn't a thing we talked about.

At Cambridge

My first degree was in English, at Cambridge. I think that, like many people, I'd use that time much more wisely, and take more of those opportunities if I could go back *now*; but in those days – you just have to live with who you are. I fairly quickly developed a close friendship with a clever woman in my year who was also reading English; who became very quickly engaged to a chap in another college. So that I again felt a little unusual. But we went on being just very good mates (we still are), and I really tried to look after both of them – because they were very happy together. And again, again, again we talked and argued about ideas, and books, and plays... and that was that. So, not much there, really; except this sense of discontinuity with everybody else. Well, it's difficult to define, because I'm never at all sure whether I'm really a lesbian, or whether I'm transgendered, or one of these mixed-up in-betweens. I've never really come to any fixed conclusions, except that I'm a bit odd; not like other women.

By that time I was somewhat more sophisticated, and although I didn't know any women who were like me, I did know quite a lot of men. I'd got together with one of the boys in my class at school, we'd had a little talk about things, in a sort of *misty* way, and understood one another. He did National Service, and then came up to Cambridge, and then of course he discovered a lot of other gay men, and so I got to know them too. But I never knew any more women at all, ever. Well, not until I found UA.

I was one of those people who tried everything at university, and I belonged to quite a lot of groups of people. There were poetry groups, and I knew these gay men, as well as members of the SCM (Student Christian Movement), and CICCU (the Cambridge Inter-Collegiate Christian Union, which was the fundamentalist equivalent of SCM): they were all very different. There was a lot to occupy one – more than you could possibly take in. And a lot to do – those crowded, short terms – first week, second week, third week, you know how it whizzes by. Then in the third year I decided to do a year's theology, a two-year course crammed into one, so I was very, very *busy* on the learning side, too. And the friend I was fond of, she changed to reading theology too. There weren't many women doing this: we thought that a very good challenge, too. I observed all the other people going round having crushes on people and finding boyfriends and so on, but it didn't interest me. At all. It wasn't a choice: it never occurred to me to get married. I thought being married was a pretty daft thing to be. Nothing whatsoever attracted me about it – I mean, I liked men, I had men friends, but being married to one was never an idea. Later I learnt it was the same for UA, there was no question of being married to a man. It seemed a very poor outcome from a university degree.

A baptism of fire

So, that's me at Cambridge. After that I worked for a spell at the university library, which was interesting; and then I worked in London, on the editorial and information side of the Church Missionary Society, just off Fleet Street. That was much more fun than it sounds, because of all my interesting colleagues, but there wasn't enough of a challenge in it. Also, I was very poor. I was living in various digs, some more salubrious than others. I thought it would be nice to do something else, perhaps. So I got in touch with the Cambridge Careers Service (which then seemed to consist of one solitary woman). Really, about all a woman could do in those days was to become a nurse or a teacher. She said, 'There's this job as housemistress in a boarding school.' I thought, 'Well, the interview will mean a weekend away from London; I'll have a go at that.'

I hadn't been there ten minutes before it became obvious that being a housemistress was the last thing on earth I wanted to do. However, I stayed for quite an entertaining weekend, and then came back to London and devised what I thought was a suitable reply to the principal, saying no to the job – I thought that my interests were more purely academic. But maybe I'd gone down all right in the interviews, because I got a reply saying, 'Come and be interviewed for an English post.' I didn't feel I could get out of that one, and went again to be interviewed. I was appointed.

It was rather a baptism of fire, teaching. I think it probably was so for everybody, in those days. It was very strange after London, because London was the bright lights, even then, and out there in the provinces it seemed to me that everything stopped at half-past five, the lights all went out. There was only one restaurant in the place. The most you could spend on a meal was five bob (this was a government restriction – rationing was still going on). I think anyway all you could get was egg and chips. So really it was a very sober existence. I began by living in the staff house, partly for convenience, and partly because it trained you how to live within the rules and make you suitable for the job. Most young staff left the staff house as soon as they could find a flat, or anywhere else to go, but at least the experience grounded you; it gave you food (of a kind), board and lodging. It was a nice house, but extremely cold, and you weren't paid for the first two months, so there wasn't any money to buy a fire, or even a hot water bottle. It was quite a shock after being in London. And I hadn't even been trained to teach. But it seemed to me, even then, that the only way to learn to teach is to *do* it. So I did it. And the girls rescued me. They could see how hopeless I was, because they *did* know how teachers ought to behave, and so they patiently looked after me, and gently made me into a proper teacher.

Making a good impression

And then I thought, 'Well, I'd like my own flat.' So I found a flat. This was about the time that UA and I got together. I mean, we'd known each other for seven years, so it was rather a slow development, especially as she was my head of department. I was very good at being useful: I earned a lot of Brownie points, because I was good at getting my marking in on time, and all those things you do if you're trying to make a good impression. Which I perhaps was trying to do: yes, I suppose I was. Later, after she died, I wrote this poem about that time:

> I think you liked me first for my hard work:
> For doing things on time, and legibly.
>
> I liked your laugh, subversive, sudden, rich
> With possibilities of more to come, and how.
>
> It wasn't industry or jokes: just love.
> In time we dared to tell each other so.
>
> And O my love, I'm still not one to shirk.
> It's just I'm finding life without you now
>
> Uncommonly hard work.[1]

One day UA was in a car accident. So I sped off to see what I could do (again, being useful, which has always been my way of moving on) and I went to see her in the hospital fifty miles away. I couldn't think what to take as a suitable gift for her. I knew flowers wouldn't be the thing, and books *would* be the thing, but I had no idea what books she would like. And when I got there I didn't know what to *say* to her anyway, so I went to look at the remains of the car, and confirm it was a write-off. A day or two later I fetched her home. And I went on making myself useful, doing the shopping, and perhaps even the hoovering or whatever. Anyway, I was doing the hoovering one morning, when it became clear that she felt as I did. I'd

Leo (right) with UA circa 1980

gone upstairs to ask her if she'd like a cup of coffee, and she wanted to sit up, but you can't sit up without help, when you have broken ribs. So I helped her sit up...

And that was rather a surprise, to both of us. There wasn't, of course, time to *say* anything about it, because I had to go back immediately to teach (Shaw's *Pygmalion*, I think). Looking back, the whole thing was just too comical for words. It (what was 'it'?) might have happened, or it might not have happened. And it *had* happened. But when I alluded to it, very delicately, the next day, she said, 'Oh, that was when I had a high temperature.' And I thought, 'Oh, well.' But that was just UA being wicked.

And that was it. Absolutely. Finally and forever. I remember UA saying, over a Chinese lunch, 'I don't care if it's just for a fortnight.' And I remember saying – well, I know I said it, because she wrote it down, I discovered it in her diary – that she was my future, that there wasn't any doubt about it, then. As I was hers.

Nobody 'saw' us

But of course, everything went on being absolutely the same, because we were still just colleagues. We were working together, and there was every reason why we should spend some time together, but there was no expectation that we might *want* to be together.

Then we went on holiday together, and there was time to talk about it, and to try to understand what had happened. Of course there was no *privacy*, because there was no expectation that we might want it. It was just something that *wasn't happening at all*, as far as everybody else was concerned. But it was happening as far as we were concerned. How to describe it? Unglamorous? It was just terribly inconvenient. Because we were always involved, as well, in our families, family duties and commitments, that sort of thing, as well as commitments to other people. Nobody 'saw' us; they didn't *see* what it was. We had one friend, I think, who did – but we didn't discuss it, we just knew she did. She's still a great friend. There was no sort of *status* for it. There was just the reality of it, and that was unimpeachable; but *describing* it or *talking* about it, well, that just didn't happen. We were living miles apart, and that, for various reasons, couldn't change, so we still had no common ground, and we never, or hardly ever, met privately.

There were no books, there were no blueprints about this whole thing. I remember at a very early stage we came across a copy of *The Microcosm*,[2] and that was very interesting to us; it was the only book we'd read, apart from *The Well of Loneliness*;[3] that was indeed all there was. So it was a journey of discovery and adventure. There was no question about anybody else, once we'd met. Nobody (we supposed) recognised us – not until my rather wild Sister-in-law Number One came across from Australia and actually used The Word. I think it was AIDS that was happening or something, and she said, 'Oh well, you're perfectly all right, as monogamous lesbians.' And it was the first time anybody had said the word to us. But she was too diplomatic to mention it to parents, or to anyone else.

And this went on for *years* – five years – until UA left the school and went off to do a course in developmental and social psychology. I couldn't get away (by then I was marginally more senior, even useful) because that would have decimated the department, so I stuck on for another year, and then I left, and then we bought our first house. This would be '71, the end of '71. We got a mortgage. I think it was enormously difficult for two women to do so, at that time, but we met a comfortable elderly gentleman in an insurance office who said, 'Well, I expect you're going to be together for quite some time.' This was the most wonderful thing that anybody had ever said to us. He must have arranged something, and we did have a mortgage. I think it was sixteen pounds a month, or something like that. And then we had a cat: the cat just decided that she wanted to live with us. And then we had our first dog, a lurcher from the RSPCA.

Equality was important. At no point did we want one of us to know more than the other did, so I did the course that she'd done, too. In those days, one salary would do for two people. But that quite quickly became impossible. UA taught for a bit, and I must have had some money, to pay for this course, though not much. All our old diaries are full of accounts, because neither of us was any good at arithmetic. Looking through them, I came across one point where it says starkly in the margin, 'Nil in Bank.' The diaries are full of references to money, because we were always trying to keep afloat. Anyway, she had a job and I did this course, and that was fine. And then she wanted to write, so I got a job, and then (times getting harder) we thought she'd better have a job too. She didn't want a *big* job, she wanted a job that left her free to write. So she was a temp for a while in various places. And I got a job in what was then a teacher training college and I also taught on the BEd degree at the university. Over the years, the college turned into a polytechnic and then into a university. I didn't do my DPhil till '79, when I was given a sabbatical year.

Out of our hands

So, that was us. For forty-four years. We didn't go on about it much: it wasn't anybody else's business. We did meet other lesbians, over the years, and that was (mostly) nice; some are dead by now, but some remain great friends. But the world was changing, and attitudes were changing. Our next-door neighbour was the widow of the original local doctor, and we were friendly with her. A feisty woman, and a very clever woman, and brave – she'd been in the Army during the war, and she'd had quite an interesting life. One evening she came in for a gin and tonic. One of her daughters was married to a barrister, who'd just become a judge, and UA's father had been a judge, so there was a certain amount of legal chat. The talk turned to civil partnerships, and she said, 'We've all been wondering – all the family – when *you're* going to do it.' Startled by this alarming turn of events, we carried on chatting, and she went away, and we looked at each other, and said, 'Pamela expects us to get married. Perhaps we'd better.'

So – yes, we would, and we'd do it very quietly. A couple of friends were coming down to stay from Edinburgh, and we thought, well, when they're here, they can be our witnesses, so we'll have it then. We booked it. And I mentioned it to my brother, who lives in Australia, just as a matter of news. The next day he phoned and said, 'I'm coming.' Well, if you have *one* relation, you have to ask the others. We both thought: 'I don't suppose they'll come: it's short notice, and it's midweek, and they've got children, and jobs...'

They all came. And brought a wedding cake (in the shape of an open book), and well – you know, the whole thing was rather taken out of our hands.

Of course, the banns or whatever had to be displayed. We didn't take any notice of that, but that the press noticed, because UA was slightly famous, which meant that somebody in a meeting passed me a newspaper headline in large type about 'Poet Not A-Verse to Marriage' or something hair-raising like that. Dismay! After thirty-odd very discreet years together... outed.

All our parents were dead. Such a thing would not have happened – could not have happened – when our parents were alive. It was simply not a possibility. In a sense I think when they were all dead we felt more relaxed about it. The younger members of the family obviously didn't feel any worries at all. But it was something of a shock to discover that all of the town and most of the county (there were, I think, five local newspapers) would then find out. It was in the headlines, with photographs. There was even a tiny paragraph in *The Times* or the *Guardian*.

However, in this town we're used to some pretty unorthodox people: we've had a few rather bizarre characters, over the years, and I thought, well heck, if they can cope with them, they can probably cope with us. And we'd been here a long time. And obviously our neighbours had been discussing us. In any case, we didn't have any more chance to be in the closet. Everybody was terribly discreet, and shyly congratulatory, and very loving, and they all, dammit, turned up, and packed the place. We'd invited quite a lot of people, but there were a good many free-range characters who just turned up, and we weren't a bit prepared for this – I hadn't even washed the car. It was all impromptu and amateur, but everybody was amazingly nice, and so it was got over. It was all rather out of our control, if you like. Which seemed okay.

We didn't expect it to make us feel different, but we *did* feel different. In what way? Well, that's a question that I cannot answer you. A couple of my male friends were married recently, and one of them found it different, but the other one didn't know what he was talking about; so perhaps not everybody does. But we felt different. I can't say more than that.

Damaged beyond repair

That was in 2006, three years before UA died. She perhaps need not have died, had she had better medical attention. There are doctors who, if you're a certain age and a woman, patronise you, don't take you seriously, and that's really what it amounted to. It made her death quite hard to deal with, and all the medical circumstances very painful to remember.

There are always friends – but, you know, you feel responsible for friends: you can't sort of batter them around the head with your own grief all the time. I've been very lucky, I've had very tolerant, loving friends. But you have to behave properly.

> The neighbours are kind, and relieved
> That I wind the clock and feed the birds,
>
> That I'm clean and respectably dressed,
> And not at a loss for words.
>
> Shyly they ask how I'm feeling
> *Oh, better,* you know, *getting there.*
>
> (Out of the question to speak the truth:
> *Damaged beyond repair.*)
>
> Words have lost their piquancy,
> They're treacherous as weather;
>
> *Ours,* for instance, or *yours* and *mine,*
> Or *happy.* Or *together.*[4]

I think my future is really dictated by what I've got to do, in terms of all the leftover paperwork of a very busy life; and I'm trying to maintain her reputation as far as I can. It's the final task that I can do for her.

And other people have played their generous part, saying, 'Don't you think this is what you ought to do?' – or they've said the right thing at the right time; things have fallen into place. I have been *very* busy, and that has saved my life. Otherwise I think I'd have gone and dug a hole in the ground and got into it. As Dr Johnson said, 'The safe and reliable antidote to sorrow is employment.'

I still do readings and run courses and write reviews and give talks of one sort or another. Together we always knew a lot of people, lovely people, and we (that's to say I) still do, which is a blessing. And forty-four years – a lifetime – with the most marvellous, the dearest person in the world? How could one ever begin to say thank you for that?

Leo (right) and UA reading their poetry

2

INNOCENCE AND IGNORANCE

Women have always fallen in love with each other; but until comparatively recently, that love was not talked about. Girls growing up were 'protected' from such dangerous knowledge. In fact, a key reason for the defeat of the 1921 Bill to criminalise lesbianism was the argument that it might draw the attention of impressionable young women to the existence of the vice – better not to mention it. As a result, girls who experienced same-sex desire often had no words or ideas to explain their feelings to themselves. As Marguerite says in the next story, 'I didn't know the word for it.' This ignorance is a theme that I found over and over again, both in the interviews and in the written life stories. In the mid twentieth century, sex education of any kind was rudimentary or non-existent; 'crushes' were seen as a phase to be grown out of; there were no role models.

The struggle to understand oneself against a background of silence is a feature of the next two stories, told by Kate and Marguerite. It crops up again in other stories too; Silva (Chapter 6) remembers failing her biology exam because the teacher at her Catholic boarding school simply omitted all parts of the syllabus relating to human sexuality. Religion often played a part in enforcing this state of ignorance. 'Could a girl today live in such ignorance?' asks Kate. 'We were so innocent you can't believe it!' exclaims Marguerite, remembering the story of the nuns and the Tampax. Unsurprisingly, many girls got married because they didn't know there was an alternative. As Marguerite says, 'It was like going down a plughole – you just did.'

This 'innocence and ignorance' as Kate calls it, might have slowed down the realisation of who they were, but it didn't, in the end, stop them developing a lesbian identity. For both Kate and Marguerite, as for several other women in this book, education and the coming of second-wave feminism helped on that journey. One of the surprising but heartening things about so many lesbian life stories is that, in spite of the pressure to conform when they were growing up, so many women were able eventually to be themselves and, like Kate and Marguerite, to find happiness in their relationships.

JT

~

KATE

'So how *did* you come to be living in Amsterdam?' called the shopkeeper cheerfully in a crowded English village shop. By now I was almost out of the door. 'I married a Dutchwoman,' I called back. Nobody turned a hair. Suffolk phlegm? Or a genuine change of attitude to what once would have created closed faces if not downright hostility? Since I've chosen to live in the Netherlands, in a city renowned for its liberality, I'm perhaps not the person best suited to measure changes in attitude towards British lesbians. But I did spend the first sixty years of my life in the UK, I am a very frequent returner and I notice a new and pleasing indifference to diversity there too – so long, of course, as it doesn't rock the boat and has nothing to do with immigration or equal pay for women.

I was born in 1938 to a 'respectable' but single mother from a 'good Catholic family', who was stowed in a convent for the duration of her pregnancy and had no choice about the future of her baby. My adoptive mother was one of fourteen children and had been childminder-in-chief to her younger siblings and half-siblings. All she wanted when she married my father – who was a carpenter and ex-soldier – was to have babies. She lost seven before persuading my father that they must adopt. They didn't tell me I that was adopted; so I couldn't articulate, even to myself, the effect of conversations broken off when I came into the room, or some very odd looks when some of my eccentricities – being a persistent reader, for example – came into view.

So there we were as the Second World War was looming, squashed into two and a bit rooms in a semi (which, as we know from *Monty Python*, should have been populated by a bank clerk, his wife and 2.5 children). My mother used to wash up in an enamel bowl in the slip-room kitchen – no sink, no water but a geyser over the bath for our weekly baths and a copper downstairs in the landlady's kitchen in which to do the weekly wash. We slept in one room but, as the sky began to light up at night with fire and searchlights, we often slept in the back garden shelter. Do I remember it? Yes, I think I do, although I'm aware that at this distance traces of memory are overlaid by the memories of memory, and the constant retelling of the story. Was I afraid? Not often. I was far more scared of my mother's sharp tongue and constant anxiety. She told me later, long after we'd resolved our differences, that never a day passed without worry in case I 'found out'.

And find out I did. No one had expected – or wanted – me to pass the scholarship but, just in case, my father had 'put me down' for the convent. (His religion was lapsed Catholic.) When I was fourteen, one of the nuns told me that I was adopted, in the hope that knowing would mitigate my rather freakish behaviour – I was addicted, with my best friend Hilary, to carrying out pranks like tying up the Angelus bell rope or smuggling a small wind-up gramophone into the mezzanine over the assembly hall and playing jazz after 'Daily, Daily Sing to Mary'. My first act after finding out was to rifle my mother's chest of drawers and find the adoption certificate, which gave me the huge relief of *knowing* for sure that I was indeed 'different' and why. It didn't even occur to me then to wonder who I *was*.

Deeply muddled about sex and gender

If I seem to be a long time in getting round to my lesbian development, it is indeed because I was very slow to fall in to the implications of my own emotional and much disguised sexual proclivities. For example, my friend at school (and ever after) is also a lesbian, but neither of us found out about the other until we were both twenty-six, despite the fact that the nuns used forever to be telling us that our friendship wasn't quite 'healthy'. (Could a girl today live in such ignorance? I hope not. Although I don't know quite what I would have done with the information, had it found its way through my thick layers of denial.)

As a small child I was deeply muddled over both sex and gender. At some level I 'knew' what was happening in my parents' bed but it was shrouded in such secrecy and surrounded by so much punishment for me should I be awake, or if in the waking world I showed any interest in 'doctors and nurses' with my cousins, that I couldn't even begin to articulate to myself what this feverishly exciting and dangerous activity was about. I longed to metamorphose into a boy, to wear grey flannel shorts and long grey socks, to play football or Cowboys and 'Indybums', to pee standing up. I remember undressing before my weekly bath and being terrified that since the last time I looked, I had sprouted a willy, so much did I want one. Why? Was it the perception that boys were somehow more free both of restraint and entanglement? Or had I picked up at some subliminal level that my mother's last baby was a boy who actually breathed before she lost him?

So it was by no means clear to me what was happening when, at the convent, my lay English teacher fell in love with me, although somewhere an uneasy and familiar twinge indicated that it must be to do with the forbidden and unspoken world of sex. Every day DA, as I was allowed to call her, swept down the corridor in her black academic gown, fished out an envelope and thrust it at me or into the hands of the trustworthy Hilary. Every day there was a love letter and often a poem, mostly containing 'sweet peas' or 'butterflies'. Every day we walked together two miles after school, along the petrol-stinking North Circular, until I turned into my street and she caught her bus. In the holidays, letters came by post, which was later to prove our undoing. Apart from the excitement of the illicit – we both knew we mustn't be caught – there were some very substantial gains for me. Someone recognised that I was clever and a writer. Someone loved me, it seemed unconditionally, and for the first time my love constellated itself round a woman. Although after the inevitable crash it took me a long time to accept that my love was always going to go out to other women, I still can't be wholly judgemental about that time when innocence and ignorance exploited innocence and ignorance.

One day I came home from school and immediately picked up an atmosphere of icy silence. My mother said nothing to me; *less* than nothing. I slipped out to the kitchen and opened her bag, hung on the doorknob. Inside, a sheaf of DA's letters. And nothing was ever said, but the freezing effect of that shock caused me to 'see', as if I had suddenly put on a different pair of spectacles, what it was my mother saw: a woman of thirty-seven doing – what? – to a thirteen-year-old girl. Never mind that there was no sex, it was my first and most powerful indication that what I had felt was 'wrong' and antithetical to 'the way things are'.

What a heady brew sex – or its absence – and religion are! Nobody could fault me for being the most pious girl in the school, could they? That was my next ploy to gain the approval of the nuns, God and myself, but it didn't work. At the end of my fifteenth year, the nuns had decided that I would never make a sixth-former or be 'university material', so I had to leave. To my mother's credit, when the exam results came out and I had failed everything but English (which I didn't know how to fail) she negotiated a further term's grace for me to retake my GCEs and belatedly, I woke up and passed. By then it was very clear to me and to some of the nuns, though not to my mother, that I was sick. 'I think you have TB,' said Mother Stanislaus, 'but don't worry, St Theresa died of it.' But to my mother, who had seen her favourite sister Bella die of TB, and several of the small cousins from next door to Bella go into a sanatorium because of the disease, it was a step too far even to think about. 'Thank God for your good health,' she said, and refused to let me see a doctor.

Fortunately, on my first day at my short-lived clerking job with Westminster Council, everyone in the office went for a mass X-ray and within three weeks I was in hospital. I won't dwell on the rather primitive routines that were current then in the treatment of tuberculosis, but I was very lucky because the antibiotic streptomycin had recently been developed so my stay was relatively short – eight months and a time at home on bed rest, with another year of artificially induced lung collapse.

What a liberal education hospital was! The minute Sister went off duty up we got from our strict bed rest to 'frat' with the men in the next-door ward and with each other. Many were the parties on smuggled gin and the hilarious stories, raucous and sexual. But more importantly, I got a sense of how difficult life was for these women, many of whom had been in and out of hospital for decades, and how tough, resilient, funny and brave they were. Alas, nobody ever mentioned the kind of behaviour I would have been most interested to hear about. Had people really never heard of homosexuality? Or had I just got a very efficient filter in my ears?

A time of much confusion

As soon as possible, and much against my parents' wishes, I left home to start nursing at St Helier Hospital in Carshalton, Surrey. We worked a basic forty-eight-hour week, and invariably much longer – but the bliss of going to my own bedroom in the nurses' home more than made up for that. Then began a time of much confusion. I still daydreamed about marriage and children. I had 'boyfriends' – not many, and none who persuaded me beyond the bounds of my convent puritanism. At the same time I was developing passionate attachments to a number of women, some of whom became friends for life, but none of whom was able to tempt me into any sexual activity, even if they'd known what and how to do it. (My old schoolfriend still says I should write a memoir entitled *Bosoms I Have Been Clasped To*).

I'm sorry to say that at this time of my life religion really was a substitute for sex. I flexed the muscles of my intellect a little by thinking my way out of the Catholic Church and into the Anglican Communion. That may not seem very adventurous but, to an underdeveloped twenty-year-old, brought up on hell fire and infallibility, it was adventure enough. Also, I was surrounded by 'unlit lamps' which suited me very well. However, by the time I began my midwifery training and fell deeply in love with midwifery, I had also met a major in the

Royal Army Medical Corps and woken up with some shock and horror to the possibility that I might be a lesbian. Once again the person concerned – a fascinating and complex woman, whose marriage to a well-known poet had failed – insisted that of course she had no such transgressive desires. The pain of that bewildering chapter is still a very sharp memory, but I began to wake up.

Not only was I increasingly aware that I loved women, but I also became conscious of the fact that I was barely educated and badly needed to use my brain and my nascent skill with words. Instead of taking the risk of getting A levels and going for a university education, I took the easier route of teacher training. At least we had an excellent English department, although by now, since I was back in the bosom of Mother Church (what a cave-in!) there were yet more nuns.

There, too, against all the odds and rather against my own desires, I met my partner of the next thirty-three years. Here I'm going to sound rather narcissistic and self-absorbed, because I am very unwilling to provide any details that will identify my former partner, so whatever I say is going to be partial and one-sided. I'm also unwilling to dissect our relationship and where it eventually went wrong, for much the same reasons.

Our early days together, at a Catholic teacher training college, were both a deep revelation of what had been missing in my life and understanding, but also excruciatingly painful. My emerging sexuality crashed head-on into my guilt at being a sexual being at all. I was physically sick after sex, I had to scrub myself clean, I was haunted by a profound sense of what I can only describe as 'wrongness' and it wasn't until the founder of the Samaritans, Chad Varah, began the process of getting me sorted out through counselling, that my partner and I could begin any sort of life together. That we could and did is a tribute to her patience and to courage on both sides. It's worth mentioning that I looked for psychiatric help, and was told by a 'Christian' psychiatrist, 'I suspect you know that what you are doing is gravely wrong, but I can give you medication to reduce your libido, if you like.' Another – I was nothing if not persistent – told me that God had sent him a vision of me, married to a doctor and with several children. It's only now that I realise how brave the Samaritans, led by Chad, were, and how much they swam against the mainstream.

Swaggering in bell-bottoms

And what a heady time it was to be venturing into the lesbian world! There was Kenric:[1] as I recollect, a rather middle-class outfit, which provided genuine support and new friends, although it was far from radical. During and after the Flower Power '60s came the first – to me – intimations of a far more radical feminism. However, although my partner, always the more intellectually adventurous, was fired up by this, I was far more conventional and cautious. I liked to swagger a bit in my bell-bottoms, to dance at the Gateways,[2] to enjoy the thrill of being 'outside' what I still thought of as the norm; but I was not prepared – yet – to adopt the root-and-branch critique of a male-directed world which was gradually emerging from the maelstrom of new feminist writing.

So what changed? Here I am in my seventies, profoundly committed to the vision of those early feminists, who could not have known, then, how deeply the world will need to change if the earth and her creatures are to survive climate change and the current lethal brands of fundamentalist and consumerist politics. I wish, very much, that I had woken up sooner.

But that is getting ahead of myself. First there were long years in London and in Lincolnshire, making a home with my partner; going twice, late, to university to acquire a qualification and profession in the conservation of antiquities; beginning to write...

Even in deepest Lincolnshire, we were not totally immune from the activism of people who wanted to improve the lot and perception of gays and lesbians. We had a close man friend who ran the local CHE (Campaign for Homosexual Equality)[3] group. At a conference in Nottingham we encountered for the first time a rather angry group of women who wanted to set up NOW, a lesbian-only organisation. Slowly, slowly, I became comfortable enough in my own skin to be 'out' all the time – though not to my mother. Is somebody who assumes her mother 'knows', as I'm sure mine did, ever truly out? Friends, yes, co-religionists, yes, employers yes, but the acid test is surely your mother.

However, by the time my partner and I returned to London, both of my parents had died of lung cancer. I was free to begin my last and biggest job as head of English Heritage's research laboratories, with my lesbian identity plainly identified. I became the person of resort for people who had suffered any kind of sexual harassment or gender discrimination – not a difficult task, as English Heritage was on the whole a civilised place. With hindsight though, I now see that gender definitely influenced management styles and decisions. The guys positively enjoyed ranting and verbally rough-housing each other. It was difficult, even at senior management level, to make a quieter, more nuanced voice heard or taken seriously. The temptation was to out-shout them – something that is still an unsolved dilemma for those relatively few women who make it to senior levels.

In 1993, I met Tonnie, who would become my Dutch wife, at a conference in Washington. It took us until 1997 to realise that we loved each other – mainly because, as one of the tortoise persuasion, I inched my way so slowly towards facing the fact that I wanted to leave my long-term relationship and indeed, that I was capable of doing it. It was a grievous decision. Not only the abandoned suffer loss, grief and anguish over what should have been and wasn't. Like so many other women that it is almost a lesbian cliché, I was helped to understand the truth about my feelings by the work of the lesbian poet Adrienne Rich. And in 1997 I came to Amsterdam to live with Tonnie. In 2000 we were married – the same year that I discovered I had a biological mother alive in America (she was then 86 and died a year later) and a brother in the UK. He is perfectly accepting of our marriage, but he's not quite so keen on my being a poet.

I realise, coming to the end of this account, that I have said very little about poetry, the quiet but perhaps most formative impulse of my life. I have written it since I was eleven years old but, in common with so many women, never thought my work 'worth' publishing. I have Lilian Mohin of the justly famous Onlywomen Press to thank for instantly recognising my work, after a chance encounter, and publishing a collection in 1999. What a risk-taker she is! It was Lilian who pointed out that much of my poetry is about and for women. My fourth collection, *The Silver Rembrandt*,[4] has a lesbian as main character in the long poem that forms the core of the book – better late than never!

So here I am, barrelling along now, as one does, towards age – no more time for tortoise-ing – and towards, I hope, more connection with other women who care, more friendship, more insight, more love, and more poetry that might make a difference. I have been immensely lucky in my life, especially with the women I've known, and who've helped me come to terms with my own identity as a lesbian and a woman. I thank them all, living and dead – and especially the very much alive and loving Tonnie.

Kate

MARGUERITE

I was a 'baby boomer' – born in 1946. My father had just got back from being in the Eighth Army in the war; he was suffering from post-traumatic stress, but you didn't know that in those days. I was the eldest of two girls. We were a church-going family, which is reflected in my interests now, though it's been a long journey – and therefore I was sent to an Anglican girls' convent school, where I stayed till I was eighteen.

Being in an all-female environment, I thought that everybody felt the way I did about females. I didn't know what it meant – and of course, I didn't know the word for it, either, then. Realisation came much later. On the whole it was older girls, rather than my contemporaries, that I was drawn to, and sometimes it was a member of staff. Nothing *happened*, and I never saw anything happening at the school, despite the fact that by the time we left we were into the 60s, where apparently licence reigned. And you look back, and you think, 'How could you be so dim?' There was nothing about it that worried me, though. I just sailed on, oblivious, I think because I knew nothing about it at all, and also because I thought it was just the same for everybody else. Girls had crushes on older girls, and they carried their shoes and all that kind of thing. (Can you imagine it now? No.) But whereas they were all in love with any chancing boy or young man who might have been seen on the premises, it never moved me. So my feelings weren't troubling to me, which in a way I do feel I've benefited from, as my life has gone on; but it was a long time before I realised precisely what it was.

We knew nothing about sex of *any* kind. The nuns were very keen on us keeping our virginity, I remember; and once they found out that some girls were using Tampax. I was, because my mother had given me some to take back to school. But they never said, upfront, what was wrong with it. So we said (we were so innocent, you can't believe it), 'What's wrong with it?' And they said it was because it would 'interfere with our purity'. We still didn't understand; we thought it was germy or something! And they said, would we send them back to our parents, through the post. My mother was absolutely stunned when she got them back. And we *still* didn't know what was wrong with it. Of course, it was all about sex, as it turned out, with boys. In fact, there were a few girls who'd 'done it', but it was disassociated from anything the nuns had told us, because it was all so weird, and so hidden.

Like going down a plughole

I went straight from school to university, to read theology. I didn't enjoy university particularly. The work was okay, but having been at school with people I knew very, very well, I was in a hall of residence with people I didn't know well, and who had come from such different sorts of lives. And also I experienced quite a lot of anti-religious feeling. For instance, I had an acquaintance who was a monk, and he came to the university where I was, to give a talk about theology. He came to surprise me in the refectory and, in full monk's dress, came up and gave me a big kiss in front of all the students. It horrified the people around me. It did not go down well. So that was troubling. And everybody was getting boyfriends and all the rest of it, so I thought I'd better do the same. Not that I'm known for my conformity, but it's like going down a plughole: you just do. And then I decided to get married: partly because I wanted to get away from home. My parents lived in deepest Cornwall by that time, and I had never found home very easy, because my father veered in and out of depression for a lot of the time. Nowadays people get treatment and counselling for the sort of depression he and lots of his contemporaries suffered from, but they didn't.

Deciding to get married was a big mistake. I was good friends with the chap I married and – still very dim! – I mistook that for what was actually going to happen. I was extremely frustrated and unhappy. My relationship with my husband was never sexual except when we wanted to have children. The sex was definitely for having children and, even then, we only did it a few times, both times. Luckily, I turned out to be very fertile. But I had bad depression and I couldn't, again, get to grips with why it could be. I didn't know *why* I just did not feel right, and I didn't feel fulfilled – still not equating it with what was up with me.

My husband and I both became teachers. I think it must have been during the first year I was teaching that there was a very bad winter. There was a lot of snow and we had to dig our cars out from the car park at school. My wedding ring got lost, in the snow. And that was it; I never wore one again. After we moved to West Sussex, about 1971 or so, I got a job at a highly academic girls' grammar school. The women on the staff there were something else! First generation to university, first generation to Oxbridge; lesbian, a lot of them, but unacknowledged. What I felt about women came back then; very much so. I became close friends with a couple of them. And then – I think in 1977 – I left because I was pregnant with our eldest daughter. I didn't go on maternity leave, I left completely, because Richard was a head by that time and we could cope on his salary. And that was truly terrible, because I was at home in a small village all day, with no transport, a bus only once every so often, and I really knew that I was going to have to do something about myself. So I joined a WEA class.

Falling into place

And that was it. I began to work with the WEA, but also I joined a women's consciousness-raising group. (Who knew they even existed? I didn't, certainly not in West Sussex.) There I met women who were very, very into feminism, which interested me, and later on meant that I taught feminist theology for the WEA. I was opened up to new ideas that I hadn't had before. And so things fell into place, and I met the first woman I had a relationship with. That was traumatic because, although she'd had relationships with women before, she was married and she did not tell her husband or her children about me. Now I was quite willing to set up home together, to be a breadwinner, because I've always done that. But she didn't want to do that, because she said her husband would go for custody of the children, if he knew. It was a fear for me as well, and I did go into it far more carefully than she did, but I don't think my husband would have gone for custody. Anyway, he knew what was happening to me, because I told him. Not that he was chuffed to bits about it, as you can imagine!

So that was traumatic for me, because it was my first relationship, and it was the real thing as far as I was concerned, but I hated the subterfuge. What happened in the end was that her husband got a job at the other end of Sussex, and they moved. She said it would make no difference to our relationship. Well, you clutch at straws when your whole life is falling apart, so there's me thinking, 'Okay then.' There followed a couple of years, I suppose, when we met occasionally in various places, but it was all getting less and less satisfactory, really, because she was establishing a new life, and I was going on with what was left of mine. So I thought, 'For the sake of my mental health, I've got to draw this to a halt.' Now at that point I would have said, 'Enough's enough. Say goodbye.' But she was very distraught about that, and said we must remain friends. Whatever that means. Painful. So we went on meeting, and still do. It was very difficult. It isn't so difficult now, obviously, because I'm in a fantastic relationship, I've been happy for over twenty years, and that's all fine. There are still sometimes little threads of anger, when things come up; but I don't think about what might have been, or anything like that. It might have been a complete disaster, anyway.

I became a tutor-organiser of the WEA for a time and, one dark night, I was standing in Chichester Cathedral, with a tombstone in front of me where I was taking money for a class which was happening there, and a woman came through the door, with a stick, very smartly dressed. I said, 'Can I put your name on the register?' – and she was fantastically rude.

I thought, 'This is typical. We are all volunteers, and we've turned out on a rainy night in November, and this bloody woman...' Anyway, our policy was to ask extremely annoying people like that to come on the committee, just to see what it was like. So at the end of those sessions, as was our habit, we asked if anybody would like to volunteer to come on the committee, and I asked her in particular, because I thought, 'You'll get a taste of your own medicine, madam!' And it turned out to be Jean, who is now my partner – and is delightful, and only has this brusque manner because she's very shy. She had just retired, and was trying to get into life in Chichester. She came onto the committee and the meetings were often in our house... We just went on from there, and that was that!

So then, we had to buy a house together and all that kind of stuff. That part was easy. The children by then were fourteen and eight, and Jean had spent a lot of time with us, getting to know them. She wasn't purposely being careful, she is just a careful kind of person, but they grew to know her very well, and they were fine, absolutely fine. Richard and I had been living separate lives for ages. There was never any suggestion that the girls wouldn't be able to see him, or that he wouldn't be able to see them. But what happened, which I could never have expected, was that they didn't really want to spend any time at his house. They'd go out for the day with him, but they would never stay there, or go on holiday with him and his new wife, or anything. So we had them, full-time. Jean was retired by that time, because she took early retirement (she was a senior consultant, a pathologist and then a microbiologist, and taught medical students) and we just led a normal family life.

One thing about the middle classes in our part of West Sussex is that people are terribly polite. So they don't out-and-out criticise you in any way. Actually, the only blatant homophobia that we had was from church people. Not at our church, but at others, where we were sent letters saying, 'You're doing terrible damage to your children, they'll turn out to be lesbians.' (What research *that's* based on, I can't imagine.) And, 'They'll have prejudice against them for the rest of their lives.'

We always had friends to our house, all the kind of things you do when you've got children, and funnily enough, of course, children don't take too much notice of what the situation is, because they're just interested in themselves. And, to be fair, the parents didn't really make any fuss about it.

Before my elder daughter went to university, we said, 'Just be a bit careful about what you say.' You know, you give them the old sex, drugs and rock-and-roll type talk before they go. But of course, she was absolutely fine. She came home from Lancaster, which is where she did her first degree, and said, 'I don't know why you gave me that lecture, because we're really boring. Nobody else has to sit round at mealtimes and have conversation, and their parents don't go to WEA classes.' All this resentment came out. And she said, 'They've all been divorced, and their mothers have got boyfriends who've sexually harassed them, and that kind of thing.' So *her* life was obviously all dead boring, and it was all our fault!

Being looked at

While she was at university, she met the love of her life. They've been together now for about ten or eleven years. After a few years they got married, because they wanted to start a family, so he had to explain to his parents about us. When he said that he was going to have two mothers-in-law, his mother said, 'Well, you'll have deformed children. The daughters will turn out to be just like them.' She said a lot of other things as well. We couldn't do anything, we couldn't speak – we'd never met them, anyway, at that point. But they got married, and, luckily, we had a lot of input into it, because we were the bride's parents.

They would have been married in the cathedral here, because that's the congregation we're part of, but the Lady Chapel was being done up. In the end, they were married in Arundel Parish Church, where there was an interregnum, which was good because we never wanted any old vicar to marry them; we wanted our great friend, who's gay, to marry them. And he did.

But we felt that we were being *looked at*, at the wedding, and I didn't like that at all. (Jean always feels she's being looked at, so she didn't like any of it much.) But I thought that was pretty horrible. We didn't know whether to dance at the reception, because we thought, 'Oh God, they're going to be looking!' And it still lingers...

They soon had a baby, and she was baptised by the same friend, in the cathedral – much to the amazement of our son-in-law's parents. They find it very difficult to grasp the fact that we are totally acceptable there, and what's more very much part of the congregation. Actually, on the day of the baptism, because I was the granny, I was on duty as a lay minister, with the chalice. They didn't understand any of it, really. But now there's a granddaughter. She's lovely, and obviously will grow up without any prejudice whatsoever, because children are like that, they accept what there is. And when they come and stay with us, she comes into bed with us in the morning – she will talk about that freely, in the future. Other gay friends of ours have had this too, particularly when they haven't got children themselves, with nephews and nieces. That seems absolutely fine.

Hanging on by our fingernails

I've never felt a conflict between my sexual orientation and my faith, because I do feel that I was lesbian from the start, and it somehow wasn't any kind of choice. So I can feel a sense of sin about a lot of other things, but not that. But the attitude of the Church to homosexuality – that is a conflict for me. It's going to be a conflict for a good many years, I imagine, and I've thought about it a lot. You hang on by your fingernails, for years and years, then something happens and you have to think it all through again. I particularly thought about it when a friend of mine was passed over for promotion in the Church because he was gay. At that point I thought, 'This is it, this is finally it.' And I emailed him and said I was so sorry; I said, 'This could be it, for those of us who've been hanging on by our fingernails, this really could be it.' He wrote the most fantastic, encouraging letter back, and said, 'It's our Church as well. And if they force us all out like this, what will be left?'

And I do feel, myself, that I am made in the image of God, like everybody else is; and that I'm made in the lesbian image of God. So, I hung on. Actually, since I've retired, I've got even more involved in the church, because at retirement I don't have to worry about things like the parents of my pupils latching on to it. I wasn't out to many people at school – only to the other lesbians on the staff (I could always find solace in the PE Department) – but since retiring, I have got more involved, and I do speak about it. People say, of course they've known. And of course, they have; Jean and I live together, after all. Plenty of people don't want to even think about it, but they're fine with us.

Waiting for the Queen to sign it

We registered our civil partnership in 2005, right at the beginning. In some ways, we weren't bothered about doing it, since we knew we couldn't have a religious ceremony. But then, of course, Jean's ten years older than me, and you'd got the whole pension situation and everything, so we could see the business aspect of doing it. We weren't massively into going up to the registry office – you can imagine, in Chichester – but the children were absolutely adamant that they wanted us to have a ceremony and they wanted to be there. So I went into the registry office to book it.

I wandered in, and I said, 'I've come to book a civil partnership ceremony.'

And she said, 'Oh, we're not doing those!'

I said, 'What do you mean? We want to book a civil partnership ceremony.' Luckily this was in a reasonably open office, and there were a couple of other people there.

She said, 'No, we're not doing those, you'll have to go to Brighton.'

I said, 'We can't go to Brighton, because the law is that you have to go to your local office.' And I'm thinking to myself, 'This is very weird, I didn't think there was going to be any problem.'

She said, 'Anyway, the law hasn't been passed.'

I said, 'Yes it has.'

She said, 'No, we're waiting for the Queen to sign it.'

I said, 'She's signed it.' I was getting quite angry by this time.

She said, 'Anyway, we haven't had the training.'

I said, 'What training do you need? It's exactly the same as when anybody else comes in here.' I was going to go, because I don't like making fusses, but I thought, 'This is outrageous.' So I said, 'Has anybody else been in here to ask you about this?'

She said, 'Oh yes, we've had a lot of enquiries.'

Well, I thought, 'This is the living end!' Because I do know that there are people in our area who've lived together forty-odd years, and this is… people just don't seem to understand what it means to them.

So I said, 'Would you get your appointment book out now. I want to book it.'

Another woman came across, got the appointment book out and booked it for me.

I said, 'I don't appreciate your attitude towards this at all,' and I left.

But later that day I had a phone call from the chief registrar, deeply apologetic. She said, did I want to make a complaint?

I said that I felt I had made my feelings clear when I was in there, but yes, I would like to make a complaint.

And she said, 'I would like to book another appointment to see what you want,' and all the rest of it.

When I went back, that woman wasn't there, so I don't know whether she'd been transferred or binned off or what, but anyway, she wasn't there. The chief registrar turned out to be a really nice person, and she more or less said we could have what we liked; we had to keep off anything blatantly religious, but we could have what we liked. We had written our own things that we wanted to say, and we used other people's words as well.

Marguerite (left) and Jean (photograph: Abigail Saffery)

She performed the ceremony herself for us. She cried, we cried, the whole assembly cried, particularly my elder daughter, who always cries at everything – she used up loads of tissues. Afterwards the registrar said to us that she had actually conducted all the civil partnership ceremonies up until that point, and the first one she did was for two old guys who'd lived together for fifty years and couldn't get over that they could be united in this way. She said it was deeply emotional for everybody. And she said that, to be quite honest, all the civil partnership ceremonies she had done, she knew that it was the real thing, and lasting relationships. She felt it was a better experience than all the ones she did on Saturdays for heterosexuals who were only going to be married five minutes and that was that.

To our surprise, we did feel different afterwards. Even after all the years, it was very real and did affect us very much. I think we felt that, somehow, we were more legitimate, because in the eyes of the world we could be totally upfront. It's strange... And we could feel safe that if one or other of us died, there was going to be absolutely no problem about what was going to happen to our assets and pensions. We were able to say we could be responsible for each other in the way that everybody else can.

I know that, for many, the civil partnership is enough, but marriage has a theological significance, so I am now married. After more than twenty-five years together *and* a civil partnership, we wondered if we would feel differently again – and we did. Having a proper marriage certificate handed to us was amazing: now our relationship was properly recognised in law and the sight of God (not the Church yet, of course). When we turned up to the registry office it could not have been more different from the first time. The woman doing the paperwork – which is all it was – said she didn't understand why we could not have been married in the first place. A nice touch was that it was called a 'conversion'. So we are now duly 'converted' into respectable members of society – perhaps normal ones?

3

ALWAYS LIKE THAT

In spite of the conspiracy of silence which kept so many girls ignorant of even the existence of lesbian desire, a minority of the women I studied said that they had identified as lesbians from an early age. The next three stories are about girls who recognised their sexual orientation in their teens or earlier. This usually brought shame and fear, and the knowledge that what they felt was 'wrong'. Pip describes vividly the loneliness of this feeling and the terror of being discovered; Val expresses the experience of many a baby dyke of the time when she says, 'I thought I was the only one.'

Very often – though not always – this sense of not belonging was strengthened by gender non-conformity. Pip describes herself as 'the classic tomboy'; Val remembers that she had 'no interest in the things other girls were interested in'; and Crunchy says, 'The reason we knew we were lesbians was that we just thought we should have been boys, really.' Sometimes their 'wrongness' was heavily punished. For Val, the sense of being an outcast was strengthened when she was discharged from the RAF, aged only eighteen. 'I had lost everything,' she says, 'my job, my friends, my home. I swam in a sea of despair.' By contrast, Crunchy's description of her teenage self is uncharacteristically cheerful: a self-identified lesbian while still at school, she had the unusual experience not only of having lesbian friends but also of role models in the shape of older lesbian women. Later she found the ideal milieu for her butch self in the Army; and, unlike Val, she managed to escape being found out.

'Growing up without role models was difficult,' says Pip. Yet, against the odds, all three of these women went on – eventually – to lead happy lesbian lives. The idea that lesbians and gay men have developed coping strategies that make them more than usually resilient is not a new one; reading these stories gives an insight into the battles in which that resilience has been forged.

JT

~

Pip

PIP

I was born into an Air Force family, which meant lots of moving house and changing schools; my mother was a teacher and took jobs wherever my dad's career took us. In some respects, my childhood was pretty free: as long as we turned up at mealtimes, we were left pretty much to our own devices. My mother was very creative and made toys and costumes for us to play with; she was also remarkably free about gender roles and was happy to make me a cowboy outfit, to let me wear trousers and shorts and have a penknife and toy guns. My favourite 'girl's' clothing at the time was a kilt with a proper pin, which I used to wear with a little brown leather bag wrapped around my waist as a sporran. I was the classic tomboy.

Everything changed when I passed my eleven-plus. As we were on the move again, I was given a place at a state boarding school, to give me stability for my secondary schooling. It was a co-ed grammar. I was initially quite excited at the prospect. After all, I'd read the school stories and fancied the idea of midnight feasts and jolly japes. Little did I know what the reality would turn out to be. In those days the school was still based in an old American army hospital: rows of black-painted, corrugated-iron Nissen huts linked by concrete walkways. New buildings were gradually constructed over the seven years I was there, and when I left, in 1964, all pupils lived in fairly comfortable boarding houses. But imagine my horror as an eleven-year-old arriving in my first dormitory: a Nissen hut with thirty-two iron bedsteads and lockers, with thirty-two complete strangers aged from eleven to fifteen who all seemed very confident and cool. I cried for two weeks, got lost, lost my PE kit, found it difficult to manage my clothes, made the mistake of asking whether we shared bath water...

The school was like a prison. We were not allowed out, unless on supervised Sunday walks or if we were playing in a sports team. In the senior school we were allowed to have one Saturday afternoon a half-term to go to one of the two local towns – the boys went to one and the girls to the other! There were no telephones and our outgoing letters were read over by staff before they were posted. No visits were allowed. Discipline was harsh: the boys were beaten and all of us had to develop a hard carapace pretty fast, in order to survive. As I was 'clever' and good at games, I was reasonably accepted, although I do remember being criticised for using long words. I developed a role as clown, to be acceptable but also maintain some distance.

Just before I arrived at this school, I was aware that I was starting to have romantic feelings for other girls and crushes on them, but nothing more. It was during my first couple of years there that I felt completely sure of my sexuality as a lesbian; it freaked me out, but I was sure of it. I was very afraid that I would give myself away or that it would somehow be visible to others – I was tall, somewhat androgynous looking and a late developer in terms of periods, breast growth and so on. I was obsessed with my body and used to inspect it regularly to see if I was turning into a man. I used to join in with everybody else telling jokes against lesbians and gay men to try to cover my tracks. I can remember dreading anything concerning homosexuals appearing in the news, in case I was somehow spotted. Yet we all used to 'practise' kissing with each other for hours – something I joined in with enthusiasm.

There was one girl, Susan, the same age as me. We had a passionate obsession with each other, although it was no more physical than holding hands sometimes, but we wrote notes and used to gaze out of the window at each other and tried to do after-school activities together. It all ended badly for me, because some of my notes to Susan ended up in my housemistress's hands (I never discovered how) and I was called in for a very uncomfortable interview. I don't know why I wasn't expelled on the spot – I suspect it was to do with maintaining the school's reputation – but I was demoted from being a prefect, and Susan and I never communicated again. In terms of my school life, particularly in secondary school, being a lesbian definitely affected my academic achievement. I was obsessed about not being discovered, could not concentrate on my studies, in spite of being in the A stream, and just more or less gave up and escaped to the library and read and read. I managed to scrape together eight O levels and a couple of A levels, but by no means fulfilled my potential. Being in what we regarded as a prison for seven years made me independent, but alienated and with no self-esteem at all.

My first real sexual experience

Because I was a good sportswoman, I decided to become a PE teacher (I didn't know about the stereotypes then) and got a place at Chelsea College of PE in Eastbourne. More boarding school, but young women! I suspect quite a few of the lecturers were lesbians, but they were all very aloof and formal. There were one or two lesbian couples who everyone knew about, but it was very much frowned on – so, lots of double standards and hypocrisy. I was, in retrospect, extremely depressed and self-hating at this time. I hated the way I looked and was afraid of people thinking I was a man; I was constantly checking my reflection in shop windows, although in fact I was a perfectly presentable young woman.

In my second year at college I was the captain of the table tennis club, where I met another Susan, to whom I was very attracted. One evening, I asked if she would like to stay on after the coaching session and have a game – we were both about the same standard and quite competitive. We stayed a couple of hours and then walked back to our residences together. This happened a few times and it became clear that we were both really into each other. We hatched a plan to see each other at the approaching half-term in Leicester (where she lived and I could visit my cousin who also lived there). We decided not to go until the Saturday, so we could have Friday night at my digs when all my housemates had gone away. We spent most of the night listening to Dusty Springfield and snogging each other's faces off. But it felt too scary for her to actually stay the night, so we met up next day and went on the train up to Leicester.

We arranged to meet up nearly every day and came back down to Eastbourne together at the end of the break. Back at college, it wasn't possible to see much of each other (like at school, there was no reason for the years to mix), but thank God for table tennis! We spent the whole Easter holidays together, first at my parents' house and then at her mum's, and spent a great deal of the time having sex. Considering it was my first real sexual experience, it felt very easy and fantastic. I remember wondering for the first time, how could something so fantastic be wrong? Going back to college was tough (no table tennis in the summer) but we spent most of the summer holidays together. The next year was my final year and that meant a long teaching practice away in Wiltshire. Sue and I had devised various ways to spend time together with friends, male and female, so that our cover wasn't blown, but it became clear towards the middle of that year that Sue was cooling off. She was aware that I wouldn't be there the next year and she was running for president, so had to be seen to be squeaky clean. Basically, she dumped me. I was heartbroken.

Something was happening between us

I got my first job at a co-ed grammar school in rural Somerset, teaching PE and English. The school was about to turn comprehensive and for four years I had a really interesting time there. The most important thing that happened to me was realising that I could do it: I had the makings of quite a good teacher. For the first time for ages, I started to get some self-esteem together. I made some really good friends and had fun. It was also brilliant to have money for the first time in my life. I learned to drive and, after a couple of years, bought a second-hand Mini. My social life was almost exclusively with the staff at school, and mainly married blokes. I had no idea how to go about finding other lesbians in deepest Somerset.

And then, during my third year at this school, I was invited to play on the staff tennis team. This was a social event where we played tennis with the staff of other local schools. I thought, 'Why not?' It was great fun, and Dave, one of my colleagues, introduced me to Jess, an attractive woman about my age. At some point I was chatting to Jess and she said, 'Pity I didn't meet you sooner, we could have watched the World Cup together.' I felt a slight frisson and said, 'Maybe next time.' She then told me she was about to emigrate to Canada the following September. Oh no – hopes dashed. But during the course of a fairly alcohol-fuelled evening, it became clear that something was happening between us.

We met several times and started a sexual relationship. We spent the whole of that summer together, staying briefly at both our parents' houses and camping in Cornwall and in Brittany. This was a happy time in some respects, although Jess was even more firmly in the closet than I was, and I always felt there was some secret or distress in her life. She was often withdrawn, but it was also tinged with sadness because Canada loomed ever larger. It is strange looking back at those days from the perspective of the twenty-first century, where communications technology abounds, but neither of us had phones in our digs and I remember once when she was in Canada, I was desperate to talk to her and had to break into school at the dead of night and ring her on the staffroom phone. We communicated by letter and reel-to-reel tapes. Gradually the ones from her dwindled to nothing. I was frantic and couldn't talk to anyone about what was going on. I heard nothing for months and then received a very garbled tape from her. She had had a breakdown and possibly tried to commit suicide. I tried to persuade her to come home and get a job near me and we could set up together. However, she had decided to go on a long trip around Canada in a camper van, with a friend who, I later realised, was her new lover. We maintained some sort of irregular correspondence and I always hoped that sooner or later she would return. A year later, in 1971, I got a new job near to where her parents lived, thinking that if she did come home, I would be near.

The new school was a hotbed of radical educational thinking and an exceptionally exciting and demanding place to work. There were a lot of youngish single teachers and we all worked and played really hard. I decided I would give being heterosexual a shot, and had a few relationships with some of the young men, but really couldn't hack it. I had an on-off sexual relationship with another young PE teacher. I was increasingly fed up with being in the closet and decided to start telling other people where I was at. I told some people that I was bisexual: a bit of a cop-out, but it was the bravest I could be at the time.

Jess did return to the UK, in 1972, and we resumed our relationship, but it was extremely fraught. She was constantly running away and finally decided to get a job in Oxfordshire, so there was lots of to-ing and fro-ing, mainly by me. She was quite depressed and was desperate to have children. I argued that it wasn't necessary to be married, or even in a relationship with a bloke, for this to happen – but she wanted her parents' approval. In fact, she was having a string of relationships with blokes that I didn't know about. It was really only when I went to Lancaster four years later that I was able to say to her, enough. Years later she would still get in touch from time to time, wanting me but not wanting me. She had married and had two children, divorced and ended up living as a lesbian, but didn't seem any happier and was still playing 'push me, pull you'.

Coming out

I remember seeing an advert for CHE (Campaign for Homosexual Equality)[1] which I cut out and had on my desk for about a year before I plucked up the courage to do anything about it. I went, by myself, to a particular pub, took a deep breath and dived in. Imagine my horror when it was full of blokes! Very friendly and welcoming, but blokes. Eventually four women came in, in couples, and were very suspicious and unfriendly – and I was a bit alienated by their obvious butch/femme role-playing. I left feeling even more isolated and depressed and decided I would rather be alone. But I gave the pub one more try and met a bunch of women who were a bit more friendly. They were all soldiers or policewomen who were based locally. We didn't have much in common. One evening they invited me round to someone's house and we were all hanging out and chatting when one woman said, 'Right, the men are going down the pub and the girls are doing...' (something else – can't remember what). There was a pause, and to my horror I realised they were waiting to see which way I would jump: off with the 'boys' or stay with the 'girls'! I ran.

I did go to one other formal meeting, mainly because a woman was the key speaker. Long story short, we did have a sexual relationship; but the best thing about this liaison was meeting some of her friends, who were lovely and not into roles and who reassured me that there were alternatives. This was also my first introduction into organised feminism, which was very exciting. I can remember reading Sue Sharpe's book *Just Like a Girl*,[2] and being blown away by the fact that she only used the feminine pronoun – it was as if the earth had shifted on its axis.

It was at about this time I made a decision to come out to my parents. It felt like the ultimate test of whether I was really secure and happy in my lesbian identity. I felt it would be easier for my mother if I wrote and told her, and gave her some time to absorb the news before coming up to see her. It was a slightly nerve-wracking few days waiting for a response; in fact she rang me, and was quite positive about it. But although she was quite positive to my face, she said some pretty awful things behind my back. She did tell my dad, who in true conservative fashion said, 'I don't mind what you do, but why do you have to make a fuss about it?' My dear old gran, who was in her eighties at the time, said that she didn't really understand it, but if I was doing it, it must be all right. Quite right, Gran! My brother, who was the only person I had come out to before this, had volunteered to come up to see my parents with me after I had told them, and we spent the whole weekend not addressing it at all, until at the end of the weekend, my brother lost his cool on my behalf and said, how could they just ignore my courage in telling them? It wasn't very satisfactory, but at least I had tried. In fact my parents were always charming to all my girlfriends and lovers when they came to stay and my mother was quite fond of some of them.

A late adolescence

At this time I was applying to university to do a degree. I decided to go to Lancaster, as it then had a reputation for being gay. History was repeating itself in some respects, because I had started a relationship with Abby, who I had known and really liked for several years: the catch was, she had to go to the States to qualify for citizenship. Anyway, we had a glorious summer together and she said she would come up to Lancaster with me until she had to leave in the October. I found some truly horrible digs in Morecambe, a sort of flat above a garage, but that is where we settled for the time she was in England. We found out where the 'scene' was and plunged in. In retrospect, I look on this time as my adolescence. So many lovely women, a great social scene in the town and the uni, intense political awareness-raising and activities – demos, conferences, workshops.

Abby had to leave – we agreed to the orthodoxy of the times, not to be monogamous but to stay loving friends and see what happened. After she left, I was approached by the women who lived in two of the big lesbian houses with an offer to move in. I was bowled over by this group of 'normal' women, not role-playing or aping heterosexual norms; and to develop a political understanding to match what had just been gut feelings for so long was fantastic. I threw myself into everything wholeheartedly. A friend cut my hair for me – standard short, spiky dyke cut, but for the first time in my life and at the grand old age of thirty, I actually looked good – how I had wanted to look for years. Abby continued to write to me. She was getting into all sorts of relationships, which was quite hard for me to deal with, but gave me permission to do the same. I did go over to the States to visit her. She was in a steady relationship by then, and I think they were worried I would upset their apple cart, but while it was great to see her and the USA, I didn't want to start anything up again.

In some ways I did bow to peer pressure in Lancaster and did some things that I now regret: starting smoking; drinking too much; developing a simple-minded separatism... I wanted so much to be part of this group that I was pretty ungrounded and did not behave in a way I would now. One issue was the potential to be lovers with every woman around rather than developing friendships. When I say it was my adolescence, this is what I mean. There was also a kind of ranking: those women who had 'chosen' to be lesbians out of some sort of political correctness, and those of us who felt we had not had a choice. I found this deeply depressing. I also had a lot of flak because I wanted to work again when I got my degree; a few women had a go at me for 'wanting money'. My feelings were that it was fine being politically radical in a ghetto, but there was a whole world out there which needed changing and that is what I wanted to do.

Life in London

In 1979 I moved to London to train as a Media Resources Officer (MRO) for the Inner London Education Authority. I got a place in a lesbian household in Camberwell – aargh, those excruciating interviews for new housemates! I turned up on the first day of training to discover I was the only woman on the course. Not what I had expected at all, and certainly in at the deep end in terms of changing the world. I survived and got a job at a girls' comprehensive in Hackney, where I lived in another shared house with three other women. This was very nice, as it immediately gave me access to a new group of lesbian friends.

This school had predominantly women staff; some were lesbians and I was out to everybody from the start. We had a lively women's group who did a lot of anti-sexist and anti-racist work and I was in an excellent position to support their work with the students. I believe that those of us who were out were good role models for the lesbian students, too. We were also actively involved in the Greenham Common protest and in the anti-racist campaigns of the time.

There was a local group for other people working as MROs in east London and here I met my first women doing the job. Four of us set up a women's group within the MRO grade and ran a conference for other women in the grade. That developed into training workshops on equalities – race, gender, sexuality, disability and class. It was an immensely productive and creative time and I felt incredibly lucky to be doing this sort of work. I did not want to separate the different parts of me off into, say, work, sex life, politics and living in London; and doing the work I was doing, it all became possible. I spent seven years at this school, completely out and enjoying every minute of it. I had several lovers, but only one at a time! My relationships were slightly chaotic, but one in particular, although it only lasted for a few years as a sexual relationship, ultimately lasted as my truest friendship: over thirty years and still going. I seemed unable to sustain relationships for more than two or three years. I decided to go into therapy and try to sort myself out. It was through this work that I realised how cut off from my true feelings I was.

In 1987, I moved to a new job at a further education college in North London. This was around the time of the shameful Clause 28, preventing local authorities from 'promoting' homosexuality. In fact, what this pathetic and bigoted law did was to galvanise the whole of the gay community, and radical men and women worked together for the first time since the 70s. Although our protest failed to prevent the clause becoming law, and although a lot of teachers thought it meant they could not teach about sexuality in a balanced and inclusive way, it also gave rise to a lot of excellent work with school and college governors and showed what a large and powerful group we are. During all these ten years, I was completely out, at work and everywhere else. I made a point of selling myself as a role model in my applications and at interview and didn't have a problem getting the jobs I wanted. Without vanity, I know I changed the institutions I worked in, and hopefully helped a few students along the way.

During this time, I had a major change in my life. From years of living in collective houses, I was actually able to buy my own flat and live by myself. It was wonderful. I lived there for eighteen years. After three years at the college, I got a job as an advisory teacher in an East London borough. Although this was theoretically a promotion, and although it was interesting, it wasn't really what I wanted to be doing. An opportunity came to set up the learning resources department in a brand new secondary school in Tower Hamlets, so I applied and got it. But this was a time when Thatcher's policies had really started to bite and a lot of the collective politics that had gone on were under attack – as were teachers in London. Also, for the first time, I was the only out lesbian in school, and although a few gay men joined the school as it grew, I really missed having that sort of connection at work.

I was exhausted

At this point I had a few years when I didn't have a sexual relationship. In retrospect, I think I was quite depressed. Work was demanding and my social life fell away somewhat. I then met a woman quite a few years younger than me who had a young son (he was six). It felt great to be in a relationship again, and great too to be sexual, and for a year or so it was wonderful, although her ex-husband was a real problem for all of us. But my partner would not or could not commit to me, and her mental health was deteriorating. After five years of intense pressure, I realised that I could not cope with the load I had taken on. I became very stressed and anxious, lost my sense of humour, felt angry and impatient, culminating in going into school one day and bursting into tears. I had a very supportive GP, who recognised the signs of stress and told me to take time off. From being an easy-going, happy, productive, sociable and energetic person, I was a frightened, timid, miserable wreck.

It took nearly five months before I could go back to work, but although I put some strategies into place to make life a bit easier, my previous years of enjoyment and enthusiasm for my work had all but disappeared. I was exhausted and my life consisted only of work and recovering enough to go to work again. I became a virtual recluse apart from work and saw very few people.

Then, in 2003, I was diagnosed with anal cancer. Although it was a great shock and I had many moments of utter fear, two really important things happened as a result of the diagnosis. One was that I could not go through this alone; I would really need my friends. And, luckily for me, they were brilliant: I was able to open up to them and accept their help in a way I had never done previously. The second was that I made a decision that if I survived, I would give up work for good. In the event, school were really supportive of me getting early retirement, although the borough made me fight for it, and only finally agreed on the very last day of me being paid any salary by them.

Finding my authentic self

When my treatment had finished and I started to recover, I went through a rather Pollyanna-ish phase of loving life utterly; it was so good to be alive, to be feeling better and, most of all, to be free. Having the time to do one thing at a time, to look after my health, was a complete joy. I had also seen a healer since my recovery, and that turned into talking therapy, which I still do on a fortnightly basis. It was really time to find my authentic self. I now feel more open to any opportunity that may present itself, and less inclined to be dutiful. I had always known that when I retired I would move out of London; I am a passionate gardener and love to be outside as much as possible, swim in the sea and rivers and walk the countryside. While I was wondering where to go, a friend in Essex said, 'Why not come here, where you have friends?' So I did. It was important to have at least a couple of other lesbians living in the same place and to move to a place with some sort of cultural life going on.

This is that place. I have nine lesbian friends living here, have made several other straight friends and am involved in a lot of local activities. I live by myself quite happily still and find it hard, now, to imagine having another sexual relationship – although I still feel like a sexual being. In a way, forming and sustaining real friendships has become more important to me. The most important thing to me now is to be outside, roaming the coast and estuaries and countryside and tending my garden. I really hope for good health for as long as possible, and to hang on to my independence. I absolutely dread being forced once more into institutional living – the shadow of boarding school still looms large. I am aware that my body is slower and creakier, and that I sometimes sleep in the afternoon, but I do more now to maintain my health than I have done since my sporting years: swimming, gardening and walking, eating well, growing my own food and being outside as much as possible.

Growing up without role models was difficult. So many of us grew up thinking we were the only ones, and I hope my generation of feminists and lesbians have done our bit to change that for those who follow, but there is something to be said for striking your own path, and I feel quite proud of that. Thinking over my life as a lesbian, I guess the major change has been from my younger days, when I lived in constant fear of being discovered, to now when I assume everyone must know who I am, and I celebrate and am completely secure in my identity. What other people think is not my problem any more. Being a lesbian has underpinned a very great deal, but now it is just taken for granted.

VAL

I was born in May 1944. I have no idea who my natural parents were. At the age of nine months I was adopted by a railway engine driver and his wife, who lived in Leeds. He was fifty years old; she was forty and a housewife. Just after my sixth birthday, George died, leaving my mother a single parent. She had to go out to work, and I became what was known as a 'latchkey kid'. The first meal I had to make for myself during the school holidays was baked beans on toast. On her return home, she asked how I had managed. Apparently, my reply was, 'The toast was okay, but I made a bugger of the beans!' I had dropped them onto the coconut matting in the kitchen.

When I was ten, I came home from primary school one day to be told by my mother that she was getting married the day after to 'Uncle John', a family friend who was widowed with three grownup children. They resented my mother as much as I resented him. The fact that I was very unhappy for years was no fault of John's. He was a good stepfather to me, kind, caring and never interfering between me and my mother. My typical teenage behaviour was not improved when I discovered, at the age of fifteen, that I was adopted. I had never been told and the shock can be imagined.

It was around that age that I had my first lesbian experience. I had always been a tomboy and had no interest in the things other girls my age were interested in, such as clothes, makeup, music or boys. I had passed my scholarship (the eleven-plus) and attended a high school in the centre of Leeds. It was primarily a commercial high school and if one did not shine academically then the commercial stream was where one ended up, learning typing and shorthand. I passed five O levels and left school to begin work in an office, which I hated. I left there to work at the Post Office as a telephonist, merely passing time, however, until I could join the Royal Air Force. In those days girls did not leave home unless to go into the forces or nursing, where accommodation came with the job.

Double bunking

I loved the RAF. I knew that I would have to keep my sexual orientation hidden from the hierarchy, but we girls soon found each other and formed our own little cliques. Unfortunately, I was discovered in someone else's bed – 'double bunking', we called it. There was no official term for it, because it did not exist as far as the upper ranks were concerned. They did not want anyone discharged for being gay, because that would have led to the belief that the forces were a hotbed of such practices. (They were, but not to be acknowledged!) I was discharged as 'medically unfit for Air Force service'.

I was not allowed to return to my own barracks to get my belongings; I was told that they would be sent to me when I sent my uniform back to them. I was left wearing my working blues: battledress and beetle-crushers. I had one week's wages – four pounds – and a ticket to London. How I was supposed to obtain civilian clothes, I had no idea; even my knickers were Air Force issue. I got on the train to London and spent some time there. I was eighteen years old, and I had lost everything: my job, my friends, my home. I swam in a sea of despair, keeping out of serious trouble only because of women I met on the gay scene who were very kind to me.

Eventually I ended up back in Leeds and in due course, on the rebound, I agreed to marry a man, much older than me, who was kind and who understood me and who loved me despite my sexual preferences. We married and I became pregnant, giving birth to my daughter when I was twenty-two. Three years later, my husband died very suddenly and I became a single parent myself. I was glad enough then of my mother's help and we were somewhat reconciled. Stepfather John became a very loving and loved grandad to my girl.

I went into nursing, working as a psychiatric nurse at one of those old huge institutions from Victorian times, and found myself once again with a friendship group who were lesbian. It is strange how certain professions seem to attract gay people. I lived for five years with a woman I met at the first gay club to open in Leeds. We nearly split up after one year, but she got so upset I agreed she could stay. I was not, however, faithful to her and we grew further and further apart, until eventually she plucked up courage to fend for herself and moved out. Six months later, Rita moved in with me and we were together for almost thirty years, until her death in 2002.

I moved to Scotland after Rita died. I was devastated at her death. I was able to nurse her at home with the help of our GP and the district nurses, until she died at home, quietly and without pain, as I held her hand. I became ill and it was obvious to my loved ones that I was not going to cope on my own so my family asked me to move up to Scotland to live with them. My daughter, her husband and their daughter lived in Perthshire, and then they moved to a small village on the Moray Firth. Here my grandson was born, five years ago. I am devoted to my two grandchildren.

Interesting times

If I had not been a lesbian, I think life might have been easier in some ways, but much less interesting. Due to my lesbianism, I have met some very interesting people, been in some interesting organisations and become involved in some very interesting situations. (Interesting, as in enjoyable – but also in the way the Chinese saying has it: 'May you live in interesting times!')

I became involved with the Campaign for Homosexual Equality in the early 70s, and with gay societies at Leeds University, where I trained for the certificate of qualification in social work, which led to me becoming a probation officer. I was out at work from the start, because I had decided that I would not deny Rita. When everyone talked about their husband, wife or partner, I was not going to fudge the pronouns and I wanted her to be part of my life in all its aspects. I never had any trouble at work. Some people did have trouble, and at a conference of the National Association of Probation Officers in Southport, I became a founder member of a group for homosexuals, which went through several names before we settled on Lesbians and Gay Men in Probation. I worked with them until my retirement.

I still spend a lot of time with different organisations now. In the last five days, I have driven to Inverness (round trip, seventy miles) four times, for meetings of different groups, both gay and straight. One of them, Moray LGBT, was formed last year and we meet three times a month for drinks or a meal. I also attend Girlzone in Inverness, a casual group of lesbians who meet for lunch.

Times have changed; but I still work at trying to change attitudes, even though there is now much more acceptance due to civil partnerships and so on. I am a founder member of Highland Rainbow Folk, a group working with Age Scotland and the Terrence Higgins Trust to educate and enlighten members of the caring professions for older people. Our next performance is for the Humanist Society of Scotland, Highland Group, of which I am a committee member. The one after that is for LGBT History Month when once again we will take over the Town House in Inverness.

I cannot imagine what life would have been like if I had not been lesbian, because it has never really crossed my mind that I could be anything else. When I was young I did not know that it was possible for women to love women – except for myself, and I thought I was the only one. Despite thinking that, I was not about to be a shrinking violet, so I decided to attempt seduction whenever I got the chance. That was after my first time, when, because of missing the last bus home, I had to sleep with a school friend. She was compliant and we shared a few encounters for the last year of our school life, although it was purely physical – there was no emotional connection. I completely lost touch with her until I saw her in the street years later, only to find that she too had joined the RAF and was now openly lesbian – at least when in mufti away from her base!

Hopes and fears for the future? I am not well physically, but I hope to be able to continue to get about, with my disability allowance and Motability Scheme car. I am content with my life and my achievements, and I enjoy being involved with so many different groups and so many really special people.

~

Sadly, because we lived at opposite ends of Britain, Val and I never met; she sent me this account of her life by email early in 2011. So I was shocked to hear of her death the following year, at the age of only 68. Her story is included here with the permission of her daughter.

JT

CRUNCHY

I was a little bit of a tomboy, right from the beginning. My father's fault, entirely! He had vertigo and couldn't get up the apple trees, so he'd send me up there to pick all the apples. And anything else that wanted doing: if the roof was leaking, I had to go up through the skylight, see what was blocking it, and all that. When he rewired the house, he'd put me down underneath the floorboards and say, 'Here's the wire, now go along and you hand it up to me.' He was a carpenter and coach-builder, so I spent lots of time in his workshop at the bottom of the garden as well; and it was just lovely, really. So, all those practical things, and yet I liked cooking with my mother as well.

I was born in 1939. I was an only child but, in the house in Devon that we lived in, we lived upstairs and my father's sister and her children lived downstairs, so they were like my sisters, luckily. It was my grandmother's house and she lived there too. When she died, my father took the house on, and my mother did bed and breakfast then, instead of going out charring, which she used to do, to get me my school uniform and stuff like that. It was a lovely, happy childhood.

I had my first girlfriends at grammar school. There were two other lesbians at school with me, and the reason we knew we were lesbians was that we just thought we should have been boys, really. When we were in the third form, there was someone in the sixth form who came to school every day with this very manly looking woman in a mac; she used to stride along. And they wrote their life stories and lent it to us! Unfortunately, my mother found it, and she nearly took it up to school, but she ripped it all up instead. So I got into trouble with them, because I don't think they had a copy of it. But that's how we first knew what lesbians were. That was the word we used, 'lesbian': it wasn't 'gay' or anything like that.

When we were playing hockey, the three of us would yell out things, because we didn't think anybody else understood: 'Hey, Lez, here, pass it over!' One day the gym mistress came and got us all and said, 'You're not to use that word, it's not very nice. You're not to use it on the hockey field.'

We three all had our little girlfriends at school. It was amazing really. I remember there was one of my girlfriends, she would run up to me and say, 'Crunchy, so-and-so tried to kiss me!' I'd say, 'I'll sort her out in a minute.' It was terrible really, and we used to laugh about it of course, the three of us. I'd say, 'She says you tried to kiss her.' 'I did, she wouldn't let me though,' she'd say. It was just stuff like that...

I was always like it. I even fancied my Sunday School teacher, when I was very, very young. I know I used to blush when she came near – I think I must have been seven or eight. And I'd do anything for them, I really would. I was terrible at school, because if there were mistresses at school that I fancied, I'd follow them home, pushing my pushbike, carrying their cases – and they would try and stop me, but that's how I was and that's how I grew up. I used to play with boys, but I didn't want one as a boyfriend. I was their equal, I used to feel. So it was just always somebody at school. One of them knitted me a pair of gloves for Christmas, because we went carol singing and she said my hand was cold when she was holding it. I wasn't a bad-looking kid, actually: I had dark curly hair, and I was cheeky and got on well. I was very good at sport, you see: I was in all the school teams, I was school games captain and stuff like that, and I was happy.

Joining the Army

I didn't really want to leave school, I'd had such a good time there, but I decided to go to Bedford College and teach PE. Then our two games mistresses went off to some sort of county games and this poor old soul came to do a locum. She must have only been about forty, but she had shorts like a pleated skirt down round her knees, and horn-rimmed glasses, and she wasn't a bit like they were. We played her up dreadfully. Well, it suddenly came to me: 'That could be me one day.' And I went right off it. Completely. So then I thought, 'Well, I could be a nurse,' and I enjoyed that, once I was. I was seventeen and a half when I went nursing.

I tried to have a boyfriend, because I thought maybe I should, and there was this nice fellow. I had a motorbike and I said, 'I'll give you a lift home.' He was on the back of my motorbike, with me with the L-plates off, and we got picked up by the police. So I thought, 'I'll stick with him till he pays my fine!' But he was a nice fellow, actually, and never tried anything much – gave me a little kiss now and again. He used to take me in his boat on the river, salmon fishing, stuff like that. We had fun and that was nice, but I knew I didn't want *much* to do with him.

I did orthopaedic nursing. I did my prelims, but then people started to die, and I couldn't cope with it. So I thought, 'I've had enough of this, I'm not going to do nursing any more.' And I thought, 'I know what I want to do, I'll go into the Army.' I went along to the recruiting office to have a look, and they said, 'You've got to get your parents' permission.' Well, my parents wouldn't sign for me to go in the Army, no. As far as they were concerned, it was the worst thing I could have done. So I waited till I was nineteen, when I wouldn't have to get their signatures, and then I went down and signed on. I looked at what the options were and I saw 'physical training instructor'. I thought, 'How lovely, I'll do that.' I had to have a second choice, so I thought, 'I'll be a vehicle mechanic, that'll be all right. Very butch.' Because that's how I looked then: I was very thin, I had dark curly hair, I was very sporty, and that's how I identified at the time. So that's what happened. I went into the Army, and I passed out to go to the school of physical training. I loved it all. I had a good time in the Army. I went to Cyprus and did lots of lovely things there, skiing and everything, in the Troodos Mountains...

I had a girlfriend while I was in the Army. But you had to be very careful. I nearly got thrown out twice. And I only got off because basically I lied my back teeth off. You had to lie, you really had to. The first time was when I was still in training: I'd only just joined the bloody Army. I'd had my hair cut really short, and I had a married woman back home who was my girlfriend then. Naughty woman, she was! I had to get away from her – it was like joining the Foreign Legion – because her husband nearly found out. She used to send me these letters with a big lipstick kiss on the back, with 'SWALK' written on them. Luckily, the two women who were in charge of my year, the sergeant and the corporal, were having a relationship.

They got me in and said, 'Is this from your girlfriend?' and I said, 'Yes.'

They said, 'Well, you know what it's like in the Army.'

'No, I don't know.'

So they told me that you're not allowed to, you can get sacked. Well, I'd heard a hint of it, from a couple of people that had been in the Territorial Army, but I thought it was if you had a relationship with somebody who was in there. Anyway, they said, 'Write and tell her not to put that on the back, and we'll make sure that we get your letters first.' It was very good of them.

A close shave

Now, one of them had a motorbike. She was fiddling around with it one day and I said, 'You want your carburettor cleared.' So, I repaired it, and she said, 'Well, give it a trial run.'

You couldn't actually go off camp, to start with, but I did – and the bloody sergeant major saw me. I had an Army shirt on, and an old pair of trousers of mine that I'd brought with me, and she had me up for it. She didn't like me, anyway, because I had short hair and she thought I was a dyke. (I reckon she might have been one herself, but we never knew.) The charge was 'riding a motorbike around the camp in mixed uniform' and I had to go before the commanding officer.

Of course, my mates were all worried, and they pressed my uniform, they buffed my shoes up, got me all ready. Then I'm *left-right, left-right*, in before the OC. She looked at me, and looked at what I'd done, driving a motorbike around the camp, and she immediately thought I was gay.

She said, 'I don't know that we want young tomboys in the Women's Royal Army Corps. We want young *ladies*.'

And I felt like saying to her, 'Well, fuck that!' but the corporal was looking at me, the one who'd buffed up my uniform and talked to me about my letter, and she was making a warning face. So I said, 'Sorry Ma'am. I didn't mean to do it, Ma'am.'

And she said, 'Well, I'll give you another chance, before I decide whether to sign your papers to go to the Army School of Physical Training. But until then I will *not* sign them. See me in a week's time, and you've got to look very different.'

Bloody cheek! But I did. I went to the hairdresser's: it was a girl I'd been at school with, who was also in the Army, but didn't know that I was gay. Well, she got all these bits of hair, and she put it all in grips, to make it so it looked more girlie. And somebody else did my face. I couldn't open my eyes for makeup, it was terrible. Every morning we'd have to get up early to do it. It was awful, my eyes would stick together, I had lipstick on, I'd never had makeup on like this in my life.

So for the week beforehand, I'd been stuck on parade like this: trying to open my eyes, and feeling as if I had no hair on the top because it was all pulled out to the side, with my beret in the middle, so it looked as if I had lots of hair. The day I had to go in, *left-right, left-right*, to see her, I was looking like that. They're always writing away when you go in, and then they look up at you, and she looked up at me and nearly died.

'Ooh,' she said, 'Private, you do look different! Do you feel different?'

'Oh, I do Ma'am, I really do,' I said, 'I do feel different.'

Anyway, she said, 'I have great pleasure in signing your papers to go to the Army School of Physical Training.' So she signed.

And they got hold of me, shoved my head in a basin of water, scrubbed me, got all this makeup off me, and we all had a big old rave-up. 'Cause she'd done it then, see? And at the PT school they didn't want me to wear all that makeup, anyway. I had a lovely time there. While I was in training, I didn't have a girlfriend, except the one at home, but I had a couple of relationships at the PT school.

An even closer shave

The second time that I nearly got thrown out was in Cyprus. I had a girlfriend then, and she used to come into my room, and we used to talk poetry a lot and stuff like that, and it was really nice. I had my own room, because I was a corporal and then a sergeant, when I was in Cyprus. She was a private – she was in the next room to me.

I was on duty one night when one of the RAF girls (who was also gay) went missing – and we found her at the bottom of a cliff. It was me that saw her at the bottom of the cliff when we all went looking. I shouted, 'Quick, quick, quick!' She wasn't dead, but she'd got drunk or something and slipped over.

Anyway, because I was on duty that night and she had been down to our canteen area, they were questioning me: had I known her and did I know that she was a lesbian? And I said no. They thought I might know something about it because I'd been on duty that night when she'd gone missing. I can't remember the exact details of it all now, but they searched my room. They found some letters – from the same girl still, from home. I used to see her when I got home. It was over four years she'd been writing, and they worked out that she was my girlfriend. She'd written, 'The love that I have is all that I have,' and stuff like that...

The next thing was, they said, 'We want the Special Investigations Board in.' They weren't interested any more about this poor bloody woman who'd fallen down the cliff, they were interested in *my* history, then. I was under investigation. Somebody must have told them that my best friend was a private, and she was in the next room to me, so they thought that was a bit suspicious, too. I'd given her a Picasso picture out of one of my books that she quite liked.

I thought, 'My God, I'm going to be thrown out!' Again. Luckily for us, there were two Military Police blokes who were gay. They used to take us off to dinners and stuff that they had to go to; they knew we were gay.

So I said to this SIB bloke, 'Can you let me, or will you, phone my boyfriend?'

He said, 'Who's your boyfriend?'

I gave his name, and I said, 'Military Police at Paphos.'

Anyway, they phoned him, and he came down. 'Are you all right?' he said.

I said, 'Yes, but try and find Mary if you can, because she's all upset. They're making terrible remarks about us, just because we're going out together, as friends.'

And it all got dropped, just because I managed to think of that. Now wasn't that lucky?

It was awful in the forces in those days. Just awful. I'm talking late 50s, early 60s, because I came out of the Army in 1963. I didn't have *many* relationships when I was in the Army, only a couple, and apart from those incidents I was okay. I can laugh at the first one now, but the second one was a bit worrying. Because you get a 'red book' when you leave the Army that is your reference, and if it's not signed perfectly, you could never get a job. That's what happened to some of the poor women that went with a 'dishonourable discharge'. How dare they? 'Dishonourable discharge'! That's what it was called. When I got out, I met up again with two friends who'd had that, and they had an awful job to get work.

But I got a good report, luckily, and off I went, to train as a remedial gymnast. It was a conversion course for ex-services physical training instructors. They called them 'remedial gymnasts', which was exactly the same as a physiotherapist, really, but you didn't do electrical therapy. You could do it in two years if you'd been a PT instructor; I suppose they thought if I could control service personnel, I'd be all right with people that had poorly backs and knees. So I did it in two years and passed well. I was a mature student of twenty-three by then.

Keeping it secret

I came down to London immediately I qualified, and ended up in a general hospital in North London. I was living in a bedsit, and it was most unhappy, really, because it was a house with all bedsits, so I used to hear people, but I never used to see anybody. And I'd had people all round me before. It was really difficult. I was ill the second week I was at the hospital, and couldn't go to work, because I get bad chest infections. There was no phone there or anything, and I thought, I'm going to die. I'm just going to die in this little room. Anyway, one of the orderlies, who lived nearby, actually came and got in somehow, banged on my door and I let her in, and she looked after me, got me food. There are lovely people around. I got on well there; and then I took a job in neurology, and that's how I ended up head of services for neurology.

I semi-retired when I was fifty-five, because you could, and I worked for a housing charity, as their adviser for putting in rails and things like that. Then I got head-hunted by a health authority that ran a day centre, and I ended up working there. So I didn't really retire until I was sixty, and then I retired completely. I'd had enough. My mum was ill then and I bought a place in the West Country (an 'immobile home', we called it, on a residential site) near my mum, and I looked after her then. I stayed down there until she died, and then I came back here. And that's about it, really.

I never felt that being gay was wrong, because I was enjoying any relationship that I might have been in. But I was *worried* most of the time, and I had to keep it a secret. My father, I'm sure, knew from quite an early age, because he told me he did, when I was in a relationship in London. But my mother never found out until she was in her seventies. And then she was fine. I'm sure she always knew in a way, and would always stick up for me. No, I didn't feel it was wrong at all. I never, ever wished that I was different, either. I've done all right work-wise, and I've had a happy life, I suppose; and, apart from that time in the Army, I'd not been singled out as being different, really. All the time I was in the Health Service, I had to be *careful*, though.

The love of my life

I'd had little affairs but not serious ones, until the first person that I lived with. Rosita was a little Spanish woman I met when I was working at a gay club. I used to work behind the bar at the Robin Hood, then at the Raven.[3] You used to look at people from behind the bar, and there was this nice little woman so I went up to her and said, 'Hello, would you like to come to a party with me on Saturday?' As you would. And she said yes. And from that day on, we went out together, and we eventually lived together. Then I was very naughty and I went and had an affair, and we split up.

But we kept in touch, and then we went back together again; and that was lucky, because she was ill then and I hadn't realised how ill she was. In between, I'd had two other relationships. I'd lived with one of them, who was very young (she told me she was nineteen and I told her I was thirty-nine, but she was only eighteen, and I was forty). I'm still in touch with her – and her mum! We lived together for four years. And then I had another relationship, though I didn't live with her.

But I always kept in touch with Rosita, so when Joy and I split up, I went round there even more, because she only lived round the corner from here. I said, 'Are you not working now?' Because she had no money or anything. It turned out it was because she *couldn't* work. The blinking doctor had told her, 'Get on back to work, you're just putting on weight,' and she had a bloody great *swelling*.

Anyway, I took over, there. I got the phone put back on and everything else, and I said, 'Come on, we're going to get a second opinion.' So we did. He sent her off to Hammersmith Hospital and she was diagnosed. They said they'd operate, and they opened her up and found that it was everywhere, you know – she had a great big metastasis.

It was awful. I couldn't cope with it. In that way I was no

good to her at all, because I just used to burst out crying. But she wouldn't face it, though they told her many times, with me there, that she only had about a year to live. Awful. Just terrible; but I was so pleased that my life worked out so that I was around to look after her, because she wouldn't have wanted anybody else bathing her and stuff like that.

So I was off work a lot when Rosita was ill, and what they do then is they make you see staff health. Well, I had this wonderful doctor. She gave me this form to fill in: 'Do you think you're depressed?' Well, yes, yes, yes, all the way down!

She was a bit funny with me to start with. She said, 'My goodness, you've ticked a lot. Come in!' Then she said, '*Why* do you think you're depressed?'

And I immediately came out with it: 'My girlfriend's dying.'

She was so lovely. She came out from her desk and hugged me. Oh, she was lovely. She said, 'Tell me all about it.' Of course, I was crying my eyes out by now, and she said, 'Right, you're not to go back to work. I'm signing you off now, with reactive depression. And you're not to go back to work at all, you go home and look after her.' What a wonderful woman.

Rosita used to laugh, because I was on permanent sick leave then, and I used to get a Giro sent to me, and she used to say, 'You got your pay cheque, eh?' and I'd say 'Yes!' I'd stay round there most of the time; she was only a couple of roads over. I built her a little greenhouse, a little lean-to greenhouse so she could go out, because she loved plants. I was used to helping people, because I'm a physio. We used to get in the shower together, over at her place, and I used to get drenched; I'd make her laugh. I had to get a stool to get her in, and a stool to get her out.

Social Services were quite good really. They'd come round and they'd say, 'Now then, would you like someone to help you with your shopping?'

'No, the Crunchy, she do my shopping,' she'd say.

And they'd say, 'Right, what about cleaning?'

'Oh yes. The Crunchy, she no good cleaning!' she'd say.

Then it was, 'What about cooking?'

'No, no, the Crunchy's a good cook.'

'And what about bathing?'

'No, Crunchy put me in the shower,' she'd say.

And it was lovely, really. It was sad, but in a way it was lovely. Eventually, because I'd been off sick for so long – a good six months, I think it was – I had to go and see another doctor. He said, 'Well, why are you off sick?'

I said, 'I've got reactive depression, because my girlfriend's dying.' And then I cried again, because every time I talked about it I cried, it was just terrible. And he signed me off, saying, yes, I should be off sick. I've never had money off the state in my life before, apart from that.

Eventually, Rosita just got worse and worse. Then, one day, I was round there and it was just awful. She was crying out with pain – I'm sure I overdosed her, really, on morphine. I wouldn't be a bit surprised, because she was in so much pain. And then she said, 'I think I need to go to hospital.' So we called the ambulance and off we went. She was lying on the stretcher and she said, 'I am going for the angels.' Oh, it was awful. Terrible.

The sister at the hospital was lovely. She said, 'Well, who are you?' and I said, 'I'm her relationship, we're a gay couple.' And she put her arm round me – she was a lovely sister, lovely – she put her arm round me, and they took her up to the ward. Unfortunately, I was out having a fag when Rosita actually died. I saw her immediately afterwards, and she was still warm.

I went to her funeral eventually. She was buried in Spain. You never think you'll get over things like that and you don't, you never really get over it. You never think about it without getting sad. It was about sixteen, seventeen years ago now. It might even be more than that. I still know two people that knew her, and I still see them regularly. They'll say, 'Remember that time, with Spanish Rosita?' Because she was so funny, she had such humour, and her language used to get mixed up. She'd ring up friends of ours in Yorkshire, and she'd say 'Hello? Put your skating rollers on, that Crunchy's having a party!' And somebody would be 'nap kipped', not kidnapped, if we were looking at the news. She was lovely. She was the love of my life, actually. We used to share everything.

Glad to be gay

I didn't have a proper relationship after that, until very recently. I was on my own for years: I was sixty-nine when Maureen turned up. I didn't keep thinking that I *wanted* to – I certainly don't want to live with anyone again, and I don't want anyone to live here with me again. But that was good with Maureen, because she didn't want anyone to live with her either. And she was only twenty minutes away. It didn't work out, though, and it's hit me hard, I think. But I'm looking to the future, I'm going to Eastbourne for the tennis, and you never know who I might meet down there. I'd like to have someone special in my life again, now that Maureen's whetted my appetite. And I've had a reply to my advert that I put in the Kenric[4] magazine, but she lives in the Midlands – too far. And there's this woman that fancies me; keeps ringing me up and everything. But I don't fancy anybody at the moment, really. It's too soon. I'm not saying that I won't. I'm incorrigible!

I keep busy. I play badminton once a week, and for almost a year now I've done watercolour painting and I really enjoy that. I do voluntary work taking people shopping. I'm a member of the Tate Gallery, so I go to exhibitions now and again, and I can take a friend with me. I'm also a member of Kew Gardens, so I can go there and take a friend. Apart from that, I socialise. The local Kenric group meets once a month; we've got a newsletter, and we have events and outings. And of course, in summertime we go over to the Ladies' Pond, and we have barbecues. I've been in that group for years; sometimes there's only half a dozen there, other times maybe twenty will turn up. After Rosita died, it was very nice to mix with people there. I found two people in the group who knew her, as well, which was lovely.

So I'm all right, you know, I'm okay. I'm glad I'm gay, and I think I always have been really, even when I was frightened and a bit worried about being gay. I didn't ever want to be heterosexual, really. There are lots of people who've been married, bless them; they've been married all that time, and they did it really because they thought they ought to. Well, but for the grace of God, that could have been you or me. Especially me, being brought up where I was. My goodness, it was like a village down there. If I hadn't gone away, who knows, I might have got married because I thought it was the thing to do. But I went and joined the Foreign Legion, didn't I? Got away! So that was all right.

4

WIVES AND MOTHERS

As part of my original PhD research, I carried out a large-scale survey of lesbians over sixty in the UK. Nearly four hundred women filled in the questionnaire and just over half of them said they had been married to a man. In the over-eighty age group, this rose to two-thirds, which perhaps reflects the strength of social expectations at the time when they were growing up.

The most common reason for getting married, given by sixty percent of those who had done so, was simply that 'it was the expected thing'. More than ten percent said they married mainly because they wanted children. Some respondents hinted that they might not have married at all if they had had a better understanding of their own sexuality; but others did realise, and married anyway. A very small minority (five percent) said they had married because they thought it would make them heterosexual. But it is also important to note that four out of ten of those who married said that they did so because they were in love with their husbands. Not many of us have been always or only lesbian.

So my research participants included women who had been happily married and women who had been unhappily married; women who had had significant and loving relationships with men, and women who had had unimportant or downright bad relationships with men; women who had only ever had relationships with other women; and women who claimed a lesbian identity although they had never had sexual relations with anyone.

Would it be more accurate to describe some of these women as bisexual? My study had set out specifically to recruit self-identified lesbians, which might be one reason why only a tiny minority of respondents said they would use the word 'bisexual' to describe themselves, even though the large majority had had relationships with men at some time in their lives.

Current research suggests that women's sexual orientation is potentially fluid, but not all the women in my study would agree. When asked, 'Do you feel that being homosexual / lesbian is your choice?' one in five said that, for them, it was not a choice at all. However, nearly a third said they felt there was some element of choice involved, and nearly half said it was entirely their choice. Some, like Julia (Chapter 6), do see their sexuality as potentially fluid, and feel they have chosen one path over another. Others, like Marguerite (Chapter 2), whose lives might appear to an outsider as bisexual narratives, believe that they were 'always gay' and either suppressed the knowledge or took time to understand it.

The next three stories give a flavour of what it was like to be married when you knew you were really gay. The reasons the narrators give are typical: Jude, like many other women in her situation, married partly to escape the guilt and misery of knowing she was a lesbian, and partly to please her mother. Linda married because she was pregnant and forced to marry the baby's father. Brenda married because, in her words, 'This is what you do.' These three stories, told with honesty and humour, involve struggle and pain. Yet, as with so many of my contributors, they also demonstrate our power to save our own lives.

JT

~

JUDE

New Year's Eve, 1944. If I'd been the first baby born in the new year, my mother would have won five pounds (which was a lot of money in those days); but I was born at ten to twelve. So our relationship as mother and daughter got off on a difficult note, even then. I'm the eldest, and there's five years between each of us. My brother is the youngest, the *boy* in the family, and he arrived just as I was going to school. I was extremely jealous of him.

Maybe it's because my brother was so adored that I thought perhaps I should be a boy. I used to think, 'Oh, wouldn't it be good!' When I was very young, I used to try and pee like a man. Of course, it didn't work. But I always felt more comfortable in male clothes. That's another thing my mother didn't like. I was allowed a pair of tartan trews, but apart from that I had to wear skirts. I remember cutting up my liberty bodice and my vests and throwing them away, because I didn't want to wear them.

The best thing was having my hair cut, though. I went to the hairdresser's on my own, because we lived just round the corner, and I said to them, 'My mother says I can have my hair cut. She'll pay you when she sees you.' They said, 'Yes, how would you like it?' and I said 'Short!' I daren't repeat what happened when I got home. My father had a cane, which he kept in the kitchen cupboard, and I got a caning for that, at the age of about five or six. That's what they did in households like ours. Very strict, Welsh, brought up Chapel; children should be seen and not heard. You had to have the correct table manners and all that sort of thing. My mother wasn't particularly loving; she was always busy. They rowed and she'd throw stuff at him. I'd sit on the stairs crying, because of them rowing and all the threats to kill each other. It was crazy. I just couldn't cope with it.

My father was first of all in the RAF, and then he was in the reserves, and then he got a teaching job. We had to come out of

Wales because there wasn't enough work, as everyone came out of the forces together, after the war. So he came up to England, to get a teaching job. He was the 'boy made good' out of the Valleys. Everyone in his family had been coal miners, but he won a scholarship to grammar school and his mother borrowed money to take up the scholarship, and to put him through college after that. And he did extremely well. He became a head teacher; in fact he was one of the youngest head teachers in his area. We moved when I was about three, I think. I missed all my cousins and so on, because there were quite a few of us, and we all used to play together. We used to go back every holiday, for six weeks we'd go back down to Wales. Dad would go off on RAF reserve training, and I'd go down to Wales with my mother, on a 'pouff-pouff', as I called it. It was the Red Dragon; it would go steaming out of Paddington and I'd be sick with excitement, nearly. And of course, then I'd be able to play and be with people all day long... because I felt very lonely as a child. I still feel as if I've gone home, when I go back to Wales.

I had a lot of people in my friendship circle at primary school, but I never made a really close friend. I knew a lot of people, and it was the boys I got on most with. I have to say I was a good-looking girl, with blonde ringlets, and the girls I think were maybe jealous of me. Anyway, I found them quite spiteful, so I felt safer with the boys. I didn't get on very well at that primary school. I was bored, to be honest. When I was about nine, my father took me into his school.

I remember very distinctly something that happened soon after I went there. It just sticks out in my head. I was out on the playing field with a group of girls and they were all looking at their breasts: 'Are you growing any yet?' We were comparing them, and talking about the latest dolls, the latest this and the latest that. And I'm thinking, 'You're boring. Is there something wrong with me? This is *so boring*. I don't want to be doing this.' I got up and said, 'I can't be bothered with all this stuff!' and I went off and played football with the boys. I can remember the exact spot on the playing field where I thought, 'There's something different about you...'

Lovesick most of the time

When I went on to secondary school, my feeling of being an outsider increased. I loved it, but I had so many crushes that I was lovesick most of the time, all the way through the school. I had crushes on girls in the fifth year and the sixth year, never on anyone my age, always older. And when I reflect back on it, most of the teachers were living together, though we never cottoned on to what that was about. To be honest, in those days the word 'lesbian' wasn't uttered. I didn't know what it was, until somebody told me one day. Even then, I'd heard that you grew out of it. I don't know where I'd heard that, but apparently you grew out of it. Well, there's just no way *I* was growing out of it: I'm still having crushes! I had these terrible *mooning* times, especially at the weekend when I wasn't seeing the object of my desire. So I buried myself in sport. I was horrified, to be honest, to think that I was like that. When I was about thirteen, it was announced that gay men would no longer go to prison. I didn't know quite what the law was with women, but I remember thinking, 'Oh, thank God for that, I won't have to go to prison!' I remember thinking that. I realised that it was something you had to keep very quiet about. So, I was in denial and I had boyfriends. At one point, when I was sixteen, I probably had six on the go at once. I was intrigued, I suppose, as to what went on; but in love, no. No way. There was only one I thought I had a lot of feeling for. We were going to get engaged, but then I went to college and I thought, no.

I was absolutely sport mad, and I knew from early in the lower sixth where I was going – PE college. My mother was furious. 'I'm not having my daughter go to PE college, it's full of funny people, they're all, you know...' She meant everyone in PE college was gay. She must have known about me, but she wouldn't actually say it. 'Don't you get involved with any woman, just think of your father, what it could do to his career!' That stuck in my head forever.

Anyway, off I went – with great glee because my mother disapproved of it so much – and I was one of the first intake, one of the first thirty to get there. And, wow, all those women! It was like going to heaven, though not being able to do anything, because it was still so frowned on. After a term, we were allowed to choose who we roomed with. There was a girl that I really fancied, Hilary – I spent most of my time there with her – and I thought, 'Ooh, yes.' But it was a three in a room. Now, you try and do fumbling while there's a third person around! But she didn't move away, let's put it like that: she didn't move away. I thought, 'Oh, this is bliss!' But we couldn't do anything much about it.

So we got to the second year, and we shared a room, just the two of us. But some more students came in then, another intake, and one of them had a crush on Hilary, and one had a crush on me, and they spent their whole time sitting in our room, so we still couldn't do anything. It was the most bizarre situation. I knew a lot was going on – other people were less scared than me. *Everyone* knew a lot was going on, and those people that were straight, one or two of them would almost blackmail you: 'I know all about you. I could blow the whistle any time.' So nothing much happened, really, at college. Actually, I was seduced by Hilary's mother. She let me sleep with her and didn't mind a cuddle. And because she was so nice to me, I was completely smitten with her, then, as well.

That ended when college finished. That's one of the reasons I felt so down when I came out of college. I lost all that camaraderie, as well – being at a girls' PE college and playing in a team is wonderful, if you're into that sort of thing. But then I set myself adrift. I was still in denial and extremely lonely. My first teaching job was down in Brighton, away from everybody. I chose the hardest situation to put myself in: teaching in a secondary modern school, straight out of college. The principal told me that Cheltenham Grammar wanted somebody, and said, 'Don't you think it would be more appropriate for you to apply for that post?' I said, 'No, because I don't want to teach people that want to learn, I want to teach people that don't want to learn.' I'd already done special education as a second subject at college.

Why had God picked me?

There was another lesbian on the staff at my first school, but
that made my life very difficult, because the object of my
desire was the object of her desire as well. It made life very
uncomfortable for me, to say the least. Then I hurt my back.
And then, well, I had a bit of a breakdown. I was so lonely.
There was no one, no one at all I could tell anything to, about
how I felt. And I still thought it was *wrong*. It was terrible: why
had God picked me to be like that?

I did go to the doctor eventually, and I did tell him that I
thought I was gay, though I said, 'Please don't write it down in
the notes.'

He said, 'Look, it doesn't matter.'

I said, 'It does to me.'

He said, 'Some people go up one path and find it doesn't
work for them, so they take another path, and that one works.'
He was a firm friend of mine forever after that, he was so lovely.

So anyway, he sent me off to Hove Hospital for some seeing-
to in the brain: counselling and anti-depressants. I was still
going out with fellas, but I didn't want them touching me any
more than was necessary, and the thought of anything else
horrified me. Dressing in dresses, or frills of any sort, I felt as
though someone had put drag on me. It just wasn't working.

Eventually, I found someone: she was another PE teacher
from a different school. We had an absolute zinger of a sex
life then. It was wonderful! Except that I'd already taken to
drink when I first went to Brighton, to fill in the hours between
getting off the bus and getting back on the bus in the morning.
I saw no one, and where I was living was not a good area to go
out on your own, one way and another; so I'd taken to buying
cheap sherry, to try and tell myself that I was normal. Then I'd
toddle off to school. Eventually I had this affair, but there was
a third person in the flat again, so it was very hushed up, we
had to stop making any sounds while we were making love, in
case the girl next door could hear us. But then quite soon my

NOW YOU SEE ME

girlfriend started to be abusive, especially when we'd been out and had a couple of drinks. She'd say, 'You're as queer as they come. I didn't want to be queer, and you've made me!' and stuff like that. In the end I thought, 'This can't go on. I'd better end it.' I didn't like the abuse.

Doing what Mother wanted

So that was my big fling, I suppose. I felt so awful afterwards. My mother was always on about, 'Isn't it time you had a husband? Isn't it time you got married? Isn't it time you had children, blah-di-blah-di-blah.' And I thought, 'Well, I've got to look around for someone to settle down with. If I do what my mother says, I'll be a lot happier. I'll be able to keep this under wraps. It's not worked out.'

So eventually I set out to do just that, and I found the man who became my husband. He was as boring as hell, and I didn't think he'd be too demanding. But then there was twenty years of marriage. It was terrible. For me, it was terrible, and it went on for twenty years. It was only when the boys were settled, at eighteen, that I decided I couldn't stick this any longer. For a start, I did not want that thing in me again! It made me feel totally degraded, violated, upset... I didn't like the mess, I didn't like any of it. I had to get drunk to have any sex with him. I can remember the day I conceived the twins. We went to the pub on the Sunday lunchtime, came home, obviously he'd had too many, I managed to let him make love to me – let him, that's the operative word. Then we made love again straight afterwards because he was really into it. And then, after that, I don't think I very often let him go all the way. We could go so far, and then I'd just freeze. I'd try not to make it obvious.

I had the boys then, and they became my life. They were both very ill when they were little, so there was that excuse then, because I was too busy to have sex. And then David got mumps and cephalitis, and was left severely brain-damaged. Also, I went back to teaching part-time; and then my father died, and I had my mother to look after as well, because she became senile at sixty-two, when he died. She became totally dependent on me. That meant I had my husband, who was as lazy as hell; two boys, one gifted, one disabled; and my mother. Oh, and we had my mother-in-law living with us as well. And there was just a succession of repressed emotions, really. It was dreadful. But I thought deeply about my marriage vows, and I thought, I'm not going to break them. And I must say that was when I started drinking quite heavily. Not during the day, but during the evening. I couldn't cope with it all.

Taken notice of, at last

It went on for twenty years. And then, well, I was chased: stalked, I think! Where I was teaching, we had a woman caretaker. She'd been through a couple of marriages, and all of a sudden she became extremely pally with me. And I thought, 'This is nice.' Anyway, eventually I just fell hook, line and sinker – someone had taken notice of me at last. And we got into a relationship. I was deeply in love with this woman. I lent her my car and gave her food parcels and so on, because her second husband had walked out on her. Around that time, I took my mother, my disabled son (his brother had left home by now) and my husband to Menorca for a holiday. And that was the worst fortnight of my life, I think. I spent half the time trying to hide from my husband and my mother, and get down to the phone box to phone Carol in England. I don't know how I got through that fortnight, I really don't.

When I came back, I just left home. I couldn't take any more. I took my son back to his residential centre and didn't go back. I left everything. I went to Carol's house, which was a small bungalow next to the school. So then came the point where I had to tell the head teacher that I'd moved into the school bungalow. I said it was because my husband and I were going to get a divorce, and Carol had offered me a bed, because she was also trying to get a divorce. I don't think she fell for that, for one minute.

Carol's husband was definitely in the local underworld. He

eventually found out that we were having an affair – this next bit is terrible – and my husband conspired with this man to get my son to say what was going on at the bungalow and to get him to sign it. Well, my son hadn't the capacity to do that. I went mad down the phone. I said, 'You say one more thing like that and you'll never see either of the boys again. You will not do that! You cannot use my son as a weapon against me. That is vile.'

We had the police around a lot: things went missing from the house, they were obviously being stolen. We had bricks through the window. And my beloved car that was only a few months old, not paid for even, a beautiful Sierra, was torched. Two of her sons moved out – they wouldn't stay – and went to live with their father, who was her first husband. One of them, who was eight, was in my class at school. You can't visualise a more difficult scenario than that. *And* I was a school governor! Even then, I thought, 'If I really come out and say what's going on, I'll lose my job.' I still thought that. The head was very difficult. She did her best to get me out: they had to cut a member of staff and she picked on me, even though the criteria that the education authority always used was 'last in, first out'. I was head of the special needs department, not only in that school but also in the area, and I didn't want to lose any of that. All very difficult.

So Carol and I were having this rampant affair. It had blips in it every now and then, when she was extremely abusive to me, and I couldn't work out what it was all about. It always seemed to be after we'd had what I'd call a really good sex session. I'd apologise, thinking it was my fault, and then she'd be all right for a while again. Now, I think she didn't love me at all. My mother had gone absolutely mad when she found out and told me all sorts of things that are best not repeated. She'd depended on me after Dad died, and now she'd lost me, and she hated Carol. That was part of the reason I moved away.

Then I hurt my back, falling over a dip in the pavement in the town centre. The pain was just incredible. I was fifty-one and I couldn't work any more because of it. So we thought,

'Let's make a fresh start.' I managed to get a sick package, a lump sum and my pension, and that was when we moved down to Wales. And when I got divorced, of course, I got about half the house and everything else. I had all this money in the bank and I thought, 'Well, I don't need to work. I'll have a pension coming in.' So we got down to Wales and decided we'd buy a house there. And from that moment on, Carol became extremely abusive, all the time. She made sure that all my family were ostracised and kept out of my life. I never saw my sister, I never saw my brother, she wouldn't have my mother around. (Though that was no bad thing, because she and my mother used to fight, shout at each other, and that kind of confrontation I can't take. I had enough of that when my mother was married to my father and she'd throw stuff at him.)

Eventually, having fleeced me of a hundred thousand pounds, Carol ran off with someone else. And then she wanted half the house as well. My solicitor put paid to that – but then she became very, very unpleasant and threatened to throw me down the stairs. She moved her new girlfriend in with us, under my nose, and was having an affair with her, in our house. I could hear them, even though I kept turning the music up... And in the end they went off together.

A good woman

It promised to be so good, it ended up so bitterly. I never got over that, really. Five years in counselling. What was it someone said? It's like grief, the grief of a death, with insult. Grief with insult. I used to cry all the time. I couldn't go out. But in the end, I found on the internet someone I could talk to, Jo. We met on one of these sites for older people and spent our time talking to each other, her trying to help me through. Eventually we met and decided that we were for each other. She was still married, then, but she'd been wondering about herself... She'd already had her hair cut very short, and she was questioning, wondering what was wrong with her. And we clicked. Well, honestly, I seduced her. I thought, 'Oh God, I can't be bothered with hanging around, nowadays! What's the point?' I'd found out that you can be as good as you like, but you won't be happy. So then I resolved that, come sixty, I'd be as naughty as I could be. And I'm still working on it.

Looking back to when I was young, it was such a different time. If it had been like it is now, I wouldn't have felt that I had to get married. But then, I suppose I wouldn't have had the boys. Once I was out, I realised, after a while, 'Oh, the world hasn't caved in because I'm out. We haven't had terrible thunderstorms, and God hasn't wreaked havoc in my life. Except to take my son...' That's another thing you see, my whole belief in religion was shaken to bits. I was quite a big God-botherer at one point. But then I thought, 'Well, he's not looking after me, is he? He's dealt me all these cards, plus having two children that were both severely ill when they were little, then one was permanently disabled and brain-damaged – what kind of deck of cards is this?'

And the hatred of oneself that we were taught; how awful that was! It's at a very deep level, but I think the more I do, like volunteering for LGBT causes and so forth, the more comfortable I am with myself, because I'm putting something back. And now, when I come across people that talk that homophobic crap, it riles me to such an extent, I get really angry. Did I ask for their opinion? Did I say 'Could you tell me what you think about me?' I don't remember asking for that. I didn't choose to be gay. How could you choose to be a pariah? I tried not to be gay; it didn't work. So I don't think there's a choice. I think it's hereditary. Thinking back, perhaps my father's father was gay. And my brother is, as well. Two out of three children – don't tell me that's coincidental!

I moved in with Jo twelve years ago now. It was after my disabled son died. I was devastated. It was just terrible. I was still living in Wales at the time and Jo said, 'Come and live here.' Well, I was here for a long weekend every week, anyway – I was working part-time then, so I could come up for Thursday, Friday, Saturday, Sunday. So I moved in. She's a good woman, Jo: her heart's in the right place. And in the last few years before my mother died, I finally got close to *her*, too. I was able to look after her, and get her to understand me, because she never understood me before: she just thought I was an awkward cow. And we'd only just achieved it when she died. In fact, what she said was, 'You're wonderful. You're a brick.'

LINDA

I was born in the City Hospital in Nottingham, in 1945. My dad was in the Army, and my mam worked at a factory making hairnets. I've been epileptic since I were ten. It wasn't all that bad, it was just, at odd times, I'd just go, but at other times I was all right. I knew from an early age that I was gay. I was just twelve years old when I had the inkling, because I was fancying women. There was a couple of my friends at school, they were gay, and they used to go to this gay group in town and I went there once. There was a lot of people there and I got on with them, but they said to me that, with me being so young, I'd got to make my own mind up. They said, 'You might be bisexual,' but I wasn't. I knew.

I went to school till I was fourteen and a half, then I went to work at the hairnet factory. I ended up leaving there, because I didn't like it, and I went to work with the dogs, at the racetrack. Greyhounds. I used to feed 'em, take 'em round the track, take 'em out, and when they were racing at night time, I had a uniform on, with a tag to say which dog I was bringing round. It were quite interesting. I liked that, except you had to change your clothes, of course, because you got all dog stuff on them, but I quite enjoyed it. Then I left there and I worked at a cafe. I was a washer-up there. I enjoyed that and all, until I got electrocuted. There was a big electric washer, for washing the pots. Somebody'd spilled water onto the mains, and of course when I went to switch it on, I got a shock and it knocked me for six. Lucky I didn't get killed there! But I was all right.

Running away

There was a lot of upset in our house. I couldn't get on with people, I couldn't even get on with my sister; I couldn't get on with anybody. And it was me having to do everything. My sister did nothing. I were doing the pots, doing the dinner, making the beds, making the fire first thing in the morning, making sure the meal was done when Mam came home from work, and if I missed cleaning somewhere, I used to get a belt round the ear-hole. It distressed me, so I ended up running away from home. I was just turned seventeen. I ended up in a mental hospital, then. The nurse there said that I could stay until I got my mind back together, because I couldn't get my mind sorted out. I couldn't leave until they said I was all right to be on my own.

I came out of there when I were twenty-one. And then I went home, and I still couldn't stay there, so I got myself pregnant, for no reason at all. I just did that to get away from the house. I think it was stress more than anything, just to get away from the house. Because I knew if I got pregnant, my mam wouldn't think it were funny. And she forced me into getting married to him, and that was the biggest mistake of my life. Every time my husband used to come near me, I used to cringe, and I used to say to him, 'I'll see you later,' and bugger off out.

I lost my first baby, that little girl... then I had Peter, and Stan, and then I lost a little boy at three month old. But still I couldn't get to grips with it, that I didn't really want my husband. I just didn't want him. It was a feeling, that every time he came near me, I just used to freeze up. I had to be drunk to get pregnant, and I never normally drank. That's how I did it, I had to be really drunk. Then I started to think, 'Well, why do I shut myself out?' So I was talking to my dad, and my dad said have a word with my mam. I had a word with my mam, and she said, 'Oh, you can't be, you've got kids!' I said, 'Mother, there's a lot of lesbians who's got kids. It doesn't mean, because I've got children, I'm not gay.' But my mam wouldn't accept it, because she was a Catholic. She couldn't get it round her head. But when she was dying, she told me to go out and find a girl, to go out and find a partner.

I stayed with my husband, but I didn't stay with him, because I was out more than near him. Every time he'd come in, I went out. And then I used to come back about four o'clock in the morning, I used to sleep on the settee, I never went near the bed, near him. I'd sleep on the settee and when he got up in the morning he used to make me a cup of coffee. One morning, I was with a girl – I'd brought a girl home with me! I was twenty-two.

My first girlfriend, I met her at the Dog and Partridge. I was with her about three or four year. Then she found somebody else. She was bisexual and I said to her, 'Well, I can't be doing with it. I can't be doing with you wanting a man as well as a woman, that's not going in my head.' I found out she'd got pregnant with this bloke.

I said to her, 'Well, you can have the baby, you know...'

And she said, 'Yeah, but I love him.'

I said, 'Well go to him, if you want him. Because it's not worth me staying with you. Because, you know, I'd get upset.'

I went to visit her, when she had the baby, and she wanted me back, because the bloke apparently had buggered off and left her. I didn't think that was funny. I thought, 'That's bang out of order. He waits till she's had the baby and then leaves her.'

She said, 'Will you come back to me?'

But I said, 'No, I can't, I've got somebody else.' I'd found somebody else, you see. And we got on together.

My sister passed away when she were fifty-four; she had a heart attack at a very young age. And then my girlfriend, she passed away. She had a heart attack, just after my sister. I was on my own for over three years then. I couldn't stand another relationship, after that one had gone. And then I met this other girl, Dee. She was full butch; she'd never, ever been with a man. She was more *like* a man than anything. She used to do gardening work, like making posts, for kids, goal posts and all that sort of stuff. She was ever so intelligent. But because she was that way, and didn't ever have kiddies, her mam was very awkward with her. She said, 'If you can't give me grandkids...' and they didn't get on.

After a year or two, me and her moved away. After I left my husband, I'd been living at my mam's flat. But my mam had died, and then my dad. They both died in the flat. And everywhere I was turning, I was seeing my mam or my dad. So I couldn't stick in the house. So me and Dee made arrangements to go to live at the seaside. We lived there about eleven years. We had a good life there.

It doesn't bother people

I've been quite happy being gay. I mean, I've found a lot of friends who were gay, and I've mixed with straight people. So it doesn't bother me. And it doesn't bother other people knowing that I'm gay. Well, most of the time it doesn't. There was one time me and Dee was in the pub, and these lads came over, and because we were sitting in the pub together, and we both wore trousers, they automatically said, 'Are you gay? Are you lesbians?'

So my reply was to them, 'Why, are *you* gay?' Straight out. And I don't think he liked it. So I said to him, 'Well, why come over and interrupt me and my friend talking?'

He said, 'Well, you're two women together.'

I said, 'Excuse me, but you've just walked in with your mates, and I assume they're men that you've walked in with?'

So he says, 'Yeah.'

So I says, 'You've walked in with your four mates. Are they gay?' I said, 'Don't be stupid and ask us a stupid question.' I said, 'Go back to your mates, and if they want to know if we're gay, just give them the answer, and then if they've got anything to say tell them to come over and I'll give them some more answers!'

They didn't like it. But you get some, who're just a bit... well, just because you're wearing a shirt and trousers, automatically you're gay. And like I said to 'em, straight out, I said, 'Look, there's plenty of women in here who're wearing shirts and trousers. It doesn't mean that those people who come in here dressed like that are automatically gay.'

So he says, 'What do you mean?'

I said, 'Well, I wear trousers, I've got a poorly leg. But that doesn't mean because I'm wearing trousers I'm automatically gay. I said, 'You could have offended me, I could have been with my sister!'

Which I was once, I was with my sister. We went to Skeggy once, Mablethorpe, and we went in this pub. Now my sister, she was very bonny. The pub was part gay, part straight – and my sister, she was straight as a damn, you know, but she loved me, because we're sisters.

And this bloke happened to say, not to me but to my sister, 'Oi, you lesbian get, what you doing in here?'

And the landlord heard him. (Now, *he* were gay.)

I went over to him, and I says, 'Excuse me, are you referring to me or my friend?'

(Now, you could tell we were sisters, we were very alike.)

So he said, 'We don't like lesbians in this pub.'

I said, 'Excuse me, love, how do you know we're gay? If you can't tell that that's my sister, get yourself some glasses!'

So he turned round and he says, 'Oh yes, you look alike, don't you?'

I said, 'We do, love. That happens to be my sister. And you don't think I'd go with my sister, do you?' I said, 'I may be gay, but she's definitely not. She's got a husband.'

But he was on and on and on. So I'd had enough. I went up to him and I said, 'Either leave this pub, or you're gonna wear that pint!'

So the landlord looked at me.

I said, 'I've had enough.'

So he says, 'You and whose army?'

I just picked his pint up and I said, 'Here you are, wear it! Now bugger off.'

And his missus, she was gob-smacked, because she daren't say nowt to him. She wouldn't say boo to a goose to him. Well, she just busted out laughing.

And he said to her, 'I don't find that funny. She has soaked me!'

So the landlord just went up to him and asked him to leave, because he was really bugging me. I used to be a regular in that pub and they all knew me – I was in their pool team. Most of us was gay who were playing in the pool team, even the landlady. It was a right laugh. We all had to have the same suit on, the uniform for the team. It was really good. Everybody knew us, everybody was friendly, they wasn't nasty. You just get the odd ones who don't like gays.

Coming back

I was with Dee about fourteen years, until she died. And that broke my heart. I miss her a lot. She'd made a request that if anything happened to her, she was to be buried at sea – cremated, and her ashes put into the sea. We were living by the sea, then. So I granted it her. I done her wish for her. I'll never get over her, because I really loved her, and I don't think I could ever get another partner as good as what she was. I seem to bump into people who want to go with men as well as women, and I can't. I can't get my head round that. She was just for women and that's it. It's just over four year now, since she died. So it's not long. But I couldn't go with anybody else now, because I can't see a future with anybody else.

I stayed there for another year, but I couldn't cope because everywhere I were going, she was there. Like, if I used to go into the pub, instead of buying just one pint, I used to buy two. It was all like that – I couldn't cope. Everywhere I went people would say to me, 'How's Dee?' And I'd say, 'She's passed away,' and I'd crack up again. So I decided to come back.

I was in a hostel to start with – that's a homeless place. And then I came to the housing association. You come there when you're homeless and you move on from there, like, and get a little place. I was there just over three and a half years. It's usually not supposed to be that long. And now I'm in a block of flats. I've been there for just over four months. I've got my own little flat: I've got my own bedroom, my own bathroom, toilet, I've got my own little kitchen, my own living room. I love it. We play bingo on a Tuesday night. That's a laugh, and all! I've got my head back together now, and I've been quite contented. I go out with Val, she's the voluntary worker over there: we go to bingo, and the rest of the time I mix with the other people in the place. I think they've got an idea what I am.

I don't think they'd bother, because they're all getting on like me anyhow, there are not many young ones in there. They're all sixties and seventies. I don't turn round and broadcast it; but the staff know.

I've still got gay friends round here. I went to the old pub, some of them still go in there. There's quite a few on 'em who's passed away, but I still see some of them. I only go there if I'm going into town, I'll probably nip in and just get myself an orange, because I don't drink when I'm on my mobility scooter. Get an orange, and probably see them, but otherwise I don't bother. Like I say, I'm quite content as I am. I mean, you can't get any younger, now, can you? I'm quite happy with the way I am, getting older. And I've been quite happy being gay. I've found a lot of friends who were gay and I've mixed with straight people. So it doesn't bother me; and it doesn't bother other people knowing that I'm gay.

Set in my ways

People say to me, 'Why don't you find somebody else?' But I don't want anybody else, because I'm quite contented in my own mind. I did meet somebody when I came back, but she was only twenty-seven. She had a little lad. He was ever so nice. I sometimes see her – once or twice at Gay Pride – but I don't think I could cope with anybody else now. I've got set in my own little ways, cooking for myself and doing everything for myself, I've set my sights on my own way. Except, if I win the lottery I'll be getting myself a bungalow. I always do the lottery. Well, it's only a pound. I might put a couple of pounds, or I might put three pound on it, it all depends. But I always do the same numbers. Val, my friend, who's a temporary worker there, she said if she won the lottery what she'd really like is a bungalow, and I said, 'Don't worry, if I win the lottery I'll get *two.*'

If you look back to the old days, you had to be careful then, very careful. Doesn't matter where you went, you had to be careful. We couldn't go splodging [snogging] in some pubs.

Well, you'd get the odd ones who did, and they used to get beat up outside. Especially if you went into a straight pub. A lot on 'em think they're big, they go into a straight pub and they think, 'Oh, the landlord won't mind if I kiss my girlfriend,' but they do. Because some on 'em's against it. But now, I don't think there's that many who'd mind. When you go to Gay Pride, now, you see all these little kiddies, babies and that, mams and dads bring them! And you know, like they say to them, it's a fact of life. It's the way it is now. We've got equal rights now, haven't we?

BRENDA

I was born in a seaside town in Kent. My parents were living with my maternal grandparents, who ran a hotel, and I was born there in February 1948. My birth caused all sorts of upsets, apparently, because I wasn't planned, and my grandmother said it was a ruse to get out of the work. It caused a rift and meant that we had to go and live with my paternal grandmother in South London, which was a total change from the seaside! We were in the top front bedroom, the whole four of us. And the only water was down the back of the house, in the scullery, so my mum brought all the water up for the nappies – she had two of us in nappies. That was hard. She badgered the council to get rehoused, and they were saying, 'No, no, you're living with family and they are happy to have you there.' In the end my granny had to say that she wanted us out. My mother took that and she plagued the council every week, sat there waiting for them to see us, and they moved us onto a council estate. My father, who worked in a biscuit factory, had a heart attack when I was seven. Because we lived in a top-floor flat with no lifts, we were rehoused to a ground-floor flat on another estate in Blackheath. You'd think it was a bit more posh there, wouldn't you? But really it wasn't.

So I wasn't particularly planned, or wanted, and also I think I knew from very early on that there was this whole thing about 'boys was best'. From a very early age, I wanted to be a boy. One of my earliest recollections is about getting up before anybody else – God knows what time that was – and sitting by the embers of the fire in my pyjamas, pretending to be a cowboy. I was... four, perhaps? I put my cowboy hat on, and my walking shoes, because they were my boots, and I was strutting. I remember strutting, because I'd got the spurs on, sort of making them clink. That sort of thing. Like the cowboys we used to watch on the telly.

I also remember, when I was about five, a policeman knocking on the door – he filled the door – and my mother opening the door, and the policeman saying something to my mother, and my mother ushering us into the back room, saying, 'I will deal with this.' I didn't think any more of it at that point. Then it happened again, when I was about nine, after we'd moved. Because I was older, I was more aware of what it was about. It was something to do with my dad. My dad had said something to a little boy on the estate, the little boy had complained, the mother or the father had gone to the police. I remember my mum saying, 'No, no, that can't be right, he's a married man.' I didn't think any more about it, then.

I had lots of colds. I was always snotty. I failed my eleven-plus, but I got a 'governor's place' at the grammar school, because they thought if I'd been well, I would have passed.

The school rang my mother up and said, 'She could go to the grammar.'

And my father said, 'You don't educate girls, what's the point? It'll cost us money,' because he was Victorian. He was quite a bit older than my mother (well, probably the same gap as between me and Jo, really).

But my mother fought him and said, 'Indeed we will, and I will go back to work to pay for the uniform.'

And that's what happened. It was a co-ed grammar. We got to the stage, from when we were about eleven or twelve, where people had parties for their birthdays, and all the kids from our year or form would go. But they always ended up with snogging sessions, where the boys would stay where they were round the room, and the girls would move about – ten minutes of a snog with this one, and then round you'd go. I used to have these fantasies, when I was around thirteen or fourteen, that I was going to be a much better lover than some of these boys, because, bloody hell, I could kiss a whole lot better than they could.

I didn't get on with my dad, probably because I wasn't a boy. I left home at eighteen and went off to college. My brother had already gone, he married early, so our parents were just at home together and it must have been awful. My mum had got to the point where she'd had enough and she wanted out. She moved out, and remarried in '68, when I was twenty. And then there was this little bit of a hoo-hah... It would appear that my dad had importuned a fifteen-year-old boy (which is probably older than some of the others were) and the boy had obviously gone to the police and complained. Dad had to appear in court. He lost his job and got put on probation. And I suddenly thought, 'Ah, it must have been going on for bloody years, then. Half my childhood, this has been going on!' By that time, I'd left home and I just thought, 'Silly old sod, serves you right.' But I think that somehow in my head I got what Dad was doing mixed up with how I am. In my head, homosexuality and paedophilia got all mixed up. And it took me absolutely *years* to put a name to my dad. It took me years to put the term 'paedophile' next to my father and to take that away from sexuality, my sexuality. It took me a long time to untangle that, and to decide that it was okay for me to be how I am. I was forty by the time I thought, 'Fuck it, I've got to look into this!'

The Swinging Sixties

So, I went to college. I met a friend on the first day, who I'm still friendly with, which is nice, and she took me under her wing. She was slightly older than me, and certainly more worldly-wise than I was at that time. It was the Swinging Sixties, and God, look what was happening around me! I remember this amazing party, where people were getting high on this and high on that... I'd never seen a drug or anything in my life. There was LSD, there was marijuana, there was the whole kit and caboodle, and there's me in my pink up-to-the neck pyjamas in a little sleeping bag on the sofa, surrounded by all these people bonking, thinking, 'For God's sake! What the hell is going on here?' And that was a really rude awakening to the Swinging Sixties.

Ellen and I shared a flat. When she married her boyfriend, I had to come along too, because otherwise I was going to be homeless. He was living in this great big flat in Harrow, so I just came along and had one of the bedrooms. There were quite a lot of people living in this flat and I just picked up the one that was left. That's who I fell in love with and married. That's how we did it then. You tried everybody's friends out – it was like going round the circle snogging everybody else to find the best one, when we were kids. We got married in '71. And I didn't give it a thought, I just thought, 'This is what you do.' And I knew I wanted children, so again, that was what I did. I kept putting everything away... I knew it was there, because I had these thoughts, I had these little fantasies, but I thought, 'No, no, no, I can't do that. It's not something you do, it's just not acceptable.' It took me a long time to get over that. So, I was a married woman and I just accepted that that's how life was. I trained as a social worker. We were married for five years before I had my first child. She was about two and a half when we had our second.

All mums together

I've always surrounded myself with women and when you become a mum that's very easy to do, because there's all these other young mums around. So then I got into the local ladies' group. It was coffee mornings, that sort of thing, and we were all mums together. Then there was a thing called Network, which was all about bringing young mums with pre-school age children together. I was on the committee and we had great fun – Easter egg hunts and all those types of things for the kids – and it was lovely. But then again, I was surrounded by all these women: my daily life revolved around taking the kids to nursery, going to So-and-so's for coffee, or whatever, and just chin-wagging about all and everything. Very nice. I really enjoyed that part of my life, with all these women. And again, 'it' was there, but I put it to one side and thought, 'No. These are all happily married women with small children. You don't rock people's boats and it would certainly rock yours. Leave well alone.'

There was a woman – she'd got four kids – and one day I

put my arm round her, because I'm a very touchy-feely person.

And she said, 'Oh, do you cuddle?'

I said, 'Yes, I cuddle!'

'Oh, lovely. I love cuddling.'

And I thought, 'Well, okay, I'll cuddle you.'

Then, one evening, her husband was away and she said, 'Oh, do come round and keep me company for the evening.'

Well, we ended up in bed together, though I was fully clothed and she was in her nightie. And she said, 'Oh, do give me a cuddle.'

We were cuddling and I thought, 'What the fuck am I doing?'

She said to me, 'Do you think you might be…?'

I said, 'Well I've no idea, I haven't thought about it' – as you lie through your teeth. And that was that. I just went home.

The next thing I know is, her husband's ringing me up and warning me off. After that, I remember having this dream: I could see the front of my house with the word 'QUEER' in big white letters, dripping. And I'm thinking, 'Fucking hell, what have I done now?' So, back to 'keep your head down' time. But that was the start. It was me thinking, 'What am I going to do about this, then?'

A few years after that, another woman from the same group, who'd just had a divorce, said to me, 'Could you come and help me decorate the downstairs loo?'

So I'm wallpapering this loo, and as I'm slapping paste on, she said, 'I've been having fantasies about you.'

And I'm thinking 'What? Whoa, here we go!'

She said, 'I'm having fantasies about you and I'm just wondering what it would be like.'

So I'm saying, 'Well, what do you want to do about this?'

So she said, 'Well, I'd like to try it.'

I thought, 'Well, it's being offered, and there's not going to be anybody warning me off this time, is there? So let's do it.' And I thoroughly enjoyed that. I thought, 'Look what I've been missing! This is the way to go.' Even though, actually, it was only me doing something; she didn't reciprocate. But even so I thought, 'Oh God, yeah!' It really got me juices flowing.

I was in my late thirties. And then, it was almost like a rush of things happening, because there was her and I, for an occasional, when she fancied and when I could get away either for an evening or overnight; and then, I'm at work and there was this other woman... I'm working in a special school as a social worker, and this woman came to a meeting. And I could feel there was some sort of chemistry between us, so I thought, 'Bloody hell, here we go!' And she's reciprocating, she's giving me the eye, and I'm thinking, 'Okay, what's this about?'

We were trying to rehome a boy into a school plus a foster placement, I think, and she was his social worker. We took this boy off on this trip and we were picked up in a van from the station. Well, we were in the back of this mini-van, and we were sitting and jostling, and wow! I don't really know how to describe it, it was just that the chemistry was so sort of – wow! And I remember thinking, 'What's this about?'

She said 'Shall we go for lunch after we've dropped him off where he's got to go?' and I said, 'Yes, all right.'

So we found this little country pub somewhere – and out she comes with, 'How long have you known about this?'

And I'm saying, 'Known about what?'

'That you're a lesbian!'

And I'm saying, 'Am I?'

'Yes, don't you know?'

And I'm saying, 'Well, not really, but I'm just about getting there. I mean, I'm married. I've got two kids.'

And she says, 'Well I was married, and I've got two. And it might take you a bit longer, but you're definitely, definite.' And she said, 'Can I see you again?'

And I'm like, 'Well, yeah.' I was around about my fortieth birthday, then.

If I don't do something now...

The year before, in the October, my very best friend, my soul mate, died – committed suicide. I'd had absolutely no idea that was in his head. I was so devastated over that, it galvanised me into thinking, 'What the fuck are you doing, Brenda? Life is too sodding short, you don't know what's around the corner, you don't know when your time's up – if this is who you are, for God's sake do something about it and find out!' So I made a phone call to the London Lesbian and Gay Switchboard.[1] And they said, 'Well, there's a local gay and lesbian group, and they meet at this pub on a Monday.' They gave me the name of the female contact and I rang her up.

I was thinking, 'This probably marks the end of your marriage. Is this worth it?' And I'm thinking, 'I need to bloody know. I'm forty, I'm part way there, for God's sake, if I don't do something now I'm never going to do it.'

So anyway, I go along to the first night of this thing, where there's all these women, and I find, I find that I'm just totally different, I'm outgoing, I'm just loving it, I'm lapping it up. People asking me about myself, then some woman came up and just spilled her life story out to me – I don't know whether I'd got 'social worker' written on my collar or something – and I'm thinking, 'Wow, this is, oh, amazing!' And that was it. I kept going. I didn't know then my husband had followed me. I'd told him I was off to a discussion meeting, a women's discussion group – because I'd enjoyed the ladies' group, we'd had discussion meetings there, so I thought, 'Well, I'll tell him that, that'll sort it.' It clearly didn't, though. He knew something was up.

Then, through this group, I met a woman and we became a couple. She was my 'bit on the side' of my marriage. She was closeted – she was still living at home – and it suited both of us, really. She was seven years younger than me. We were a couple for five or six years. But it got to the point where I wanted more than this closeted relationship. She'd moved out of home, she'd got herself a little flat, that became our little sort of lesbian garden of paradise. We could be ourselves there. We had friendships with people that we'd met through the pub and the group, because we didn't do anything other than go to the lesbian pubs and meet lesbian friends, so it was a lesbian life – but it was totally closeted. Nobody knew about it. Our families didn't know about it, people at work didn't. I got to a point where I was thinking, 'If this is who I am, then I need to just embrace this, and I've got to go with this, and if I lose people along the way...'

My biggest worry was, 'What if my kids don't understand?' By this time they were adolescent – my daughter was sixteen and my son was thirteen, fourteen. So I thought, 'Well, I don't quite know what to do about it.' By which time, I think Paul, my husband, had sussed. And by '92, I thought, I just can't do this any more.

So I said to him, 'That's it, our marriage is over, this is how I am. I'm really very sorry, but...'

He said, 'Fine, I thought as much. What are we going to do? What about the kids?' He said, 'You know I don't want to.' Basically, he was happy as we'd been, I think.

So I said, 'Well okay, we'll live under the same roof, but really that's it.' We had enough room so that he could have his own room and I could have mine, so that was that, really.

Spinning plates

Then in '93, I met Jo. She just said to me one day, 'There's something about you.' I was out at work by this time, so she knew that I was in a relationship with the bit on the side of my marriage. And she was so... She wasn't out, but then I don't think she would even really put a lesbian label on herself – and she was much more sexual than I was, she'd had lots of male partners, and I'd only ever had the one. She became the bit on the side of the bit on the side. And then I had about four months of *total madness*. It was like juggling plates, spinning plates – I'd got this child, that child, him at home, her, and *this* her... I was running ragged, thinking, 'I can't do this, I just can't do this!'

So, I told Christine that I was with Jo. That caused all sorts of upsets, and I'm not good with upsets, not upsets that I've caused, anyway. It was bad enough breaking my husband's heart and saying, 'I'm sorry dear, but I don't want this any more,' and then with a partner of five or six years, to break *her* heart. It was like I was jumping off some precipice, out of a relationship that was safe, and a husband who was still there, and I was living still with my kids, into a relationship where it was just going to blow everything apart, because Jo is just so – out there. She wanted to be open and honest and up there and in your face, and... I had this sort of false start with telling Christine, the other woman, that this was the end, and then I went back to Christine in the February. But Jo said to me, 'You've got to make a decision one way or the other.' She went off to India for three weeks, during which time I was to decide. I know she came back thinking, 'That's it, I'm not holding out any more hope for that.' But when she came back, I went to see her and said, 'It's you I want. This is where I want to be.'

And that's where we are, really. That was in '94. So, twenty-odd years ago, now. I came out to my children soon after that. Because, Jo being Jo, it wasn't enough for me to go over to Jo's, sleep with Jo, get up at two in the morning and go home, which is what I'd always done.

She said, 'I can't cope with this. You either come and stay with me, or I am allowed to come to you.'

And I'm like, 'But that's, that's totally separate, that's my "straight family", that's sort of my matrimonial home, I can't be doing that.'

She battened me down and battened me down and, lo and behold, got her own way. But she was so in your face, so like a dog with a new bone or a new toy: 'I want it, I want it and I want it now and I want it all the time, and yes, yes, yes!' – that's Jo.

And I said, 'Well, okay, but I've got to come out to my kids first, otherwise what's the point, they won't understand.'

No more deceit

I said to Paul, 'I'm going to tell the children, and I want you to be there for them, because if they've got questions they'll turn to you, and you need to know that this is what I'm doing.'

'Fine,' he said, 'Do you want me to sit in with you?'

And I said, 'If you want to.'

We'd been a family that had had family meetings at times of crisis, so it wasn't unusual. The kids came in and I'm – I mean, how do you tell your children? Really hard. I just said… Well, I don't know how I said it. And they said, 'Oh, is that all?' I don't know what they thought: somebody was dying, or I was ill, or something big. They said, 'We know that. We know that.' And I was like, 'Oh. Okay.' So they've been absolutely wonderful.

As a child, I grew up in a family of deceit, because my mother and father had not got on. When she finally left him, it came out that they hadn't had sex since I was two. But to all intents and purposes, as I was growing up, I thought I was the only one who hated my father's guts. Because they seemed so close. My father would hug my mum, he would fondle her breasts in front of us, and she would laugh – all of these things – and I would be thinking, 'How come they're all so happy and I'm just out of it? Why don't I fit into this thing?' They never spoke about anything that was going wrong – it was all show, deceitful. And then with me and *my* life, well, you can't get more deceitful than having a bit on the side of a bit on the side, and they're both women, and you're still in a marriage, can you? How much more deceitful can you be? So it's not surprising that I emotionally withdraw at times. Everything is so interlinked with what happens to you in that first ten years of your life. It's amazing how it all interlinks, and how all your emotions make you the person you are, and you're trying, even at this end of life, you're trying to make sense of why things happened how they did, and why you reacted how you did, and all of those things.

So, where am I now? Well, I need my shed. Jo says, 'Oh, for heaven's sake, go down to your shed!' I think she's just about got her head around this whole thing about I need my space, and that it doesn't mean that I don't love her and don't want to spend time with her, it's just that's who I am. In the shed is all my machinery, it's my woodworking place.

She used to say, 'Go and play in your shed!'

That really annoyed me. 'I am not playing, I'm making things.'

So now it's just: 'Go and work in your shed.'

But we do a lot together. I suppose because we're constantly together, as much as I can cope, we are very compatible. Because we're into totally different things, but they gel. So she's the cook – I hated cooking. We share a love of gardening – but she is the person who'll say, 'Put it there, I want it there.' (Well, she's bossy, isn't she?) So we share that. And we have a very nice life.

Jo is still of the opinion that she's with me because she loves me, not because I'm a woman. She would put it all on spectrums, you see, and say your sexuality is fluid. Although, if asked, she would tick the lesbian box, if she's not asked, she would say that she may love a man or she may love a woman, it's dependent on the person. Whereas I would say I much prefer women to men, and so I would see myself as much more up the lesbian end than perhaps she would. She's much more fluid along the whole thing. In terms of gender, she would also put that on a spectrum of male/female, butch/femme, however you want to put it. There'd be gradations in between, and somewhere along, there you are, you fit.

Now, I'm more towards the butch. I'm less butch than I used to be; and I don't know whether that's age, or because I got pissed off with constantly being taken for a bloke. I was happy to be masculine, I suppose, but I didn't want to be the whole hog. I wanted to be a woman, who happened to look a bit more butch. When I first went to the pub, to the lesbian and gay evening, because I knew nothing, my naivety was, there had to be butch and femme. And I put myself into the butch camp. Over the years I've realised that that is not the case, you don't have to be one or the other. And you don't have to be dominant or submissive in the sexual act. That's all fluid, you can be whoever you want to be – or whatever takes your fancy, you do, and it doesn't have to be one or the other. Whereas up until then – my first ever thing was me doing it unto someone else, and not getting anything back, and even

Brenda at her wedding and (below, on right) her civil partnership

the luscious woman from Hackney who was so out it wasn't true, she took from me but didn't give back. And I'm thinking, 'That's what it's about, then.' Which I later found out is these 'stone butches'. I'm thinking, 'I don't want to be a bloody stone butch! Sod that for a game of soldiers, I want my share, where's my bit?' And as I've got older, I think I've embraced my more feminine side a bit more, and accepted when Jo says something like, 'You've got graceful hands,' or whatever. I think, 'Well, okay then, if that's me, then I'll accept that.' Whereas before, I would have just put my hands in my pockets and thought, 'Sod you, I'm not showing them, then!' So it's been quite a journey.

I couldn't have done anything else

I suppose, looking at what I've said, that if someone had said to me, 'This is a life story,' I would get quite excited about somebody who had changed their whole life halfway through. Actually, when I did it, I was mad, juggling all the time with my spinning plates. But when I look back on it, I just think, 'Well, I just couldn't have done anything else.' Because it was the right time. I'd got to a point in my marriage where I was thinking, 'God, is this it? Are we just going to sink into middle age, and then old age, and is there no more than this?' Whereas when I met Jo – well, for my fiftieth birthday she whisked me off to the other side of the world for two weeks. Nobody had ever done that. It was 'Woo-hoo!' We took six months off together and went round the world. My whole horizon somehow just opened up. Because once it felt like the whole of my lesbian identity was a dark, cut-off place, not only in my real world, but also my head. It was 'over there', it wasn't real, and it was something that I did in my spare time. Whereas now – this is me. You know what you see now is what you get. I'm out, and I'm happier now than I've ever been. Happy as Larry, whoever Larry was. I hope she was a woman.

5

WEARING THE TROUSERS

Brenda's description of how she accepted, and later moved on from, a butch identity, brings us to the subject of butch and femme.

The popular image of lesbian life in the 1950s and 60s is of a wall-to-wall butch/femme club culture, soon to be obliterated by the coming of feminism. This image is strengthened by stereotypical representations, as in the film *The Killing of Sister George*.[1] Of course, history is never that simple; but I was still surprised, given the generations I was studying, to find that only seventeen percent of my survey respondents had ever identified as butch, and thirteen percent as femme. This makes butches and femmes a minority within the older lesbian minority; and one which has sometimes been marginalised within, as well as outside, the lesbian community.

Although some women who came out into the gay scene of the late 1950s and 60s did form butch or femme sexual identities, many more found the whole culture alien and unhelpful in their journey of self-discovery. As second-wave feminism grew, it offered women (like Pip, for instance) a different and more congenial kind of lesbian identity. Some of those who came out in the context of feminism rejected butch/femme identities as heterosexual role-playing, and stigmatised those who identified in that way. The political struggle between butch/femme culture and feminist politics was played out, not just in debate and writing, but in the lives of individual women.

The rejection of butch/femme culture by radical feminists in the 1970s and 80s still resonates among older lesbians today. The majority of women in my questionnaire survey condemned butch/ femme as imitating heterosexual power relations. But a minority, for whom these forms of gender expression had felt like true reflections of their own identities, considered them a 'natural' part of the spectrum of lesbian identity and desire. Opinions on both sides have softened somewhat over time. In spite of their differences on the subject, older lesbian social groups often accommodate a considerable range of gender identity and gender expression – perhaps suggesting that, as we age, community cohesion becomes more important than political difference.

It is important to remember that we tend to describe ourselves with the words and ideas available at our own particular point in history. Terms like 'genderfluid' and 'non-binary' were not available to these women when they were young, and trans narratives were rare. There are several women (like Linda's last girlfriend) who are described as 'full butch' – and who knows how they would identify if they were young now? Back then, words like 'butch' and 'femme' had to do duty for a whole range of sexual identities, as well as a range of gender expression.

So the next three stories look at the broad spectrum of what 'butch' and 'femme' might mean, then and now, from the point of view of people who were part of that culture. Philippa 'never felt like a little girl', identified with Stephen Gordon in *The Well of Loneliness*,[2] and has always been attracted to feminine women. Sandy describes her younger self as 'full butch' and, for a few years, she passed as a man. Catherine brings a less frequently heard voice to the conversation – that of a femme who always recognised her own desires, and fell in love at first sight with a woman in collar and tie. However, she nicely complicates the stereotypes when she describes how neither of them behaved in traditionally masculine or feminine ways at home, even if they appeared a classic butch/femme couple in social situations. These three narrators represent a lesbian minority, then; but a sizeable one, which is an important part of our history and demands a place in this collection.

JT

PHILIPPA

I was born in 1938, on one of the farms belonging to my family, in a rural area of Norfolk. My mother was the daughter of a working-class family from Norwich, and my father was a landowner's son; so, a very mixed marriage. (Mother said her most embarrassing experience was when they had to sign the register at their wedding, and she put down her father's occupation as 'boot and shoe worker' and Father put down 'gentleman'.) It wasn't a successful marriage; they were totally incompatible, but they stayed together for the sake of us children. Years later, when I came out to my mother, she said, 'I've always known that, darling. And anyway, I've always thought you got it from me!' I was so shocked that I never ever asked her what she meant; and she wasn't really well enough to be asked later on. She'd had a very close friend, my auntie Philippa – for whom I am named, I guess – and when I met Auntie Philippa, I did think, 'Oh yes. There could be something in common there...'

I never really felt like a little girl. I had a tantrum, aged very young, because they told me I couldn't be Lord Nelson when I grew up. My aunt used to make me clothes during the war, and I ordered a pair of dungarees, but they must have seven pockets in precisely the right places. So, you know, there was some ambiguity around there, for most of the time. And a female cousin taught me to masturbate when I was aged about seven. My parents didn't mind that I was a tomboy. In the country, particularly, you ran wild in the fields, and I was with a gang of little boys and that was it. I also rode motorbikes when I was in college; my father helped me buy my first motorbike. So they were fairly liberal in many ways. (Of course, they didn't know about my cousin.) But the other thing that might have helped is that Norfolk had always been a popular retiring ground for lesbians, because it was one of the cheapest parts of England.

So there were quite a few lesbian couples running general post offices and things, and I picked it up quite early. I remember my mother and father used to talk about the 'he-shes' down the road – and so I'd immediately go and look at them, of course. So I think I knew what was happening, fairly early on.

School was heaven

I was fond of my parents, but it wasn't comfortable. My mother also was very handy with her fists and she beat me, but never my brother. I'd been to school locally and then Mother thought it would be better if I went away to school. I was about eleven, quite late for boarding school, but it was nice to get away from the fraught atmosphere. School was heaven! It had rules and regulations, and you knew where you were, and no one was suddenly going to smack you round the ears. So I enjoyed it; I had a good time. I only came home spasmodically after that, for the holidays, and then progressed on to college.

Obviously in a girls' school there was a whole load of crushes going on. I rather thought they were silly, because I knew even then that they weren't the real thing. I never had a crush on a girl of my own age, because I knew that – well, they were playing at it, was what I thought. So I didn't display any form of crush or show any sexual feelings at all. I knew that it wasn't a good thing to talk about. I suppose I was bright enough to know that being different could cause problems. But I never, ever, felt guilty about my sexuality. I got hold of a copy of *The Well of Loneliness* when I was about fourteen, and I read it and thought, 'Yes, that's about right!' I'd read about homosexuals and lesbians before, because when I went to boarding school I read in advance of my age, so I was allowed to go into the senior library, and so I picked up a little bit in there. (I also got told off for putting down some things on the 'Please Buy These Books' lists that were eminently unsuitable.) I invariably ended up playing a male role in the school plays and things. It was quite fun, because I could drag up: that was wonderful; but I did find the love scenes a bit difficult, because I didn't want to appear too keen.

First love

Then I went to college. Everyone wanted me to go to university, but I'd had enough of studying. I thought I might quite like to become a doctor or a lawyer, but six years didn't appeal, so I became a physio. It was three years, university level, not in a hospital as such, but attached to one. And that was where I met my first love, when I was seventeen and a half. I had to go up to college early, because they felt that I should learn some basic anatomy (little did they know!) before the students who were nurses came, as they'd already done some basic stuff. So I'd been there for about a week, more or less by myself, and I went into the library one day, and there was this very nicely rounded woman, dark curly hair, wearing a bright red dress. She was kneeling on the floor leaning forward, and I had never seen such a magnificent cleavage in my life. And that was June. We just sort of hit it off. I don't know how long it took. I think I pretty soon managed to... seduce her, I suppose would be the word.

So for three years we had a relationship. I had to live out of college after the first year, so I got a little flat, and although she was supposed to be living in, most of the time she was living with me. There were some difficulties, because obviously we couldn't come out at all: physios until relatively recently would have been dismissed instantly had there been any knowledge of it. I knew that we shouldn't let our set know – the people we were training with – and certainly no one else. So it was very closet. Quite a few problems were caused by the fact that, as cover, we both had to have boyfriends. There was a fair amount of jealousy; you know, if you came in a bit late, or if she came in a bit late... It was difficult. But we got through it.

Eventually, it was all blown wide apart. I'd moved up to London – we'd separated, but we were still in touch – and I used to ride my motorbike up and down and meet her secretly. One day, one of my boyfriends also came up to London, poked around in my writing case and found a letter to June.

Whereupon he told everyone – all the people we knew from back in college. Apparently, our set had been worried about us at one point, so it wasn't an entire surprise to them. And as a result, he made me promise to go to a psychiatrist, which I did, just for the sake of it. I went to a very nice Freudian psychiatrist who, after about four sessions, said, 'I don't think there's much wrong with you, darling; I think your boyfriend's got a problem.' And that was it. So I ditched the boyfriend and thought, 'Sod it. I am what I am.'

An 'officer-lady' in Germany

I'd known from about the time we left college that this relationship wasn't going anywhere, because I wanted to travel, find gay society, see a bit of the world and have some fun; and June basically wanted to be married, which she couldn't with me. So I said goodbye and took myself off to Germany, as a civilian physio attached to the forces. It was very straight, but fun. I did some travelling, which I'd been wanting to do. I remember going to Dusseldorf, which was just up the road, trying desperately to find the red light district, I was so frustrated. And I couldn't bloody find it! I was an officer-lady, you see, and the other ranks were beyond touching; I would have been sent home. Two years. It was hard.

I did come back and see June a couple of times. I slept with her the night before she got married. Yeah, before she got married I spent the night with her. Well, she welcomed me back to her bed. The next time was when she'd told me she was pregnant, so I went over to see her. I don't know whether I was establishing my right, or pissing on someone else's gatepost. I don't know, but I did it. And I suppose… I suppose I wanted to know she loved me. The next time I saw her, she was heavily pregnant, she was about eight months gone, and her husband wasn't treating her very considerately. He wasn't being cruel, but he wasn't being a very caring husband. So I took her home to my mother and she spent two weeks there just before she had the baby, with my mother and myself looking after her.

I remember she was so pregnant she couldn't get up the stairs without lifting her belly, but I also slept with her then. She had the baby, and I remember coming over especially to see the baby and buying some clothes and things.

Then they emigrated to Canada, which I was upset about. But I was leading my own life. I was probably at that time still in Germany and having quite a good time socially – because I was always quite happy dragging up, so I was wearing the dinner gowns, the ball gowns and all the rest of it, and quite enjoyed it, it was very pleasant. I was having boyfriends, moving from young officer to young officer, for cover. I didn't sleep with them. I didn't sleep with a man till I was twenty-six and that was only to find out if I could. I've never disliked men, never been frightened of men; quite enjoyed them, in fact I enjoyed their company more than women's, mostly.

We had to get married

In Germany I met my future husband, Michael. He was a doctor in the Canadian Royal Army Medical Corps. He was six foot five and a half in his socks and looked like Gregory Peck. Very attractive – all the women were nuts for him. I was the one woman who never chased him and he obviously found this interesting. When I left the Army, I left Michael behind, having never been out with him alone.

In between Germany and London, I had gone to Malta, purely because I'd met some Maltese people and thought, 'I'd like to have a look at Malta.' So while I was there, I was introduced to a doctor who was a womaniser, and a teacher who was a woman. I had a relationship with the teacher, but I also lost my virginity to the doctor. I thought, 'Why not? He's fifty-four years old, I'm twenty-something. He's got a hell of a reputation as a womaniser, he knows what he's about. If I'm going to do it, this is surely the best way to find out.' So I did. And then I fled the island.

In London I stayed with a male friend, again a totally asexual arrangement, and by this time I'd hit the London gay scene. I was down the Gateways and the White Raven, and the Robin Hood... Then Michael came over. We went out for a drink one day and he said, 'Well, who are you going to marry? Me, or Reg?' And I said, 'You.' We'd never been out together; never kissed each other before we were married. The night before we got married, I found a note from him in the hotel when I arrived, saying, 'Gone to the Spread Eagle. Join me if you feel like it.' So I left him a note saying, 'Gone to a party. See you later,' and went down to the Gates! We met up that night, got married the next day, and went back to Germany. I was twenty-six.

I think both of us knew that we had to get married: me to get my mother and my family and society off my back; and Michael because he was a doctor, he was thirty, and he needed to marry. I think we both knew that this was probably right for us, in our own peculiar strange way. We got on very well, no problems, possibly because neither of us felt deeply enough involved to fight about much. He liked the fact that I was a fairly dominant woman. I mean, if anyone bought the cars, I did. He wasn't good at it and he wasn't ashamed to admit it. I liked him: he was good-looking, he was clean and pleasant, and he was bright. But he was also an alcoholic, which I didn't know before I married him, because he would dry out for three years and then start again.

Our marriage lasted eight years, legally; two years of actual living together. It wasn't helped by the fact that we were posted to rural Canada. I'm certain that we would have done a lot more, been able to socialise more and have a more interesting life, if we had lived elsewhere. If we had been in London, I'm pretty certain Michael would have condoned my... It was never discussed, but he knew I had gay friends, gay women friends, and he knew I used to stay with them. Some friends of mine came over. One of them was an actress and she came over to Broadway. So I said, 'I'll fly up to New York and meet you.' And he knew she was gay.

I'm leaving you, darling

So we had a hell of a time in New York, it was great fun. But after I came back from New York, it was a bit 'How're you going to keep them down on the farm, after they've seen Paree?' And I thought, no. If we were living in London, or somewhere else, maybe, but...

So I left. I just said, 'I'm leaving you, darling.'

He didn't ask why. He just said, 'Oh. Are you coming back?'

I said, 'I don't think so.' But he was an absolute gentleman... no problems.

So I came back to London. It must have been '66, the height of everything fun! And I *do* remember what the 60s were like, because the one thing I didn't do was drugs... So I hit the gay scene and progressed from there, basically. There was a gay pub in Hampstead where, if you were a reasonable-looking little butch, not too boyish to be embarrassing, and you hung out there in the lunchtimes, you met an amazing assortment of bored Jewish housewives. I've always been fond of small, dark, cuddly women. But the one I liked, I met in the Gates: her name was Gina. She was a sculptress, and married, so it was all very secret and hush-hush. We used to go to one of her friends' flats to make love. I remember one night getting dreadfully drunk. She of course couldn't leave me in the flat and couldn't take me to her home. She was married; she had to be back at a reasonable hour. She had a lot of freedom, but not that much. Not, sort of, coming home for breakfast. And it was beyond her curfew, so I was dumped on a roundabout somewhere near Swiss Cottage, drunkenly trying to hail taxis.

She was probably the second real love, after June, but I knew it wasn't going to go anywhere. She told me she had no intention of leaving her husband and, you know, one had to believe her. I've never been one for wrecking homes or relationships, or anything like that.

One night I went to a party and met a woman called Michaela. She was living in the South of France, and she was in

London to have an operation. She'd had both breasts removed and was having implants put in.

She wanted someone to drive her car down to the South of France, and my friend Anne, who was very drunk, staggered up to her and slurred, 'My friend can drive anything!'

So the next day we got this phone call saying, 'I believe you'd be willing to drive my car.'

I thought, 'Yes, why not?'

So I was taken to lunch in the Serpentine Restaurant, to see whether I knew which way to hold my knife and fork. I must have held them the right way, because very shortly I said I'd drive her car down.

That's when I said goodbye to Gina. I said, 'I'm off to the South of France.' And we said we'd keep in touch, and we did write...

But anyway, I stayed down there for about six months, living the life of Riley, being kept by this rather lovely ex-Hartnell model, and everything was fine. I helped her initially, but then I thought, 'You can't do this for the rest of your life.' Because I was knocking on by then, I must have been approaching thirty. I knew that nothing would last too long, because in that life your looks are everything, so I came back to London. Hitchhiked back, actually. It was quite fun. Didn't have anywhere to stay, no money; contacted my friends and said, 'I need a bed.' It was quite nice, because mostly they had lodgers, and as long as I didn't upset the bandwagon I could seduce the lodgers, if it was a mutual agreement... So it was always quite pleasant, coming back to London.

I wrecked it

And then I met Rachael, the third really important person in my life. I was thirty and she was twenty-one. She was great and probably much more emotionally mature than I will ever be. She came from a lovely working-class family. She was the illegitimate daughter of an American serviceman and an Englishwoman from Shepherd's Bush, and her mother married and left the daughter to Grandmother. And Grandmother was Jewish. She loved you to death, but my God, you'd do as you were told!

Poor Rachael, she had a hell of a temper, she was always losing her jobs, and she didn't dare tell Granny, so she came to stay with me. And it was great, it really was good. She ran the house for a while and I worked. By that time I was a medical rep, so I had a car and an income. Then she got a job and her own flat, and that was fine. It was great. I was really very, very fond of her. Then, after three or four years, like a stupid idiot, I wrecked it. I think I got bored. I didn't play around, but I left her for someone else. I shouldn't have done. It was a big mistake, but the woman threw herself at me and I found it difficult to say no. We tried reconciling, but it didn't work. Rachael disappeared and I heard that she got married. She was still very young, and she hadn't had that much experience.

At that stage I was so arrogant and emotionally fucked up and everything else, that I don't think I felt very much. I was just having a bloody good time; and it's not a nice thing to say about myself, but I don't think I was a very nice person. I met an American woman, Shelley. I was never really very interested in her, but I'm not good at saying no, and I took her out to dinner. She was very pretty, and nice to be seen with, but by the end of the evening, I wasn't terribly interested. So when she said, 'Would you like to come for a coffee?' I said, 'No, no, I think I'll go home.' And the next thing I knew, I was being dragged into her bed, and I never really got away.

But I think we both had problems. She'd lost her father at a very early age. She'd swanned around the Greek Islands, and got in with Leonard Cohen and all that crowd... and then realised, I think, that she'd have to come back and get down to something. She decided that she wanted to be an analyst. Now, if you're in a relationship with someone who goes into analysis – and I mean deep analysis, not just because they've got problems – things go wrong. And things did go wrong; very wrong, culminating in her going back to visit her mother in America, and coming back and saying that she'd met Hiram J

Hackenfelder the Third, or someone, and that he was coming to fetch her and she was going to get married to him! She was nuts: Hiram J Hackenfelder had two teenage daughters, and Shelley had told him she was a lesbian. Of course, he didn't turn up. He never had any intention of turning up, I would imagine. So I threw her out. And she tried to take me for half my house. I think I was almost the first palimony suit, before Billie Jean King. She got the lawyers going, but I consulted my own lawyer. So, I got rid of Shelley.

A very intense relationship

And that's when I met the love of my life. (I may have *made* love a lot, but I haven't been *in* love a lot.) Perhaps I had grown up a bit. I was forty by then, and she was fifty-five. She was absolutely gorgeous – sophisticated, smart, intelligent. She'd been around, but she was always very proper. She'd never had a relationship with a woman; and she said she'd never had an orgasm until she met me. I don't know how true that is... she didn't tell me that until she was eighty-five. Anyway, we had a very intense relationship. It was when I was with her that I bought the house in West London where I still live. She moved in, although she didn't really fancy being 'in the country'. She preferred South Kensington: to her, this was a remote cottage! She'd been married, by that stage, three times – always good relationships with the husbands, but it just sort of didn't go on. I had a great time with her, because first, she could teach me, and I like being taught, and second, I like older, fairly maternal women, probably because my mother wasn't. So I had all this, and we travelled – she'd go anywhere.

I'd say, 'Do you want to go to Budapest?'

'Oh yes,' she'd say, 'let's be off!' She'd be wonderful that way.

We'd been together for about five years, and the relationship had been ropey for a while; and then I got ovarian cancer. They didn't discover straight away – not until they'd closed me up – that it wasn't just a simple ovarian cyst. In the middle there was a little nasty. So they had to open me up again to do a hysterectomy. And she went off to Spain while I was having the op! It was understandable to a degree, although also totally not understandable. She was very hard up and she had this house in Spain, a small village house, and she'd had an offer to buy it. She needed the money desperately, the man was being an absolute bastard, and if she didn't go... But even so, I couldn't forgive her. I just couldn't, because I felt that she could have somehow or other done it without that. We gradually drifted apart after that.

But we were still in touch, until she died. Towards the end of her time, when she was in her eighties, she was getting frail. So I was taking her away for holidays, I was doing the shopping, I was making certain she was all right. I was seeing her two or three times a week. I was basically being her carer at the end. She died in January of this year, when I was on holiday. I really had got to the stage where I couldn't devote more time than I was devoting already, because it was having an effect on my life, and I suppose that makes me selfish, but I don't see that one person should sacrifice their life for another. (I've made it plain to my partner that if anything happens to me, I've got enough resources, so put me in a nice home and come and visit me as long as I recognise you; don't go beyond that.) So I'd decided that I would go away, knowing that she wasn't physically sick, she was no more physically sick than she'd been for a long while, but she was becoming frail. I'd arranged for various people to go in and see her. And I was away, I was actually in the swimming pool, when someone came and said my partner was calling me, and I thought, I know what this is... Because she had been getting so frail.

She didn't believe in God, under any guise. She didn't care about funerals. I thought, 'Her daughter hates me, I don't know any of her family and I'd have to be just another member of the congregation.' So I decided I didn't want to come back for the funeral. And that was it. But I am an executor of her estate, so I've been involved in that, which we're just about closing, I think. It was a bit hard to go back to the house.

Lost and found

I'm not dependent on a partner, in that I don't like living with my partners; but I like to have some significant other in my life, I freely admit it. I have spent several periods of two, three years, without a partner, and that was one of those times. And then – Rachael came back. Yes. She turned up on my doorstep. Apparently she'd been married twice by now: no children. Living in Berkshire, married about twelve years, had had nothing to do with women. I'd been to one of the grocer's shops up the road, and she'd been parked at the off licence at the end of the street, to get a bottle of wine, and she'd seen me. She'd got back in her car and gone home; then thought about it, I presume, and then turned up on my doorstep. And it was as if we'd never been apart. For a while we had an affair. I said, 'Look, Rachael, you're married, so no promises, no commitments, I don't want to do anything that's going to change your life.' So we did that and it was great. It was lovely. I think I like a mistress, sometimes, better than a wife.

Then, after two or three months, she went away on holiday with her husband. Just before she went away, I discovered a lump in my neck. So I was in the Marsden, having this lump taken out, while she was on holiday. It was only minor stuff – but apparently, she got worried, got drunk and told her husband. At first he said, 'Okay, get it out of your system!' But then he got tired of waiting for her to get it out of her system and announced he was going to divorce her. She went through a hell of a traumatic divorce, because he was trying to keep every penny for himself, and she was saying, 'Well, I think I deserve something for twelve years.'

But again, I think I fucked it. I think I took her for granted. She was living somewhere out in Berkshire that I found rather boring. I can't remember how it happened, but I know something upset me and I stormed out. I'm a good stormer-out, but I usually storm back in. I think possibly I had taken her for granted, and I think she needed some freedom. So we didn't get back together. She went off to America and met someone there, and that was really it. I'm not in touch with her, but I know where she is and she knows where I am. She came over last year, about this time, June, and someone I knew told me that Rachael was here and that she'd managed to get a green card and was going back to America. So I said, 'Well, tell her, if she wants to, I'd like to get in touch and say goodbye.' She did. And it was just the same as ever. But she has settled for what she's got. And I can't say any more than that. So I lost the love of my life this year and Rachael last year.

I met Julia two years after Rachael and I split up. I really wasn't ready, but Julia's very tolerant, very understanding. She's a *really* nice person. She probably has to be, with me.

Philippa (right) at a women's dinner dance circa 2005 with Julia,
whose story appears in the next chapter

SANDY

I always wanted to be a boy. I always wanted boys' toys, boys' clothes and boys' everything. So I knew very early on; but I couldn't have put a name to it. That only came much later, when I was about twenty-one. My parents used to take the *Daily Mail*, and there was an article in there by an agony aunt, giving advice for parents on what to do if they thought their children were gay. It gave the address of the Minorities Research Group,[3] so I wrote off to them and got some information. The magazine was called *Arena Three*. And then I read absolutely everything I could get my hands on. Not that there was much to read, then.

I was born in 1943 in North Yorkshire. My mother and I lived in Sheffield until the end of the war, when we went out to Berlin to join my father for three or four years. (I should say, at this point, that I was the child of an 'unmarried mother', and I was adopted when I was six weeks old so, when I talk about my mother and father, I'm talking about my adoptive parents.) Then we moved to London, where we stayed for a couple of years, and I went to a private school, which I hated because for the first and only time in my life I was bullied. I was about six. When my grandfather died, we all went back to Sheffield, where my father took over the family grocery business. I was sent to elocution lessons when we moved to Yorkshire, specifically so I wouldn't get a Yorkshire accent. My mother was rather a snob. But they were lovely people, and I had just such a wonderful upbringing, I really did.

We lived in Sheffield until I was eleven. Then my mother became very ill, and the doctor said that she'd be better in clean air, so we moved to the coast. That was where I went to the girls' high school. I hated it; I hated school. I was a real rebel, always in trouble. I knew from the age of eleven that I was gay. I had the usual crushes on games teachers and other teachers and so on; and – although it was hardly a sexual affair – I had my first relationship at age eleven. And that lasted until we were fourteen, when the girl moved away. Actually, she got expelled. I had one or two very unsatisfactory, fleeting and fumbling relationships – and then I met a woman who taught me – well, everything.

First love

I was eighteen at the time. My father had bought me horses, I'd been away and got some qualifications, and I was going to run a riding school; but I came back and fell in love with Barbara. She was sixteen years my senior and I had a relationship with her. I just let everything go: I wanted to move away, so I could be with her. I took a job working for an international three-day event rider in Gloucestershire and Barbara came down to see me during that time. Now, she was married with two small children. She had intended to leave her husband *and* her children to come and live with me, at this flat where I was working. She did come down to Gloucestershire – she actually got a job – but then she went back and thought about it, and sensibly told me that that was it. I say 'sensibly', but it didn't feel like that at the time: I took a load of sleeping tablets. I see now, with hindsight, that she *was* sensible. I was eighteen; it couldn't have worked out.

I think my father had guessed what was going on. He knew, when I took the sleeping tablets and ended up in hospital, and he came down to see me. Then I went back and lived with my mother. (My father had still got the business in Sheffield, so he used to be there during the week and he'd come home at weekends.) Anyway, I had one horse there, and I stabled it with a local farmer, who had a son, Derek, who was lovely. He was really, really lovely. He was six foot four, ever so gentle, a really nice guy; and I wanted to be like everybody else, so I got engaged to him, even though I couldn't bear him near me sexually. And it was then, through *Arena Three*, that I saw this advertisement for a gay women's group in Nottingham. So I wrote off to that and arranged to meet them, and I went down there one Saturday night. It was just amazing. Here were all these women who were like me.

It was a very drag-orientated society and you were either butch or femme – if you were anything between you were looked down on (it was the early 1960s). I was full butch: three-piece suit. The Foresters was the women's pub, but on Saturday nights you used to get all these straight guys in there who used to cause trouble, and then it was, 'Everybody out into the back yard!' and invariably we got beaten up. On Sunday morning your wounds were tended to, gently. It was silly, really, but it was wonderful.

To thine own self be true

I was still engaged to Derek at this time, and that Christmas my great-uncle and his long-term partner came to stay. My mother wouldn't have it that they were gay, but they were. My mother was absolutely, really homophobic. They lived in London. He was a floor manager for Swan & Edgar, I think, and his partner worked in the stock market. Anyway, they invited me to go down and spend a weekend with them, which I thought was really lovely, and I duly did. They took me to see Beryl Reid in *The Killing of Sister George*, then to a restaurant in Soho for a meal, and then we went back to their flat.

Reggie sat me down and said, 'I'm not going to say very much to you. I'm just going to say one thing and I want you to really think about it.' And he quoted that speech from Shakespeare that says, 'To thine own self be true.'

I went back and thought about it. And I thought, 'This is right: I can't go on with this.' So I broke it off with Derek. My mother was distraught; we had a huge row. It was on the morning of my twenty-second birthday. We had this huge row in the morning, and I went off to work; and when I came back she'd had a cerebral haemorrhage and died without ever regaining consciousness. You can imagine what that did to me. Prior to that I had been very close to her.

My father – who knew that I was gay, and was very good

about it – just said that he thought it was better that it was a broken engagement than a broken marriage. By then I'd met somebody in Nottingham who I wanted to live with. Dad rented us a house, just into Derbyshire, and I moved there with Linda and her young son, and Dad used to come over at weekends. But it didn't work out, so I went back to working with horses, away in Surrey. I worked there for about eighteen months, then got back with Linda. We moved to Southampton – where there was a big gay scene – and I was with her there for about five or six years.

After I'd split up with Linda, I went into the Merchant Navy. Wow! That was wonderful. There's something that happens to women at sea: I don't know what it is, but they lose their inhibitions. And about half the crew were gay, both men and women, so it was just a riot, a wild time. Eventually, I met somebody. Pauline was actually the daughter of the CEO of the shipping company I was working for. I knew that he was okay, but his wife wasn't at that time. I knew it would start a witch-hunt if it came out, and you can't keep secrets on a ship. So I left the Merchant Navy, we rented a flat and I trained as an HGV driver.

A young chap

I was only the second woman in the country to pass the HGV1 test. I eventually got a job, and worked there for about four or five years. And while the company I worked for, and the drivers at the depot, obviously knew I was a woman, when I was out on the road most people assumed I was a guy, a young chap. I used to get my leg pulled about being too young to have an HGV licence and that sort of thing.

I was butch anyway, and even where we were living, people thought we were a young married couple. They thought I was a guy. I had a Triumph Spitfire at the time. We were living in an upper-floor flat; there was a young couple below us and he had a Spitfire as well. He got killed in the Spitfire. He ran it underneath the back of a lorry, drunk one night. And

153

the neighbours thought it was me. They came round and commiserated with my girlfriend. But of course, it wasn't me.

But it was easier that way. It was easier than actually being gay because, although I've always been out and don't give a damn about what people think of me, it was just easier slotting into society. It was very much the real me. I suppose my thinking has moderated over the years, but it's very much towards the masculine. And if it had been possible then, I would have had the operation. I used to *pray* that I'd wake up and be a boy. It was really that strong. I've lost it over the years, I suppose, but there are still times... For instance, if I have to wear a shoulder-bag, I do it because I need both hands free because of my disability, but I don't like it. I have this little voice in the back of my head which is Linda, my first live-in relationship. If I did something that was in any way feminine, she'd say, 'Call yourself a butch?' And it still resonates sometimes. But I have fully come to terms with who I am, now, and I wouldn't want to transition even if I were younger. If I were to have my life again, I would want to come back as a gay woman – though perhaps miss out the whole butch/femme parody.

Pauline and I bought a Morris Minor and I did it up. It was a Traveller, the one with the wood trim. I used to enjoy woodwork, so I replaced all the wood, had it sprayed and everything. And then something happened that changed our lives. We were going up to see my parents, and this idiot came round the corner and across the road, and we hit him smack, full on. Fortunately, Pauline always insisted that we wear seat belts, otherwise we'd both have been dead. But it buggered up my knee and put two discs out in my back. And for her, her seatbelt broke on impact, the glove compartment came up, the windscreen shattered onto the glove compartment and she went full face into it. So she had fifty-five stitches in her face, and whiplash injuries. She had to go home to her parents for them to look after her – I couldn't, because I could hardly walk and my back had gone. Her parents were very wealthy. She was away for about six months.

I had to have a year or so off work, because of the damage

from the car accident – I couldn't stand upright – and when I was well enough, I took an apprenticeship in woodworking. I worked for somebody who did fitted kitchens. Then I saw a vacancy at a shop-fitting firm. That was hardwood joinery, which is what I'd been trained in, so I applied for the job and got it. They thought I was a lad. Until of course I started and gave them my P45, and they realised that the person they'd employed was actually female. That was the only time I really had homophobic bullying and nastiness; because the foreman really, really didn't like me.

My life changed forever

Eventually I went back to driving lorries and, because I was the newest in, I was the relief driver; so I used to drive people's rounds when they were on holiday. For two weeks, I went to a place called Porton Down. You went in through one set of manned, policed barriers, to a huge square building, three storeys high; I could see cages on the top storey. Then you went underground to deliver, and they opened these doors which were about two foot thick, they slid back and you backed the lorry on and did the deliveries. Then you went further on down about another mile, through another two checkpoints, to a huge fenced-off area where little electric vehicles were running around. These little electric vehicles had rotating vents on the top of them. It was surreal. And the people there were really odd. Normally you'd go to a place every day for about three or four days, and the people would chat and laugh with you like they do at normal places, but here they didn't. I couldn't understand what this place was; I knew it was something to do with the military, but I couldn't understand what it was. Anyway, perchance I picked up a magazine called *Undercurrents*, and there on the back page was a big advert for an organisation called Animal Aid who were holding a demonstration against Porton Down. I thought, 'Here's my chance to find out what this is all about.'

So I went to the demo at Salisbury and my life changed

forever. Irrevocably. I was so shocked by what I read and what people were telling me – about the way animals were used for research there – that I think I cried solidly for about three days. Then I thought, 'This is no use, it's not doing anybody any good, I've got to go and do something.' So I joined the local animal rights group and, to cut a very long story short, I became involved in illegal activities like breaking into laboratories. Eventually we were caught, just outside Oxford, trying to release some cats which were being bred for vivisection. And eleven of us were charged with conspiracy to burgle.

Meanwhile Pauline and I had moved back together again. She guessed that I was involved in illegal stuff, but she didn't want to know. Anyway, the night of that particular raid, she wasn't at home. She was at her parents' house – fortunately, because when they arrested us, the police raided the house and took away loads and loads of stuff. When we were released and I went back home, Pauline's sister, a trainee barrister, was there and she intimated that I should get out of the house. It was half my house, actually. I think she was just frightened that Pauline would be implicated in some way with this – and Pauline agreed with her! And I thought, at that moment, 'You don't love me.' It just came like a shot out of the blue. Anyway, I didn't go, I stood my ground and said, 'This is my home as well.' But soon after that we decided to call it a day. We agreed to buy a house together in London and convert it into two flats, where we could live together, but go our separate ways. So that was that.

Those of us who had been arrested, elected to go to Crown Court – trial by jury – and it involved a lot of procedural hearings. The eleven of us would all go up together for these things. It was during one of these court hearings that I realised I was very attracted to one of the women involved. But she was straight, and I always made a rule never to make the first move as far as straight women were concerned. (Not that that ever stopped anything.) Anyway, we were found guilty – well, we *were* guilty. I'll always remember the judge saying, 'I'm sentencing you to six months in jail.' And everybody thought, 'Aaaah!' and then he said, 'Suspended for six months.'

Shortly afterwards, about seven or eight of us went away to a cottage down in Sussex. It was lovely, a chocolate-box cottage with a thatched roof and everything. It was there that I knew I was really attracted to Jackie. But I wasn't saying anything. Then we came home and she rang me, I think it was that night, and said that she felt that she was attracted to me. I said, 'Well, I feel the same.' Jackie had been made chief exec of one of the animal rights organisations, and she said to the committee that she'd like to have me on board, so I went as their group and student co-ordinator. I moved in with Jackie, and Pauline went her own way.

A house in the hills

We were very happy and very busy; but when you're up against powerful people like drug companies and governments, an awful lot of dirty tricks go on, and eventually Jackie felt that she just couldn't continue any longer. I wanted to move to Wales, so we started looking and eventually bought a house just outside Llanidloes, in the hills, moved out there, and made wooden toys.

My woodworking skills came in useful then. I'd always remembered the wooden toys from my German childhood and always loved them, so we started to make them. It gave us a living, although not a tremendous one, for a few years. But I was driven, I really was: I wanted to make a success of the business, we were working all kinds of silly hours and never had any time for *us*. In the end Jackie said, 'I can't do this any more,' and went to work in a local shop. Then the recession came and I was offered a job teaching woodwork to unemployed people, at about fourteen grand a year, so I jumped at it, because it meant I could pay back the overdraft. I worked there for about eight years.

I lived in Wales with Jackie for seventeen years altogether. And right at the end (oh, how I regret it now!) I had an affair with somebody. It was crazy, because all the time that I was doing it, I knew that I was really in love with Jackie. She had a breakdown because of it – a nasty one. So of course, I felt guilty. We did get back together again, for about eighteen months, but the guilt just coloured everything with me, and eventually we split up again. I take full responsibility for what happened and I wish I could have my time back, but that's the way it goes.

Moving on

I moved out and rented a small flat from a friend. She was doing a medical aid mission, taking medical equipment out to a kids' hospice in Russia, and I went with her as co-driver. During that time, we talked about how she'd been to Africa on six-month trips, how she enjoyed travelling; and I said that since I'd seen *The Deer Hunter* I'd always wanted to go to Vietnam. We decided we'd do it. So I gave up my job (everyone said, 'You're mad, you'll never get another one') and we went to Southeast Asia for six months. We spent the Millennium on top of a lorry in a square in Bangkok. It was wonderful.

I did get another job, working on the shop floor of a company that made Portakabins for the mobile phone trade. They were fine. Most of the guys knew I was gay, because I never made any secret of it, but it was lovely because they treated me as one of their own, as an honorary male, I think. They used to pull my leg and kid me on, just like they do with each other. It was really good, that. But then I was offered a job by a friend from my toy-making days, who was starting up a new business, making wooden love spoons. And I went to manage that; it was only a small company.

Then I got an email from someone I'd known vaguely in the animal rights movement, back in the 80s. We met, and eventually I moved to the Midlands to be with her, to live with her. It's an odd thing, and easy to say with hindsight, but I knew right from the word go that it wasn't going to work, we were such different people. Yet I still went ahead with it, and that's why I moved here. I lived with her for five years – rather unhappy years, I must say – and eventually split up with her two and a half years ago.

And now...?

And now I live here, in a really nice area of Birmingham, and I'm very happy. I've got my own flat, with a warden, and cords all over the place. It's great. I really don't want another relationship. I suppose if somebody came along... Well, 'Never say never!' But I'm quite happy on my own. I think that as you're getting old you get selfish, set in your ways, and so on; and what matters to me most now are good friends. I've got quite a full life. I'm involved with Pink Sou'westers and the Older Lesbian Network, and I have straight friends as well. I do two art classes a week, I volunteer with an art group for people who are mental health service users. I go to quizzes here and there, and see friends. There are things that I miss about being in a relationship: the closeness, the sharing, and things like that. But when I think of starting all over again with somebody new – well, quite honestly, I don't think I can be bothered. I'd still like to travel. The woman I travelled to Southeast Asia with has been working out in Africa for about eight years with a children's charity, and she keeps saying to me, 'Come over, come over!' I'm thinking that I should go, while I can still walk.

All the people here know I'm gay – I make no secret of it – but it's still not the same as having gay people living around you. In an ideal society, there would be somewhere where gay people could live together. It would be nice to have a housing complex like this one. They've just built a very big complex in Birmingham, a retirement village. The organisation that I'm with here are hoping to do the same sort of thing: they've bought the land down the road and they're going to put up fifty-one flats. The complex will have its own hairdresser and café and so on, and you will be able to stay there until you die. So even if you get Alzheimer's or something, you'll be cared for. That's good; but it would be nice if there was something like that, just for us.

I think I've lived quite a selfish life... If I'd been straight, I'd probably have got married and had kids, whereas in this life I've done really what I liked. I've had a lot of experiences which I wouldn't have had if I'd been straight. I don't regret being gay. In some ways, it makes you more able to cope with getting older. I remember Jackie saying, when we were splitting up, 'You're really lucky, because wherever you go in the country you will have a ready-made supply of friends.' And that's true. There's always a gay community wherever you go, whereas for somebody who's straight or bisexual, it's much more difficult, when they're getting older, to find new friends. When you talk to women who come to Older Lesbian Network, you know often it's the only gay contact that they have, but at least they have that.

Sandy (photograph: Michele Watkins)

CATHERINE

I was born in 1939, so I'm just pre-war – none of your Utility stuff! We were middle-class; my father was a salesman. He was very devoted to his mother so, when she was widowed, we moved to live with her and I grew up in a city in the East Midlands. I was six then, and already at school – though I didn't ever go to school very much, because I'd had bronchial pneumonia when I was four and I've had asthma ever since. In the winter, I only looked in at school occasionally. When I passed the eleven-plus, I couldn't go to the grammar school: it was on two sides of a main road and I couldn't go outside to cross the road in winter, because of my asthma. So instead I went to a private school for people who'd failed the eleven-plus. That wasn't very nice, because I was brighter than most people in the class and I kept being held back, so I was a bit disruptive. (I know that nowadays 'disruptive' actually means smashing furniture; but in my case I just sat on the back row and muttered.)

I became aware of my difference, when the other girls at school started going out with boys and I hadn't actually noticed there was such a thing, because I had a best friend, Gill. We were very close. I would say I was in love with her. We would have had sex, only we didn't know what to do! We knew that women shouldn't kiss each other on the mouth, so we didn't, we kissed each other on the neck instead, and that was about as far as it got. We were fourteen, fifteen... I had a go at going out with boys, but it didn't work. I went out with two boys, actually, just to see. I thought, 'Maybe if I start on this, it'll work.' It didn't, so that was that, and I was identifying as a lesbian from about the age of fifteen (though we wouldn't have used that word then – I'd have said 'queer').

Then my girlfriend's father's secretary, Kay, who was gay and very sexual – one of those people who *radiates* sex – tried to seduce me. I said, 'I'll never be disloyal to Gill.' So she went along to Gill, who didn't say that. And Gill went off with Kay. Kay was in her twenties, about eight years older than us. I was hurt. I was jealous. Cross. I was rather a nuisance to them, and this went on until I was in my twenties.

I went to university, but when I got there I found I was hopelessly out of my depth, as everyone was much better educated than I was. Then I fell in love with the only lesbian in my year, who unfortunately fell in love with somebody else. So that didn't come to anything. And I had a breakdown, failed college and came back to my home town. Everybody was wondering what to do with me, then they thought, 'Oh well, she likes writing, she'd better be a journalist.' So I did that. The trouble was that I wasn't very pushy, and if anybody said to me, 'Oh no, I don't want to be interviewed,' I'd say, 'Fine!' and go back to the office. So that wasn't very successful.

A collar and tie and a hacking jacket

Then Jocelyn turned up in town. Wearing a collar and tie, a hacking jacket and corduroy trousers, and driving a laundry van. So she was a little bit... noticeable. Before that she had run a travelling library, down in Kent; and she had worked as a talent scout for a film agent – but she absolutely *had* to wear trousers, and in those days you couldn't, in an office job. So that was how a clergyman's daughter came to be driving a laundry van. I just thought she was gorgeous.

She used to deliver laundry to the place where Kay worked. So Kay thought it would be a good idea to get rid of me, on to Jocelyn. She told Jocelyn that there was this girl who worked at the local paper, who was madly in love with her! So Jocelyn was going round in her van and, as she came past my office, I happened to come out. Now *she* assumed that Kay had rung me and said, 'Come out quick, the laundry van's coming.' But I'd seen her before and thought, 'That looks nice.' So I cycled very slowly and eventually she caught me up and asked me out for a drink. And it went on from there. I was twenty-one, and that was my first real, sexual relationship. It was lovely. I'd got myself where I wanted to be: all I'd ever wanted to do was meet somebody and settle down.

Leaving home

But then, of course, we had a problem with my parents. Jocelyn was, as I've said, rather noticeable; and everybody in town knew me, and there I was riding round in a laundry van with her. She was a good deal older than I was, too – she was thirty-seven when we met. My parents raged and sent me off to a psychiatrist.

The only thing the psychiatrist said to me was, 'Now tell me. Are you sexually attracted to little girls?'

I said, 'Oh God, I *loathe* children!'

Then he said, 'Well I suggest you leave home and send your mother ten shillings a week.'

So I did leave home. We came down here to Sussex and I got a job on the local paper. I hadn't told my parents that Jocelyn was here with me, but then unfortunately I got a peptic ulcer and was rushed into hospital, and they all met round my bed. In the end, they were really fond of her, though. She persevered. And we were together for forty-eight years.

Eventually I got the sack from the paper. That was because we had a period when Jocelyn went off with somebody else. I was twenty-five, and instead of just looking the other way and letting it burn itself out, I did the dramatics: 'It's me or her!' So we parted for two months. And I didn't go into work very much, so I got the sack. Then Jocelyn just said, 'Sorry, I made a mistake,' and came back. So we went up to London and started again. And when in my turn I had two little affairs, she just looked the other way. But that was much later on. We'd been together twenty years by then and I suppose I thought, 'Have I settled down too young?' She just looked the other way until I got over it. In a long-term relationship, it's very cosy, and you suddenly see something that looks a bit exciting, you want to have a little try... I suppose I would have been in my forties.

Catherine (left) with Jocelyn, late 1980s

Butch and femme?

Well, Jocelyn liked to dress in a very masculine way, yes. And she was so good-looking that I always wanted to look nice, so that people wouldn't say, 'What's that good-looking woman doing with that little scruff?' I suppose we looked a typical butch/femme couple. But she wasn't very masculine. She didn't spend hours tinkering with the car, and she didn't have a tool box, or go into the shed or anything. She liked to do things like going up to the bar for the drinks, but she cooked. And I cleaned. We worked things out according to what we liked doing. That wasn't anything to do with being masculine and feminine. A feminine person would want to cook and feed and nurture people, but I have no maternal instinct at all. In the 60s in Brighton, everybody was very butch, very femme, and you had to play along, you know. Then when we got up to London, it got a bit more blurred.

When we first moved to London, we didn't find the gay scene very welcoming. We started off going down the Gates and we were very disappointed. Brighton in the 60s was a lovely friendly place: you'd go to a club, you'd meet up with two or three people, you'd go on somewhere else, then you'd go back to someone's flat for a party... So that first year in London we weren't very happy at all. But then we met somebody down the Gates who told us about Kenric,[4] and after that everything was lovely. Kenric had only been going about a year when we joined, I think, and we thought it was really nice – because I will say, the people we knew in Brighton were, some of them, criminals, prostitutes and so on, and it was really nice to meet people you could have taken home to meet your mother.

Hard times

In the 1990s, Jocelyn began to lose her sight and we decided we needed to move to a bungalow. House prices in outer London were prohibitive so, rather reluctantly, we returned to Sussex, where we still had some friends. The following years were hard and I prefer not to talk much about that time. As well as going blind, Jocelyn developed dementia. I cared for her until she died in 2009.

It's not easy, making a new social life when you are in your seventies and only recently single, but I'm getting used to it. I didn't have a choice, did I? Having a gay social life hasn't really worked out, though. There was a lesbian supper group I went to, but there were thirty-eight people there, and they were already in groups. One or two people were nice to me, but it was too big. I've just joined the local gay society, which is a mixed group. In fact it's nearly all men, but I like gay boys and get on very well with them. The only reason I haven't been to it yet is because I've been ill and didn't want to arrive coughing. But I'm looking forward to that.

Most of my friends from the old days have died. One lives a long way away; they have a dozen dogs and I'm allergic to dogs, so she comes down to stay here occasionally. I've got another friend or two I still see, but everyone else is dead. The trouble is, everybody is so scattered. I've got a friend in Cambridge, so

I can just about get there and get back in a day; but she's a lot older than I am and I think she'd probably find me a bit of a strain now. She rings up sometimes.

New friends

I seem to have got two straight friends now, which puzzles me a bit. I just happened to meet them and they both seem to want to be friendly with me. But it's difficult, because I should come out to them, and I haven't. You'd think people would know, wouldn't you? I say, 'I lived with a woman for forty-eight years, I'm not married,' and what would you think? But they haven't got a clue. When there was both of us, we *looked* like a couple. I think my next-door neighbour thinks I'm gay; she's made a few remarks, but she's a great gossip, so I haven't followed it up. She was very fond of Jocelyn, actually: she used to come and sit with her when I was out. And she's very kind to me. If I fell over or something I'd only have to ring the phone and she'd be round. But I don't see any point in… labouring the point.

After Jocelyn died, I started going to church again. I've got a gay curate at church. He's very open. He's in a civil partnership. I was in a bereavement group there, which wasn't particularly good because I couldn't come out in this group of respectable widows. Then he happened to mention in a sermon that he was a trained bereavement counsellor, so I dropped out of the group and started to see him privately. He's been very helpful. But he's had trouble. When he was doing the crib service, at Christmas, a lot of parents took their children away, because they thought he was a paedophile. They all went off to the next village. I've got a friend in that village and she said, 'We've got about three hundred extra children at our crib service!' I was appalled.

I think it deflated him a bit. He's very bouncy. I mean, he must have thought he'd done the right thing by being honest to people – but it would probably be better if he hadn't. He's quite lot younger than I am and he's a bit surprised, because he comes from Brighton, you see, and it's probably easier there.

I think he's only in his forties, and I felt like saying, 'I think you'd have been better not to do this.' People would have been quite happy whispering behind their hands, 'I think he's one of *those*' – but because he came straight out and told them, they didn't like it. But he can only learn. He'll be off to his own parish before long, and I hope they send him over Brighton way.

Prejudice

A lot of my relations don't have anything to do with me. I'm not in touch with them. It hasn't bothered me very much. Jocelyn's relations weren't particularly bothered about her anyway, so there wasn't a problem. They quite like me, actually: after she died, I found a lot of letters that she'd inherited among her relations' things and had kept, that said how nice it was that she'd met such a sensible woman, so that she'd settled down and got a proper job and bought a house. That was really nice.

But we were refused entry to a hotel once. It must have been in the early 60s. We went away for a weekend together, went to book into this hotel, and the receptionist just disappeared. We stood there for about an hour and then we suddenly realised what had happened. So we went off and found a bed and breakfast. There was nothing actually *said*. And I think when I got the sack from the paper that [homophobia] might have had something to do with it, because I'd been seen around with Jocelyn. But I couldn't be too sure about that: the reasons they gave were that I wasn't working hard enough, I wasn't coming up with original ideas, I'd been sick too much... My other jobs were in London and we were living away from where I worked, so people didn't see. I don't think I had any other trouble.

A funny thing happened when I was on the *Gazette*, though. We were in the Spotted Dog one night, and a woman from my work and her husband came in. So everybody pushed me down under the table and sort of sat on me. They didn't stay very long.

Anyway, the next day she came into the office and said,

'You'll never guess where I went last night. We went to a gay pub!' And she said, 'All these men in makeup, drinking cocktails, and all these ladies in collars and ties drinking pints of beer!' (Which wasn't what it was like at all.)

She said to me once, 'You wouldn't understand this, but if a lesbian walked into this room, I would know.'

So I said, 'Really? How?'

She said, 'I don't know, but if somebody walked over there, I would know.'

And I just said, 'Gosh, isn't that strange.' That's one advantage of not looking like one: you get some very funny remarks made to you.

I was never unhappy about being gay, because I just didn't think there was any option. It was just me. I did feel that I would have preferred not to have been, because I thought it would have been easier; but it was so much part of me, that I couldn't imagine, actually, being any different. I think I've had a more interesting life, being gay. But of course, if I'd been straight, I would probably have children now, whereas I've only got two cousins who really don't want to know, and no close relations at all.

Future plans

I assume that eventually I'll be able to sell this bungalow, and I've got quite a lot of savings, so I assume I'll be able to provide for myself. But when I start needing care, I do have concerns. For instance, the local Society for the Blind was definitely homophobic towards us. And so was one of the charities that helped to care for Jocelyn. The agency carers were all lovely and didn't mind about anything, but they said, 'We can't understand why every time you ask for help from these services you don't get it.' They said, 'Why are they so funny with you?' And I didn't say, but I knew. Anything I asked for, they'd say, 'Leave it with me.' And when people say that, you know it's not going to happen. I had to fight for a lot of things that other people wouldn't have had to fight for. The County Association for the Blind, they were fine. No trouble at all. In the end I got them in, and they put little spots on the door for Jocelyn to touch so she would know where she was, and everything. But the local society were definitely prejudiced.

When we were young, I just thought that was how things were, because people were... ignorant. And as long as we were together, and had lots of fun, it didn't really matter. Even now it would still depend very much where you were living. I mean, I don't think coming out here would ever be a good idea: where I live isn't a very sophisticated place.

But that's life. It's just how things are.

6

IDENTITY AND POLITICS

I have been struck, as I have listened to women telling their stories, by how many of them started out feeling 'different' from their schoolfriends or siblings, even before sexuality came into the picture. It might have been because their heritage, religious beliefs or home background set them apart; or because they were different to look at, adopted, chronically ill, or even very clever, at an age when most of us just want to be like everyone else. But we all have several overlapping identities, of which our sexual orientation is only one; and those identities take on more or less importance at different times of our lives.

In the next set of stories we will meet Silva, whose parents were immigrants from Italy and France, and who worked in the fairground as a child; Mumtaz, an Indian girl from an upper-class East African family, stranded in an elite girls' boarding school in southern England; and Julia, who hesitated to invite her friends to a poor home dominated by an alcoholic and verbally abusive father. So their stories are partly about that feeling of being an outsider, even before their sexuality set them apart.

All three were born shortly after the Second World War; for all three, feminism and the liberation politics of the 1960s are implicated in their development as lesbians. This was the generation for whom the butch/femme story was no longer enough – for Silva, it was actually a hindrance to understanding who she was. Observing the position of women in society, in China as well as in her own culture, turned Mumtaz into a photographer and an activist. Radical feminism in London gave Julia the courage to take a woman lover. And for Silva, diving into politics showed her that 'I could be myself, and be a lesbian!' It was, as she says, 'joyous'.

JT

~

SILVA

My father was Italian, but was living here from the 1920s onwards. My mother was French, and they met in London, just before the war. I was born after the war, in 1947, but I was sent back to France when I was six or seven months old, all on my own, to live with my maternal grandparents. Why? Well, I suppose I wasn't a very loved child. What my parents always said was that they were just so busy building up a business. My father was a real entrepreneur, they were into making money, they were working. They were very much in love with one another. My mother was besotted by my father and did whatever he wanted, so they weren't really that interested in me; and my father, being an Italian *paterfamilias*, really would have preferred a boy.

On my mother's side, in France, we were fair people. We lived in caravans, and they used to do the fairs. They didn't travel, they just did all the fairs around Paris. They were very lucky because they had two pitches, which went with the family, in the Place de la République, right in the centre of Paris. Which was worth a lot of money. These pitches were more or less permanent, though I think at some point they used to rent them out. There were three or four large fairs in the summer just outside Paris: one in St Germain-en-Laye, which is still there, and one at Foire du Trône. There were about three or four months of big fairs, and then they lived off the Place de la République takings. They did different things – rifle shooting, the wheel, the hoopla, things like that. And my first memories were around all that. My grandmother was quite old; she tended to look after me, but there was always somebody at home, there were three or four sisters. I loved it. But when I had to go to school, I was sent to my grandmother's sister, who had come out of the fair business and lived just outside Paris, in a village. I went to school there, in a convent, as a weekly boarder. And I stayed there till I was about eleven, when I went to the *lycée*.

I used to come back to England – I was probably the youngest solo traveller on the Blue Arrow and Air France in those days: Paris to London, by myself. I did that three or four times a year, for holidays, back and forth. I was never close to my parents at all – in fact, I couldn't speak the same language as my father, because he spoke Italian and English, but not French. My mother spoke all three languages, and when I came back to London I was encouraged to speak English, although I didn't really speak it well. So to me he was this terribly moody figure who must be obeyed, basically. By the time I was eleven or twelve, I was really very unhappy in the country in France. I wanted to move to Paris, to be nearer to my relatives there. So I kicked up a fuss until they agreed to have me in Paris, and I went to the *lycée* there. But I was still very unhappy. I was an unhappy child, I can see now, looking back. The only time I was happy was at the fairs. I was getting old enough to go and help out, particularly in the summer.

My mother hated that life. She was deeply ashamed of it: she'd escaped it, basically. My father was a real entrepreneur and did a number of interesting things. He set up the ice-cream vans; that was his business. Not so much the ice-cream, but the refrigeration. He imported the first soft ice-cream machine from Italy and did very well, and was moving into refrigeration. So they had a good life and lived in St John's Wood; they'd done well. It was funny, because my grandmother used to look down on my father for being Italian, and he obviously used to look down on them for living in caravans. 'Oh, your mother, she married a Macaroni!' my grandmother used to say.

We always had our summer holidays in Italy, near the Lido in Venice. My mother used to stop off in Paris and pick me up, on the way. But I was going a bit off the rails. They were all busy, they were all working, so I could do very much what I wanted. I was not attending school. My grandmother was almost eighty then, so she was far too old to control me. So I missed school, I used to go to the cinema, and all of that. The only time I was really happy was on the fair. And when my mother found that out, I was whisked back to England.

A strict Catholic upbringing

I was about twelve and a half when I was wrenched from everything I knew, taken back to England, and bunged in a boarding school immediately. The first boarding school was in Ealing. I got thrown out of there. The second one was in Norwood. I got thrown out of there as well. I would never know why. 'Dumb insolence,' they called it, whatever that was. They were all convents. It was quarterly boarding; you only came back at half-term. The third one was in Sussex, and I was okay there. In fact I thrived: they made me head girl. I did all my O levels, and a couple of A levels too. So that was a success in the end.

At that last school we were allowed to watch *Top of the Pops* or *Ready, Steady, Go!* or whatever it was in those days. We did the usual screaming at pop stars and all of that, but boys? I just did not meet boys. It was a very strict Catholic upbringing. Kids nowadays are allowed out of school, but we were never allowed out; and when I came home, it was the same. The expectation of my father and my mother was that I would leave school, maybe go and work with them in their business for a couple of years, and then get married and have kids. My father was already lining up would-be husbands for me. I knew that was the expectation.

But I think I was a very late developer: I didn't know anything about sexuality at all. It's strange, when I think about the kind of knowledge that young people have today, but we knew nothing. We used to kind of speculate... but I didn't know about willies, I didn't know I had a vagina. I knew *nothing*. We did O level biology, and every single girl in the school failed, because the nun who was teaching us would not take us through the last chapter on the human reproductive system, and the whole exam was about that. We looked at the drawings, but it just didn't make any sense. I must have had

175

hormones, because I had my periods young, when I was about ten or eleven, but I was a very asexual kind of young girl.

I was very bright, I'd done two A levels at the same time as my O levels, and the nuns were saying 'You should go to university!' but I wouldn't have it. I could not wait to get out of boarding school, and for me, going to university was just more of the same. I agitated my parents to let me leave school and they were absolutely fine with it – my father didn't see the point of educating me. He agreed that I could go to Pitman's College to become a secretary. And then he died, of thrombosis, just at the end of the school year. He'd gone back to his village in Italy for the first time since he'd left in the 20s. He'd gone back there, had a major thrombosis, and died within a few minutes. My mother was just completely and utterly distraught, she almost had a nervous breakdown about it. But it had all been agreed that I would go into Pitman's College, and I'd already been enrolled, so that carried on.

I didn't even know the word

It was great fun. I immediately took up with Kathy, an East End girl the same age as me who was at the college. We were best friends, we used to sleep in the same bed, and I was allowed to stay over at her parents'. There was no sexual thing at all there, we were just best mates. But my first sexual relationship was with a girl. If my mother had known, she would have hit the roof. Kathy and I used to go to pubs and Portobello was just starting to be a trendy place to go. I could walk there and we used to go on Saturday. We went to this pub – I can visualise it like it was yesterday – just at the top of Portobello. We were standing outside and there was this young woman, the same age as us, standing over there. She and I took one look at one another... well! I didn't even know the word lesbian. I went over and chatted to her and we just – I don't even know what it was, it wasn't sexual, but Kathy kind of realised and I could tell she didn't like her. She was the same age as us, and she didn't look like a dyke.

I can't remember whether she phoned me up, or whether I phoned her up, but it was within a couple of days. She lived with her parents, like we all did, in a council flat in the East End. We used to go out, and I asked permission to stay at her house. I was given permission, because her parents were there and that was all okay... And that was my first sexual relationship. We just went to bed. We'd never said a word about it; we didn't say, 'Let's do this.' We went to bed and just did it! It was amazing. It was absolutely wonderful. That relationship carried on for about six months. We never spoke about it, we never held hands or anything, it was only in bed, and I kept it very secret. I didn't even tell Kathy that I was seeing her. Nobody knew. We knew we had to keep it *absolutely* secret.

We carried on this relationship until one day she phoned me up and said, 'Oh, we're in terrible trouble! I didn't tell you, but I've been keeping a diary.' And she said, 'My mother found it – she's going to ring up your mother. We must stop.' And I never saw her again. I lived in absolute terror. But she obviously never did ring. For me it was a big secret, all of that; and after that I didn't go out with any women, I was so scared I would be found out.

Leaving home

Around that time, a member of my family raped me. That, again, was a big guilt trip, because it was 'all my fault', and so that had to be kept hidden, too, and I did not tell anyone. Then I ran away from home. My mother wanted to send me away to Italy, to another boarding school (I was well below eighteen, still) so I left. I'd just about finished my first year at Pitman's, though it was a two-year course. I left home with about ten quid. Somebody helped me find a bedsit in Swiss Cottage. I got myself a job as a secretary, on the strength of my one year at Pitman's and the fact that I could speak languages – it was an Italian shipping line. And that was it. I'd left home.

Then I think I finally realised. I used to go to a pub in Fulham Road, where I became aware of a few lesbians. They were women about the same age as me, maybe a few years older, in their early twenties. I fell in love with a woman called Vanya, but it was totally unrequited. She was an Asian woman, which was very unusual, and she was *so* out, she was outrageous. Her parents had an Indian restaurant. She used to go up to straight women and kind of touch them up, in the pub! I've never known anything quite like it. And I used to follow her like a little puppy, but she never looked at me. So, there were a few lesbians on the scene and it was at that time, I think, that I became aware of lesbians (and did *Sister George*[1] come out at that point?). But I was going out with men, having sex with men, usually one-night stands, and usually when I was drunk.

That carried on till I was nineteen or twenty. I was very poor: I was earning ten quid a week, and four pounds ten shillings of that went on my rent. I was still friends with my good girlfriend Kathy and people like that, and we used to go out to discos, so I came across gay men. At one point, Kathy and I started a business: we bought string vests for just a few pennies from an Army Surplus store, dyed them amazing colours and sold them to the gay boys! So it was a way of making a bit more money. We used to quite like going out with gay boys, because they were nice and entertaining and it was no threat. It was a whole new world opening to us. It was as part of that, I think, that I became aware of the gay scene. But for me there were those few gay women I fancied, who were on the scene; and then there was the traditional gay scene, the butch dykes.

Then Kathy met this guy, and I didn't see her that often any more. The club where I used to try and go, and sometimes I used to get in, was the Robin Hood,[2] not far from Paddington Station. It was very hard getting into it unless they knew you – you used to have to get someone to sign you in. And I might have looked younger than I was; there was a whole thing about being under twenty-one, it was really difficult. You'd wait there, hang around the corner waiting for somebody, to say, 'Would you sign me in?' Then I met this woman, Alma, who took me to the Gateways.[3] She was a very, very traditional bull-dyke, much older than me: she must have been in her forties then.

She was an antique dealer, and she had a house down the New King's Road, and I'd got the impression that she had a steady girlfriend who was a nurse, but I stayed at her house loads of times and I didn't see the girlfriend – so maybe they didn't live together. And she took me to the Gateways. I must have been nineteen, and it was an absolute revelation. I was horrified, really. I saw it all on Saturday nights – that was when we went there, so everyone was dressed up, and I'd never seen women who looked so much like men. What we'd now call bull-dykes, with a femme. But then, I was in that scene, too.

Swinging London

Alma was very butch looking, though she didn't quite wear the suit and tie. And she didn't have the *very* short hair; but she was still butch, and she expected you to be femme. One drank such a lot in those days, there was so much alcohol, and I used to drink... One didn't drink wine or beer, it was spirits. So, there was a lot of drinking. And I ended up with this woman – with Alma – and I thought, 'This is it, then.' I wasn't happy. I didn't like the sex with her either, the sex was really not very good. She was, I feel now, looking back on it, very repressed. It wasn't that wonderful, sensual experience. It was very like with a man, really. But this was the gay scene and I thought, 'Well, this is what it's about.' So I carried on going out with her.

She had a group of American women friends that used to come round fairly frequently, and they were in the horse business. They were horse trainers, rich women, one of them had a house in Montpelier Square. We used to go there and, as I said, I was drinking a lot, everybody used to drink, and they used to talk like blokes, talking about their women and what they did to them, and all of that. I was just this little girl – I was very pretty – this little girl in high heels and mini-skirts, and I lived like this, with this woman, just waiting to go out with her every weekend. We had nothing in common. Then, one day, I decided, 'No, that's it, I'm not a lesbian. I can't be a lesbian, I hate it.' Because it was also so old-fashioned. You had

Swinging London... and then you had all of this. I knew there was something else because, as I said, Vanya and her friends used to come to the Gateways and the pubs, but they tended to mix with a much more trendy set. Her girlfriend was a DJ in this quite trendy disco, so they mixed with pop stars and all of that crowd, which I wasn't into. I knew it existed, but... So I said, 'That's it.' I finished with Alma – she wasn't really bothered – and I thought, 'Well, I'm obviously not a lesbian!' It was very disappointing.

I carried on with my life. I had affairs with men; nothing ever lasted, it was mostly one-night stands. Then somebody I knew gave me a job in a second-hand shop selling antique clothing. By now I was a bit more secure in myself, but still not very happy. It was the 70s, and very much the days of sexual liberation. Everybody was sleeping with everybody else. I was friendly with a woman called Diana and she knew a lot of quite famous people. I used to go over to her house in West Hampstead. What happened then was that, while still going out with men, a lot of the women were sleeping with one another. Whenever there weren't any men around, we used to have sex. I had a period of a few years when one used to sleep with one's friends. But again, the 'L word' was never mentioned.

The sex with women was always so gorgeous, so enthralling, so sensual! It's what you love doing. The sex with men was – well, I remember many years later saying it was like rape. But for me it was only ever when I was very drunk anyway; I could only ever relax and do it properly when I was drunk. Or in those days, stoned, I suppose: we were smoking dope and taking pills, and then doing all that kind of thing. Yes, the sex with women was absolutely gorgeous. As soon as the men were out, we all used to do it – but then, although the environment was fairly liberal, it was still kept quiet. Some of the men knew and just shrugged it off, because it didn't matter to them, as long as the women were available to them; but we never spoke about it. It never had the 'L' label on it. You never told your other friends, women who disapproved.

I then entered into quite a long relationship with a French

woman, Solange. She was a manicurist; I've never had such beautiful nails as I had then. My nails and toenails were simply gorgeous. That lasted around eighteen months, which was a long time. She had her own place – most of us were sharing flats, and she had her own self-contained studio flat, just off the Kings Road. So that was good, because then we could go there and do what we wanted. But again – hidden. At that point I was sharing a flat with a woman called Jane, who was completely heterosexual. Oh God, she loved men! She loved fucking men, and she was working her way around the world: she wanted to go to bed with men of every single nationality, age, height, width, you name it. Completely liberated, sexually. I remember, she used to say to me, 'What you need is a good fuck. The reason you're like this is because you're not fucking enough, Silva. That will release you.'

She didn't like Solange. But I was quite happy with her. I wasn't in love with her. At that point, apart from my first girlfriend, and maybe Vanya that I was besotted with, I don't think I'd fallen in love with a woman. But you know, it was a good sexual relationship and we were good friends. Solange had been badly abused physically, as a child – tied to chair legs, starving, very bad – and she was fairly emotionally damaged. When we split up, she came around one day asking for me and I wasn't there. Jane didn't like her and told her I wasn't there. She was wanting to wait for me and she told Jane the whole story, how we'd been lovers and everything else. Jane didn't believe her.

When I came back she said, 'That bloody Solange's been here, and she's such a liar, isn't she?' And to this day I feel guilty, because I said, 'Oh my God, did she really say that?' I felt really, really embarrassed. So yes, it was completely secret. In those days of (supposedly) sexual liberation for women, you could just do anything you wanted, except that. So that was my life, my sexual life, until feminism happened.

Before that, I went to live in Spain. I'd got slightly hung up on drugs and was just about managing to hold myself together. My friend Diane was a heroin addict by then, two or three people I knew died of heroin addiction, and times were bad financially. Jane had spent six months in Ibiza and she came back and said, 'Oh, there's jobs to be had, it's a lovely life. I know this guy we can go and work for, selling jewellery to the tourists. Let's leave London, let's go and live in Spain!' What drove me was to try and get away from the heroin, because I wasn't addicted, but I was taking it. So we went to Ibiza. In those days, there were very few drugs in Ibiza, because the Spanish prisons were very tough. Tino, the guy she worked for, gave me a job immediately, just selling junk rubbish jewellery to the tourists, and I spent a year and a half there.

Eventually I thought, I don't want to carry on doing this, I've got to get back to London. I came back and things were still quite bad: I didn't have a job, didn't have any money, didn't have anywhere to live. I went back to see my friends, and people were still in the same position, they'd not moved on, and I thought, well I can't go back in that cadre. Somebody got me into this squat. I didn't know what squatting was, but I ended up squatting, claiming benefits – and I'd never claimed benefits in my life, I didn't know they existed.

Radical politics

But I got into that life and into the radical movement – and all of a sudden it all changed. I got politicised. As part of that, there was the campaign for homes in Central London (where I was squatting), Save Covent Garden, feminism, lesbianism – all the -isms were there: anti-racism, the abortion campaign, all of that was there. I was having an affair with a man who was quite nice – one of the few that lasted a little while – and I told him, when drunk, how difficult it was to have sex with him and about my affairs with women, and he actually told me I should come out. All around me I came across lesbians who were out, and they were women like me. It was joyous.

Once I found my feet and started getting involved, I got a proper job in the rights environment, giving advice, and there were lesbians everywhere. You could be what you wanted. I was friendly with a woman called Carol. She didn't look like a lesbian, but we were talking about something one day and I said, 'You're a lesbian, aren't you?' And she said, 'Yeah. I don't like labels, but that's what I am.' And I thought, 'Ah, God, so I can be a lesbian!'

Of course, there was opportunity – they were everywhere, at conferences, it was just like being in a sweet shop. After all those years! I've never looked back, really. It was wonderful. I could *be myself* and be a lesbian: I didn't have to look like that any more. Having said that, of course, I got the gear, I looked the part. I cut my hair short, I didn't quite have the dungarees, but almost. I looked like a lesbian, and all the women I was going out with looked like lesbians. They had short hair – and we didn't wear makeup then, didn't wear high heels. I'd been a very femme girl, very pretty, totally into clothes; and for me that was also part of it, because men used to always go for me because I was such a pretty girl. For me not to have to look like that, and still be a sexual being, was really important. I could cast all of this away and still be sexual, and there were other women like me. I've never worn a dress since, I don't own a dress.

Eventually, I got a job at the GLC (Greater London Council), and I always remember – it was much later, it must have been in the mid 80s – I was walking along Piccadilly, going to a club on a Saturday night, a lovely summer's evening, with a girlfriend. This guy, part of a group, just stopped, and I thought he was going to be aggressive. He was young, a yuppie dressed for the office.

He looked at me and said, 'Let me tell you something about yourself: you're a lesbian, you work for the GLC, and you live in Islington.'

And I said, 'Yes, well done!'

And he went, 'Yeah!' and they all clapped.

It was so funny. So I looked the part. In those days, being able to recognise one another was so important, to be able to identify. They were good times. I had a good job, working in local government, I was out to everyone and had a permanent girlfriend by then, I never had any hassle or discrimination, so I was living the life, really. But I must say, I was horrible. I talked about those 'lipstick lesbians', and looked down on feminine lesbians, and all of those labels we used to give one another... I remember in those days you could not wear a leather jacket in the GLC-funded Gay and Lesbian Centre and there was a huge separatist movement which I was on the edge of. I was part of that. Looking back, I think a lot of us during that period were quite sexually repressed in bed by the 'political correctness of it' – trying not to emulate straight relationships and heterosexual behaviours – in fact I think my sexual life was probably more varied when I was sleeping with my girlfriends, before liberation, without the politics of it. Nevertheless, it was good and suited me. Later on, it was labelled 'vanilla', I believe.

Lucky to survive

Well, one had a fabulous life, as long as one carried on living that life, going out, being young and having the energy to be able to do all of that. I've changed since then. I stopped looking like that, grew my hair, moved out of central London to what is almost countryside. I had a twelve-year relationship; that finished in '97. After that I had a couple of short-term relationships and one-night stands, but nothing since – my job was very full on and stressful and did not leave me much time or energy. I'm not a relationship person, I believe now.

Since I moved here, I can't go out to bars and, with age, have outgrown them; my gay milieu is getting smaller and smaller. Where do you go? I don't have much of a social life, full stop. I have some friends, but it's not a huge crowd and maybe that comes with age? Also, it's about retiring. I did a full-on job in local government all those years. I managed housing services for a borough. I was very busy. I'm still involved, I do a bit of consultancy and I support a small housing organisation, so I still see quite a lot of those people. But obviously, work took so much of my life, and a lot of the people that I was involved with and knew were work-related. Having taken the decision sixteen years ago to move out here, well, it's not Hackney! In

Hackney, you look around and there's lots of lesbians. I saw two dykes the other day and it's the first time I've ever seen them around here. I almost rushed over to say, 'Hello!'

I think I need to make an effort to widen my circle of friends. I attend Meetup groups when they have something interesting on and I can never make up my mind if I want or need to go out more, or if I value my autonomy and freedom to vegetate and entertain myself more. I almost know more gay men than gay women: I've got lots of good gay men friends here.

But I've done well. My friends think I'm quite together, and probably I am, because survival was my priority. I've put that ahead of relationships, perhaps. I don't necessarily view my lesbian life as a success, and that must be my fault. I wish, in those early days... I wish I'd known then what I know now. I wish, when I tried to come out that first time, that had worked. You know, with a different type of woman. There must have been other women like that. I would have saved myself a lot of grief, I think. I don't generally look back, I'm not that type of person, but I really, nowadays... When people talk about, 'Oh, those days down the Gateways,' and how great it all was – well, it actually wasn't for me. It was an underworld type of life, wasn't it? Later on, I went to a couple of Gateways reunions, and now I tend to look at that life with fondness, if you like, as part of our heritage – but it didn't do *me* any good, I must say.

I've got this idea that I probably won't live for that long. None of my family lived to be very old. And I've never been a planner – people used to call me a real existentialist. I've never looked ahead. I've made a decision on one day, and my life's changed; I've always lived like that. Now, I think I've got a much wider perspective on my life, who I am and why I'm like this, but that's quite a recent thing. I was always a very inward-looking person, a scared person. When I left home, I had no support system at all. I didn't speak to my mother – I spoke to her probably about half a dozen times after I left home. So survival was always very important for me. I've always just been lucky to survive.

MUMTAZ

Life is never separated from history, and the effect of history on my life is extremely important. My family is an old East African family; we had moved to East Africa from India during the early nineteenth century and settled in Zanzibar, which became a British Protectorate. The British did not allow Indians to buy land on the mainland. But after the First World War, Britain was granted mandate over Tanganyika, which had previously been colonised by Germany, and property there was being sold off as a result of Germany having lost the war. This meant that Indians could buy land in Tanganyika. By this time, Zanzibar was clearly losing its position of dominance in East Africa, and my family, being very well established and wealthy, decided to buy some of this German property and shift to Tanganyika.

So by the time the Second World War came along, we were well established, business-wise, on the Tanganyikan mainland. But there was the possibility that Germany might win that war, and then what would happen to all their properties that had been sold off? So the decision was made that the majority of my family, particularly women, children, and most of the young men as well, would move back to India. And the business was re-established in India, just in case, because no one knew what the outcome of the war would be. That's how I ended up being born in Bombay, in 1950. By 1952, when I was about two years old, everyone had moved back to East Africa.

We were very segregated there. We lived in tight-knit communities and, because of the nature of my family and their 'standing', I actually didn't have friends beyond my cousins. My first schooling was in East Africa; then I was sent to an English boarding school in Sussex. It was a school for young women of the aristocracy, not an academic school. I had two older sisters who were already there: my oldest sister had been sent two years prior to me, and my middle sister the year before me. I had never wanted to leave East Africa and I was extremely unhappy. It wasn't so much that I didn't want to leave my family; I didn't want to leave Africa. I really, deeply, did not want to leave that country. It wasn't about nationality, because it was a very colonial country, with all the trappings of colonialism. It was much more to do with the land, and my connection with the land.

The year I arrived in England, 1961, was the year of Tanganyikan independence. It was the first of the three East African countries to become independent, and Independence Day fell in early December. I'd only been at the school three months. My dormitory at school was a large one, I remember, about eight or nine of us. I had all the girls in that dormitory up at midnight, Tanganyikan time – I was absolutely astonished that they did this – and I sang the Tanganyikan National Anthem, and we marked Independence Day. I was determined I was going to do it, and they were going to do it with me because they were in the same room – and they did! I was eleven.

A protected girlhood

I spent much of that first year, I realise with hindsight, being ill – not really ill, but ending up in the sanatorium because I had been so unhappy. Eventually it became all right – I got used to it. I remember one girl at school who would always invite me home for half-term and things like that, if there were no family members in this country for me to go to. Almost all the pupils were English. In my eldest sister's class there was an Iraqi woman, and apart from that, as far as I can remember, there was only me and my sisters and my cousins. Most of the rest were getting ready to 'come out' – meaning to be presented at court, find a husband and get married. But I wasn't. I grew up in a so-called progressive and secular Muslim family and although it was clear that as a woman I too would eventually get married, I never did.

When I left school at sixteen, I went to Germany. My step-grandmother was German, I already spoke German, and I

187

had decided I was going to do languages. I hadn't been able to do any A levels at school. They didn't do them there, and somehow it just never came into the frame that that might be a possibility, or that I might go to university. There was no guidance. So, I left school in many ways rather uneducated; and certainly very innocent about sex and relationships. I had no knowledge, for instance, that women could love each other. That awareness I suppose grew within me, only as I became more aware of the women's movement and stuff like that, later on. So, I left school and went to Germany. I was always very protected. I lived in a hostel for young women in a suburb of Hamburg; there were business friends of my parents who were supposed to be keeping an eye on me while I was there. I went to a private language school, to learn German.

The girls in the hostel were older than me. There was one girl, who I still know, who is more or less my age, but the two women with whom I shared a room were five years older than me. Bearing in mind that I was sixteen and they were twenty, twenty-one, that was a considerable age difference. I would go out with this group of young people to places like jazz bars, and there were always men around, but somehow all the men were very protective. I thoroughly enjoyed that year in Hamburg. I certainly went overboard with drink, but everybody was drinking – and it wasn't actually totally overboard, you were exploring your limits. At the time, I felt like a big person and I felt I knew what I was doing. But when I reflect on it, it seems astonishing. And I didn't really know very much at all. I pretended I knew.

History intervenes again

I came back to England, trained to be a secretary, and started work. Then my mother became ill with cancer and came to England for treatment. Just as I was finishing the secretarial course, she asked me whether I'd go back home. And I said yes, I would. I guess, on reflection, it was for mixed reasons. My mother and I had always had a very difficult relationship: that has to do with complex female relationships in the household, between my mother and my paternal grandmother, that I got caught up in. Unconsciously, I think I went home because I wanted to try and repair that relationship, but on another level it was also an opportunity for me to get back to the country I'd never wanted to leave in the first place. It was a complicated couple of years. It was the time when I certainly became aware of my sexuality much more, of the way it was building up in my body, but not having any way of expressing that.

Eventually, at the end of those two years, what happened – and again, this is history playing its part – was that Tanganyika was going down the socialist road, with Julius Nyerere and his policies, and they were nationalising everything. I went back in '69, and in '71 there was, basically, the exodus of the Asian community from Tanzania. I and my middle sister both travelled back to England by ship. I was coming to the end of my two-year work permit. I had some VSO friends, and one of them took my parents' belongings out of the country as his own. My parents had left overnight. My mother was seriously ill, and it wasn't easy to get tickets out of the country by air. A couple of cousins of mine were getting married to men from Nairobi in Kenya, and those two men gave my parents their tickets. So it was extremely traumatic. I haven't been back to Tanzania since then. At first it was just difficult, and now it's much more to do with my disability and my lack of finances.

Just to bring my relationship with that part of the world to an end: bizarrely, many years later, when I was living in London and working as a photographer, I was invited to an exhibition opening just down the road from where I lived. Amrit Wilson, the left-wing activist, writer/researcher and so on, came to the opening. She is also from East Africa, and she came with this elderly man. She knew who I was, because of my name; anyone of my generation who came from East Africa could automatically place me because of my name. She introduced me to this man, and he was one of the leaders of the Zanzibar revolution. Just after Zanzibar became independent, there'd been a very bloody revolution when the large majority of the

Arab population, as well as many South Asians, were killed. The only member of my family still living on Zanzibar then was a great-uncle, and he had managed to escape, again at the last minute, with his wife and daughter. So for many, many years, my family had not been able to go back to Zanzibar.

And there in Haringey, in the middle of this very small opening, I meet Abdul Rehman Babu, and he looks at me, and he says, 'Are you related to this person, and this person?'

And I say, 'Yes, that is my grandfather,' or whatever. And I'm obviously a little bit disconcerted and uncomfortable.

But he just said to me, 'Don't feel ashamed about your family. They did what they could, and they were good people.'

In one fell swoop, he managed to reassure me, heal this thing that I'd always had to live with, a family that had got very caught up in colonial politics, with all the consequences. I had felt embarrassed and uncomfortable about them.

There was another person from East Africa living in London, who also clearly recognised who I was. She asked me once, 'Have you had any repercussions here, because of who you are, within the women's movement?' Now, she was talking about class, and the effects of class. They didn't object to what my family had done; but I was the rich kid and what did I know about life? It was part of that 'hierarchy of oppression' business within the women's movement, which wasn't just about gender, but was also about class and race, and all sorts of other things.

I think class attitudes are pernicious. I'm not minimising prejudice towards working-class people, but I think class attitudes can also be used, just as racism can be used, in other ways. Because I'm from an upper middle-class background, I feel there is very little understanding of the struggle of some upper middle-class women, in terms of having to find their own way in a world with which they're totally unfamiliar. Just to become financially literate, for instance, you have to work at it, you have to learn. Men don't give you those gifts, whether they're your family or anyone else. They don't teach you, and learning how to do that is difficult. You may have grown up with so-called comforts, but that didn't teach you how to survive in the world. I'm not minimising what other people have had to go through, but I feel strongly that putting labels on people is very, very limiting – whether it's a class label or any other kind. We don't see the person for the label.

Photography and politics

After I came back from Tanzania, I started working for Amnesty International, at the International Secretariat, as a secretary. Eventually I got very frustrated, as I felt I wasn't moving or shifting anywhere. So I decided to study languages properly – at the Polytechnic of Central London, because they offered a degree in Chinese. I was going to do German as my second language. I chose Chinese because of the link with Tanzania; at the time we were leaving, their presence was strong in Tanzania. And I had always had a left-wing bent. So off I went, as part of my degree, to spend two years in China: 1978 to '80. One day when I was travelling in China – they were just getting televisions – I was in a department store, watching the Brixton riots on the television. As I was watching the Brixton riots, I was saying to myself, 'I've got to make a choice here, that England is my home.' Because up until then I hadn't made that choice; my home was in Africa. And I thought, I'd got to make the choice where it would be. So I came back with that conscious choice in my mind.

I had to start getting involved with things, and where was I going to do that? One of the first things that I did when I came back was to get involved with an Asian women's group that were producing a magazine called *Mukti*. At that time I also changed from being an academic to being a photographer. My whole intention behind that was not to take pretty pictures, but to transform the ways in which people had been viewed. I had realised, when I was in China, that nothing I had read about or seen was true to the picture I experienced when I was there. It was also obvious to me that the way in which the Third World and my own country was depicted wasn't true either. While I was growing up, it was westernised men within our communities who were the ones who were seen as the most progressive. Because traditional perspectives on women within our communities were more restrictive, it was always seen as though the women – my mothers, my aunts, to personalise it – were controlling, were 'backwards'. And gradually I learned to hold different perspectives. I taught it to myself; I didn't learn it in discussions with other people. I also became highly sensitised to the situation of Chinese women. It was one that I related to, because there was a double standard going on – the double standard of the Communist party against the reality of what their lives were.

It's not that I was unaware of women loving women by then, it was in my consciousness, but this is when it was becoming a reality to me. I don't think we realise how much we've internalised, on all sorts of different levels – whether it's the internalisation of 'being the good girl', and just behaving like the good girl, or of all the colonial teaching, that tells us that our cultures are backward, that there's nothing good in them, that everything our mothers had to teach us was wrong... That's what colonialism said. And I *am* a child of the British Empire – I inherited that. Underlying all that is what still goes on here, today. You don't have to scratch the surface very far to realise that the ideals that informed the liberation movements of the 1970s have not gone very deep. Whether it's the women's movement, anti-racism, gay liberation – I do think a lot of the time people just pay lip service to those ideas. I think what's happened is probably what's happened throughout history, that the establishment has been very good at co-opting revolutionary ideas... And they've taken all sorts of bits and pieces from the women's movement, the gay movement, and everybody's supposed to be okay now. But, actually, it isn't okay, and you don't have to scratch very far beneath the surface to find that out.

I've been thinking about the women's movement, in the context of sexuality and sex, and also in the context of where we are now. What has changed, if paedophilia, child trafficking, women trafficking, prostitution of all kinds, is worse now than it ever was before? People talk about things like the sexualisation of children as though it was something new – but in the early 90s, when I created a piece on sexual abuse, I found a double-page spread in a newspaper on the sexualisation of young girls, through the kind of clothes that they were wearing. What has changed, twenty years down the road? If anything, it's got worse. What's become acceptable is for young women to go and do pole dancing for themselves, as an expression of their sexuality!

Independence

Throughout my life I've looked for intimate relationship, but I was never very successful at finding it, whether heterosexual or in the lesbian community. I don't know how people find their partners, but they seem to find them, and I never did. I found one: I had one relationship with a woman which was important to me. It didn't last. I was brought up so confused by my body, I was brought up to think that my body and its expression were not right. And not finding a relationship that could turn that around, I live with my body myself, now. I've decided it's just not worth the effort, and I'm quite happy to live a celibate life, in the sense that I live singly and I choose not to express my sexuality with another person. I think what I'm saying is something about myself that runs deeper than the issue of sexual orientation, and for some reason it's not been part of my life to be in a relationship. What I've found as I've grown older is that that's another oppression: the way society is structured is that we should all be in relationships. It was a very strong part of the cultural script that we were given, and it continues to be, for economic reasons if no other.

I'm not even sure, now, whether I can call myself a lesbian. I've lived such a long celibate life, not in an active intimate relationship to another woman. I think I would feel differently if I was in a lesbian community, but I'm not. I thought I might be; it was one of the reasons why I came up to Liverpool, to try and be in one. I knew a couple of women here, I knew there was a community established here, and I was looking for a community. It didn't work out, though. When your health isn't strong enough for you to constantly be going out to whatever, there's very little that comes back.

I can never stop being a woman, whether I'm part of a women's community or not; so, does that hold true for that part of me that is or was a lesbian? I don't know the answer. I simply know that I don't feel part of any community, whether it's a women's community, whether it's my family community, whether it's my ethnic minority community, or whatever. And I think that's something that's to do with me, and my life's journey. Sometimes it's very tough. At other times – well, this is the way it is. It's not for want of trying. But I've given up the trying, and all I can do now is simply be. It was actually a great relief to turn sixty – I could stop trying. I could just be.

I've given up trying to make plans. It just seems to me now that I live from day to day. My mobility's very poor; I walk with a stick. I refuse to use a wheelchair – I don't know if I could, because I don't know if I could lift the wheelchair into the car if I needed to go anywhere. And what I've noticed is, every time I've taken on an aid with the intention of helping me, I've got a little bit weaker, or it's taken me in a different direction. So I think what's becoming more and more important to me is to find a way of working with my energy – and that probably, for me, means in yogic terms. When you feel your internal energy, you also feel your sexuality, and you begin to feel alive in a completely different way.

It's very frightening for me to think that I might end up in a home, because I would totally lose my independence. I work off and on for Age UK, as what they call an 'expert by experience', visiting care homes. Those places frighten me. Whatever has happened to me, I've kept myself going in whatever way I've been able to. Thank God for the power of the internet! I really don't know how people survive isolation if they can't communicate. So I'm concerned that I would lose that kind of independence. If there's anything that's crucial to me, it's my independence.

JULIA

My home circumstances as a child were very difficult. I was born in January 1948, in a suburb of London. My maternal grandmother's family came to East London from southern Ireland. My father was from Belfast. Unfortunately, my father was a drinker – I suppose you would call him an alcoholic – so that was a problem throughout my childhood. He had ill health, and my mother said that was the reason he drank. So he never held down a job for very long and we were always really short of money. My mother worked part-time, but in quite low-skilled jobs, so that didn't bring in any significant income. So things were very tight. He wasn't a violent man, but he could be verbally abusive and the house was always in a shambles. Things weren't great.

I was quite a bright child, and I passed my eleven-plus and did fairly well, but I think it was at that stage that trying to cope with the difficulties at home actually told on me, and my studies suffered. I was supposed to go to university, but because things were so bad at home I flunked my A levels, and that was the end of it. My father had had a couple of blood clots and strokes, and at one stage when I was taking my A levels he was on what they called 'open order' in hospital, expected to die at any minute. And I just don't think I was emotionally strong enough to deal with it.

I had boyfriends while I was at school, but they weren't sexual relationships. I don't think it was that usual, then, for that to happen when you were very young. But as young as five, I had quite intense one-to-one friendships with girls. I can remember saying to friends, albeit in a child-like way, 'Oh, why can't we go to a land where girls can marry girls?' And I remember my friends looking a bit perplexed at that, as though they didn't quite understand it. I didn't mean anything sexual by it, at all. But I remember saying it, I think because of their response to me. A strange look seemed to come across their faces – they didn't quite know how to answer me! It's their reaction I remember.

I think one always does have one or two special friends. And again, I think this particularly relates to my upbringing and how things were at home. I had to trust somebody extremely well to bring them into my home; it wasn't the best of homes. I had to be sure in my own mind that that person was still going to accept me when they saw the background I was from. And that's why I tended not to go around with huge gangs of people. I was always in a one-on-one, or with two special friends.

Julia (right) aged six, with friend

A bad time and a good time

I knew that I wanted to get away from home and, rather stupidly, within six months of leaving school I'd met and married somebody. I realised at the time that I was doing it to get away from home. I was eighteen, coming on nineteen, and it was a mistake. I was from a Catholic background and I married an Orthodox Jew. Although my parents were okay about it, his parents were very much against it – understandably, but that made him all the more eager to be rebellious and marry me. And that's what we did.

The marriage lasted about three years and during that time I had one child. That was part of the problem, because for my son to be a Jew, I would have had to convert. My husband tried to persuade me, but I wasn't prepared to do that, partly because the marriage wasn't working anyway. When I met him, I thought he was very protective. He used to tell me to do things, like put my coat on if it was cold, or take care of myself in certain ways – all the things my father hadn't done. I used to think that was quite protective, but once I married him, he became very possessive and domineering, and actually became violent. Not breaking bones or anything, but I had a couple of black eyes and things like that. I just realised I had to go, because he was so jealous and so possessive. He wanted to know my every move, and I didn't think that was going to work out. Things came to a head and I left. I took my son with me.

It was sort of a bad time and a good time. My father died when I was about twenty-one. There was part of me that didn't know how to react to the death of my father, because I always wanted to be rid of him. That sounds awful, but that's how I felt. Yet I can remember going to his funeral and – I know this sounds very melodramatic, but I felt I wanted to throw myself on top of the coffin when it went into the ground. I felt extremely sorry I'd never had any relationship with him, but I also felt extremely relieved that he'd gone. And in just the same way, I was very sorry that my marriage hadn't worked out, but I was extremely relieved to get out of it.

At that stage I was to all intents and purposes still a straight woman, and I remember going to the Catholic priest to explain what had happened and try to get somewhere to live. He was very helpful and suggested that I try to get an annulment. It was the priest's suggestion; I would never have thought of it. Basically, it was because my husband was a Jew, and it's something called the Pauline Privilege. Because he wasn't baptised and I was, and because he was trying to stop me from practising my faith, I did actually get an annulment of the marriage. I was still a believing Catholic. I mean, he'd stopped me going to Mass and everything, but I was. I wasn't intense about my faith, though I had been as a teenager. I think I'd turned to religion because of the situation at home, and at one stage I wanted to be a nun.

Once I was free of the marriage, and my father had died, I tried I suppose to have some kind of youth; and I probably had four or five boyfriends, each one lasting for a couple of years. There were a couple of men that I was really passionately in love with, but things didn't work out. The men that I was attracted to were usually ladies' men, a bit of a villain, you know, 'wide boys'! It still brings a smile to my face now. I could never fall in love with a nice man, and I don't know if that's because I never had a good relationship with my father. I could not have a relationship that interested me emotionally and physically, in any way, with a nice, straightforward man. It was my pattern.

I think I'm gay

What happened to me next was a chance thing. I was going out with a guy, not a sexual relationship at this point, but just one of these decent guys that I felt absolutely nothing for, and I decided to go to college. I thought it would be good if I trained to be a teacher. I would then have the holidays off with my son, it seemed a sensible thing to do. So I went and studied English and drama at a college in the London area, external to London University, and I walked into a den of gay men and lesbians. It was a small college, but probably three of the men in the English department were gay, the art mistress was gay, the principal was gay, half of the education department... and I really liked these people. I just liked them as people, they were open and friendly to everybody, they were open about their sexuality. Obviously they didn't foist it on us, but we all knew what they were and the way they lived their lives. As students we would socialise with them and have a drink in the bar, and as we got on – year one, year two – we would go to their houses.

I was a mature student, about twenty-five, twenty-six. I was coming home with this guy that I didn't fancy one night, and he was trying to sort of push me into a more sexual relationship. I knew I wasn't going to do it, I wasn't interested.

I thought, 'Why am I wasting my time? I just cannot bear this, I've had such a boring evening – I've had far more fun talking to these gay men and women. I go out with other straight people from the college to clubs with them and I enjoy the evening, I really enjoy it. I really like those women – the only thing I haven't done is have sex with a woman. Maybe if I meet other gay women' – because I wasn't thinking of having an affair with my tutor! – 'maybe if I meet other gay women, and I go with an open mind, maybe I would like sex with them. Why don't I just go about with them a bit more socially and see what happens?'

So I walked into college, went to one of the tutors and said to her, 'Susan, I think I'm gay!' And bless her, she didn't look at all surprised or shocked, considering I was quite a glamour puss at that stage. I had long hair down my back, I wore high heels, you know, the makeup, the works, everything. She said, 'Why do you think that?' I explained to her, and she said, 'Well, why don't you come out with us when we go to some clubs and stuff, and I'll find you the names and addresses of some local women's groups you could go along to.' Which she did, and I went out a few times. I went to some of the local women's groups, and while I was there I met my first partner.

I remember the first group I went along to, where I met Renate. I walked into the house and there was a poster on the wall with a big pair of garden shears hanging beside it, and it said, 'Free Castration on Demand!' I looked at this, and because I'd come from this straight background, it seemed to me very extreme. But that was the only point where I wondered what I'd walked into.

Consciousness raising

I remember they had a consciousness-raising group going, and my not really understanding why only the people who were already in the group could carry on with it, and some of us, who were newer, couldn't. Also I think they would examine their vaginas with speculums, there was all that sort of thing. And there's me thinking, 'I don't know, is that quite...? That sounds a bit odd.' Because you've just been catapulted straight into it, you've walked into someone's house, the front door has closed, and you think, 'What the hell have I walked into?' It was a bit odd. Then I kind of realised, okay, that was some little part of them, and they were just trying to forge a different way for themselves. I suppose because I wasn't in the consciousness-raising group and I wasn't expected to get a speculum out and do all this, it was okay. But it was quite a big step.

Renate was a German woman who was studying graphic design at St Martin's. We started to go out just a little bit together socially, and I really fell for her. She was good fun, she was exciting. It came to the point where we were going out one night... she lived in Willesden Green, I lived in Hayes, and it was going to be quite difficult for both of us to get home, because neither of us drove. She said, 'Well, you can stay at my place for the night.' So, me coming from a straight background, I thought, 'Oh, this is it!' because no way would a man ask you to stay the night unless that was going to be the start of the sexual relationship. So that's what a straight woman from a working-class background, in that era, would think – you stay the night with someone, that's it.

But her coming from a sort of lesbian feminist perspective, it was just, 'Oh no, I really like you, but I'm just offering you somewhere to sleep for the night.' Basically, what happened next turned into a bit of a farce, because she said, 'Well, here's the bed, I'll sleep on the couch,' and I was absolutely horrified, you see, because I'd been building this up, this was going to be my first big experience.

I said to her, 'Renate, come over here and get in this bed with me!' So in the end, I more or less seduced her, which was really strange, because I was expecting it to be the other way round. And it was fun. It was just fun. I was sexually turned on by it, so I thought, 'Well, it works, I can be gay. There's part of me that is gay!'

I never think of myself as bisexual, though. I think of myself as totally gay. But having said that, were circumstances different, I could probably have lived a straight life all my life. But I would never want to swing both ways. For me, I know that wouldn't work – I have to be one or the other. And once I took that step, at twenty-five or twenty-six, I never looked back. All my relationships have been with women since then. I think once or twice I've met a man and thought, 'Oh yes, I could be sexually attracted to you.' But I would have to go all the way the other way again, and – it might sound a bit prudish – but it would just confuse me too much, to sort of do one thing one year and something else another. I know you can do them simultaneously, but I couldn't do that either. And I doubt that I would have a relationship with a man now. I had relationships with men for five or six years of my life, and I've had relationships with women for thirty-five years. But had I not met these women, and had I not been in a difficult marriage, possibly I could have stayed straight all my life. Though I can remember, when I was married, and I had my son in the pram, a very obviously butch woman coming up and looking at him and saying, 'Oh he's a real boy, I bet you're proud of him.' And I was so fascinated by her, this sort of 'other' thing, and knowing what she was...

So I was always a little bit fascinated by the idea, but not really feeling that it applied to me, until I met this crowd of people and knew that they were just like anybody else, and I could really get on with them and be open with them. I didn't have to role-play with them, I liked that. At that time, I'm sure it's not the same now, but at that time, if you were straight, it was the chap that rang you, and if you were interested you had to look immaculate and have your makeup on, and your high heels and whatever – whereas with them, I could say what I wanted, I could wear what I wanted.

Julia (right) with Antonia circa 1980

Coming out

I told my mother that I was gay. She was absolutely fine. But because my mother had to put up with so much from my father, she was a very passive person. Rather colourless; but a very kind person. So I knew that there would be absolutely no problem from her. One would almost have liked a bit of interest, but it was, 'Oh, all right dear.' And she accepted Renate, and indeed Renate and I lived with her for a while. She was very fond of Renate, so I should be grateful really. My son loved Renate, because she'd do all the boyish things with him, you know, building boats and things. We didn't try not to be affectionate in front of him, we'd hold hands and so on, but he came in once and caught us kissing; not a sexual kiss, but a fairly obvious kiss. He probably was about five or six, and he said, 'You two are kissing. And if you're both kissing, one of you must be the man!' Now, Renate was actually pretty dykey and butch, but he turned to me and said, 'And if one of you's the man, it's got to be you, because you're my mum!' Which was a bit odd. I can only think that he thought, even at that age, that it was the man that was the most important, so it had to be his mum that was going to be the man.

I was with Renate for about three years, and I suppose things did gradually break down. At the end of the three years it was time for her to make the decision whether she went back to Germany or not – and had things been working well, she would have stayed, but we did split up and she went back to Germany.

I had lots of friends around me by that stage – gay friends – and then I met Antonia. She was Dutch, and she was also over here studying. She was doing a doctorate in psychology. And it was a similar sort of pattern really: we had a really good time when we were together, but at the end of her three years' studying... She asked me if I would like to go over to Amsterdam and live with her, but again the relationship was kind of running to the end of its course, and that didn't happen, so she went back home. There was a loose arrangement that maybe we would stay together, but some months after she'd gone back

I did meet somebody else – who was an English woman, for a change! I was with her for about three or four years, at the end of which time I met a French woman, Chantelle.

There's a shade of regret here, because I never actually sat down and announced to people that I was gay. Though when I was with my Dutch partner, I went to a social event where I was working at the time, and for some reason or another I became determined that she should come with me. So we attended this function and I held hands with her when we danced. We danced together. So what I did was coming out by action. And that went down extremely badly where I worked, *extremely* badly. I was called in, interviewed, and told that this wasn't really thought to be decent or appropriate behaviour. It wasn't a function at the workplace itself, it was a twenty-first birthday party at a colleague's home, but she complained to the management that this shouldn't have happened, that this employee was obviously 'one of those', and that she'd been terribly upset by it. Subsequently, over the next six months or a year, it became too difficult for me to work there, so I actually left in the end.

Another incident was when I was with my English partner. We were in a pub with a group of about four or five other women, and it was a similar situation, in that I held hands with her, and I may have kissed her on the cheek or something like that. The pub landlord came over and said, 'You'll have to leave.' I can't remember what we said. I think I said, 'Why?' and he said, 'Well, I'm not having that sort of behaviour in here.' So we had a choice: either we stayed and stopped holding hands, or we'd have to leave. And I think in the end we did leave. So it's strange, but I've had a couple of incidents where I've come out by what I was doing, but I've never had the courage to explain myself verbally to people.

My whole world had fallen apart

The longest relationship I've had was with my French partner, Chantelle: I was with her for fifteen years. Because I thought, 'What am I going to do? Am I going to repeat this pattern throughout my life, of having these three- or four-year relationships, and then they finish? I've really got to make a conscious decision to work at it and stick to it. Because what will happen otherwise is that I'll go through the same scenario: year one – marvellous; year two – very good; year three – on the way out. I'll just be doing this all the time.' And I really did make an effort to work at it. I was that bit older, and she was that bit older as well, so I really did make the effort. We were together for fifteen years. But, unfortunately, she died.

Chantelle was quite difficult. She was quite quick-tempered, but she also had, from way back, a history of depression. I discovered, right at the end of her life, that she'd actually been sexually abused as a child by somebody in her village. There'd been a huge case in France, the guy had got twelve years. She was a brilliant woman, she spoke six languages, she had worked for the World Health Organisation, she was extremely interesting to be with. But she had, people told me, at a couple of points in her life threatened suicide. She got extremely depressed, because she had some physical problems, and after two years of threatening to do it, she did actually take her own life. And so I came home and found her.

When she died, it was at the weekend, and I went into work on the Monday. My gay friends tried to stop me, but I was so, so upset, I said to them, 'What can I do? I'll be at home, and I shall be in an absolute state. If I go to work, I might have to concentrate, and I might just be able to see it through.' My whole world had fallen apart, I didn't know how I was going to cope, and I suppose I thought that going into work would maybe just hold it together for me. I had been in the same job for eighteen years, all the time I was with her. I was a researcher for Price Waterhouse Cooper's, I worked in the library there. When the holidays came round, I'd say, 'Oh, I'm going away with my French friend,' because we'd go to Brittany, which was where she was from. Maybe I'd say sometimes what I was doing at the weekend, and I suppose people pick up – 'Oh, she's not married, but she's got this friend, she seems to do a lot of things with her.' I never actually said that I was gay.

I went into work, and I obviously had to say something to them, so I went to my immediate boss and said to her that Chantelle had died, had taken her own life.

She said to me straight away, 'You shouldn't be here.'

I said, 'But I've got to come into work.' I refused to go home. I said, 'I'm going to work for two days.'

There were about four or five people on our team, and she went up first and told them. I remember one of the women said to me, 'But she was your family!' And I remember thinking, 'They probably do know.' They were so sweet to me, they went to personnel and said, 'She's got to go home,' and in the end I had two weeks' leave. They were really very good. And a couple of gay friends took me in. I went to their house and stayed with them for two weeks.

I think my work did help to hold me together... and my gay friends. I was about fifty when Chantelle died. It had been so intense for the last year or so of her life, when she was ill, that it took me a couple of years to get over it. I was obviously seeing my friends, and I used to say, 'Can I give you a hug, because I can't hug her? Can I tell you I love her, because I can't tell her any more?' and they were just really sweet.

After about eighteen months one of them said to me, 'Look, there's this organisation, the Older Lesbian Network, and they meet once every month, and you don't have to book up, you can just go along when you want to, there's no pressure or anything.' And to me that sounded ideal. I think they were trying to give me a bit of a push, because they felt I ought to get to know new people. So I did go along, and it was a life-saver, a really good move for me. I used to just go along for the meetings, I didn't go on to the social events afterwards, and I was able to meet new people. I made some friends and I'd perhaps get asked to a party or something. I also worked for about a year on a gay bereavement helpline. I did that because I felt that was giving something back after what I'd been through. That was in the third year (I was on my own for about four or five years) because for the first couple of years I was grieving.

In the fourth year I was starting to go to social events, either through people I'd met at OLN, or various other scenarios. After about five years, everything was starting to come together reasonably well, I was feeling reasonably strong in myself (I was about fifty-five at that point) when, blow me down, we had a huge round of redundancies where I worked and practically everybody in my department was made redundant. So there I was: another big thing had happened. But work wasn't my life. People said to me, 'Are you going to try and find something else?' and initially I thought, 'Oh, yes I will,' but then I thought, 'No, I need some time off.' And I took the time.

I remember, on the final day at work, walking out and saying to Chantelle in my head, 'Well, there you are. I've finally stopped working, and we could have had that life in France that we'd always talked about. But I haven't got a job now, and I haven't got France any more – so you'd better find me a nice woman!' And about six months later I met Philippa.

Meeting Philippa

We met at a friend's house. They were having a social gathering. Philippa was just coming out of a relationship that had been a bit on/off, someone that she'd known years and years ago who'd then reappeared. I think I was drawn to her because she was quite witty. At one stage she just looked as if she was a bit fed up, and I remember thinking, 'Oh that's probably because she's upset about the split-up with her former partner.' I was feeling down that day, because I did still regularly feel a bit down, and I thought, 'Oh come on, *she's* being brave, *you* make an effort!' Then she'd gone out into the garden, and she looked quite alone standing there, and I thought, 'Oh, poor Philippa! We're supposed to be over here helping to cheer her up, and she's gone out into the garden, she's all on her own.' So I went out, because I felt sorry for her I suppose. I *thought* she'd gone out because she felt quite sad... and she'd only gone out to have a bloody cigarette, hadn't she? Anyway, we got talking, and we went out to a few things, and then we just got together. She might tell you that I leapt on her, but it's not true. It was kind of a mutual thing.

I think when our relationship started, my expectation would have been that we'd eventually live together, but it then became clear to me that that wasn't what Philippa did. I had to have a bit of a tussle with myself about that, because I actually think it's more fun, and less strain in some ways, to live with somebody. I think it gives a more emotional togetherness. So, living with someone is the ideal in my head, but would it work out? I don't know. It certainly won't work out if the other person is not used to doing it, so one just has to be a bit realistic about it, I suppose. I'm not used to some of the ways that Philippa likes to live her life, in that she likes to travel far more than I do, so there are a lot of separate holidays involved. I hate flying, that's a difficulty for me. And I'm not used to not living with my partner, so again that's a compromise. But I'm also old enough to realise that one can't change people, so one either has to make one's life dovetail, or call it quits – and then you lose the good parts of a relationship.

I do go on my own to OLN occasionally, and to Kenric. I'm passionate about my garden, to a fault. I've a very small garden, but I am passionate about it. I enjoy reading... and obviously we do the normal social things with friends. I do have a few gay friends of my own, but we also have gay friends in common. So we think differently about things, like not having the domestic relationship, and also not having the same idea about travel and holidays; but in other ways we get along very well. Philippa is very witty and entertaining. I think it's the entertaining aspect that appeals to me – I'm not bored! I think that's what keeps it going.

7

NOT HER NEXT OF KIN

Because the women I talked to were in their sixties, seventies and eighties, their accounts cast light on the process of ageing. As seen earlier, some, like Val and Mumtaz, are coping with physical disability; others, like Leo, struggle with the loneliness of losing a life partner – or, like Edith, of never having had one. In this chapter, two of my interviewees, Sandra and Jackie, describe a particularly distressing aspect of ageing: the fact that women they have loved for years are now afflicted with dementia.

Sandra tells a tale of growing up gay in Australia and coming to England as a teenager 'just for a working holiday'. That was more than fifty years ago – she didn't go back. The reason for her change of plan was Mara, the fascinating woman she lived with for most of her adult life. The difficulties related by Sandra reflect the times she has lived through, because the relationship was never recognised in law and so she had no legal rights in connection to her partner. The stress was exacerbated by the isolation of a couple who lived all their lives in the closet; the experience of dealing with health and social services was made even harder at first by the fear of being 'found out'.

Jackie's relationship with Miriam had no legal status, either; she had to fight for the relationship to be recognised, and to be given information about Miriam's health by the care home. Not every lesbian is able – or wants – to register a civil partnership, get married, or even come out; but, as Jackie reminds us, we can be left vulnerable if we have no recourse to law. As she says: 'It is very important that homosexual couples realise they need to take out health and welfare Power of Attorney[1] for each other.'

Jackie also mentions being a member of SAND (Safe Ageing No Discrimination).[2] This Shropshire campaigning group looks forward to a future in which old LGBT people are fully included in a wider community 'which values their experiences, meets their needs and offers appropriate personalised care'. It is a vision to which we might all subscribe.

JT

~

Sandra (left) and Mara, 1965

NOT HER NEXT OF KIN

SANDRA

I was madly in love with a girl when I was nine. Well, she made the advances to me. One evening, she stayed over at my place because her parents had gone out with my mum and dad. She was in my sister's bed and I was in my bed, and she... made advances to me. It was a bit more than kissing and cuddling. Yeah. She never kissed me, it was just inserting a finger and... yes, a bit of exploratory work there. When I was about ten, I said to her father, 'When I grow up, I'm going to change into a boy and marry Sheila!' And instead of just laughing it off, he went and told Mum and Dad. So that was the end of that friendship. Oh, I chased after her! Literally, because she only lived three doors away from me – I used to chase after her, down the road, for years after that. When I last saw her, in 1976, she was married, with a couple of kids.

But at the same age that Sheila was playing around with me, I was also being abused by an older boy. I was nine. He didn't penetrate me, but he tried to. And, well, I didn't know any different than that's what boys did. He left the area when he was sixteen, and I was only ten – fortunately, because I could have got pregnant if it had gone any further. But I've learnt to live with that.

I was the baby of the family, born in 1944, in Sydney, Australia, with an older brother and sister. My father was a taxi driver – he was an absolute bastard, not a nice man – and Mum was a homebody. Sydney was very different then. A very macho, masculine environment, I'm sure, for wives and so on: you did what your husband wanted. But it was probably the same in Britain at that time, too. I didn't see much of Dad; I didn't want to, anyway. I had a lot of illness as a child, and spent a lot of time with Mum.

When I was eleven years old, I was the same height I am now, five-ten: second tallest girl in the school. In primary school, I was bodyguard to a girl: a very pretty little thing and a mad keen ballet dancer. When it was gym she'd come into class in this tight little leotard thingy. She thought she'd have me to protect her from anybody that was bullying her. Well, kids didn't bully me, because I was pretty hefty. Then, when I was about twelve, I tried to become involved with a girl: a lot of heavy breathing under the bedclothes, and possibly my first orgasm – both of us were very physically mature. And then – it was very sad – she died. At twelve or thirteen, she had her appendix out, peritonitis set in and she died. Very sad, when you go to a kid's funeral.

I wasn't involved with anybody at high school. In fact, when I was fifteen or sixteen I went out with a couple of boys. But I was mad about the biology teacher. She was only twenty-three, so there wasn't a big difference in age. There was another, very butch, lesbian in my class and she was interested in the biology teacher, too. I felt very jealous of this other girl. She was nice-looking, tall and masculine. I went to the school fete one Saturday – I put on my best ladylike suit, dressed up, rolled up to the fete – and this other girl had turned up in a hacking jacket, jodhpurs and riding boots. I could have bloody killed her. And she looked absolutely fabulous. Fabulous. I didn't fancy her; I wished I could look like that. Talk about Stephen from *The Well of Loneliness*![3] Broad shoulders, slim hips in these jodhpurs. I went home *very* annoyed.

After school, I went to technical college, to learn shorthand and typing, business principles and book-keeping. Didn't last long. I haven't got a brain for shorthand. I went to work in chinaware in a department store. You know *Are You Being Served?* Well this was Grace Brothers, only in Sydney. My supervisor was a spinster in her early fifties – I did my best to get on the same bus home as her. I went to evening class to increase my typing speeds, and changed jobs to a large machine-tool company. I was in the import/export section, working with four guys. They soon twigged the situation, even then. The big boss's secretary, a lady in her fifties, was in charge of the mail room, and she'd go around the building asking girls to come in to open the mail. There would be about seven of us girls, but she invariably called for me, and the boys would say, 'She fancies you!' Yeah. I chased her for a long time. I think I was always attracted to older women. She was very elegant, droll and dry, and always smartly dressed. She caught the same train as me, so I was always hurrying to catch the same train home as her. I found out she was living with a lady; but then I discovered it was her sister. I still feel that she probably was... but not able to do anything about it, in her position, in those days.

At home in Sydney, I used to knock around with all the girls, and got on very well. But I started, when I was sixteen or seventeen, going out in the evenings by myself. I'd go up to King's Cross, which is like Soho in London. There was a huge club there, the Sound Lounge, a big pit of a place. It was pitch dark and had a tiny dance floor. No drinks, no alcohol allowed: they only served coffee. And I'd ask girls to dance. Sometimes they'd say yes, sometimes they'd say no. Well, it took my nerve to go up to a girl. They'd be sitting there, in this huge dark cavern, and then you'd get up onto a dance floor. I wouldn't do any smoochy dances with a girl. I knew I wanted something from those girls, but I didn't know how to go about it.

Voyage to England

The September after my eighteenth birthday, I left Australia for a working holiday in England. I travelled by ship, as flying was very expensive. We set off from Sydney and docked overnight at Auckland. And two girls came walking down the gangplank. One was stunning, with auburn hair, and her friend had pitch-black hair and alabaster skin. They were dressed absolutely fantastically. Now, Auckland in those days (we're talking about 1963) was like 1945 over here: way behind the times. So there was Barbara in her pedal-pushers, and Rina in a sort of sari outfit, and the whole of the dockside agog, looking at these two girls walking down the gangplank. I thought, they look interesting!

Next evening I went into the bar and the two girls were

there. So I went up and said, 'Can I buy you a drink?' Barbara was in her forties, and Rina probably the same. Not lesbian. Barbara was British. She was a very nice-looking girl. I can see her now, in her black strapless dress, with all the stiff petticoats of those days, and her auburn hair pulled back in a tight bun: she looked a million dollars. I don't know what Rina's antecedents were, but she was very exotic-looking, very lovely. And they took me under their wing. Absolutely. They liked me and we had a lovely time. In the evening, we'd go up to first class, because they were friendly with a man who owned a large carpet store in Sydney. We'd spend the evening with him, go back to their cabin and have laughs, and they'd have a gang in. It was really nice.

It was quite a long journey, from Auckland up to Fiji, and then Fiji to Hawaii. They got off in Hawaii, but before they left, Barbara said to me, 'Do you know anybody in London?' I said, 'Well, no, I don't.' And she said, 'I'll give you an address of a friend.' So I left them in Hawaii; and then, on to Vancouver, and San Francisco, and down to Los Angeles. I got off at Los Angeles, and I spent ninety-nine days zig-zagging right across America on Greyhound buses. Right up to the Canadian border, and down as far as New Orleans. Sometimes I stayed with relatives, or family friends; other times in hotels. I had all sorts of adventures, but eventually the time came to board the *Queen Mary* for England.

I had left Sydney on 20 September 1963, and I got to London on 18 December, just the week before Christmas. I stayed at the YWCA. Being in central London, I'd be out all hours of the night, wandering around just to see the city. It was a real eye-opener to me, 'cause it was the 60s, and I'd be walking behind what I thought were girls, but they were fellas! Because their hair was so long, by then. I'd be wandering around Leicester Square and Piccadilly Circus at midnight, and go back to the YW and the door would be locked. I couldn't get in, so I'd be sitting in the front porch until they opened it up in the morning. But I didn't get into any trouble at all. On Christmas Day, I bought a chicken sandwich and a can of beer, and stuck the can on the window ledge outside because it was so cold. That was Christmas dinner for me.

And that was it

A few days before Christmas, I had rung Mara, the woman whose address and phone number Barbara had given me on the ship. But I don't think that Barbara had told her she'd given me her address, because Mara didn't know me from Adam. She said, 'Well, I've got people staying at the moment, but give me a call after Christmas.' So a few days later, I rang again and she said, 'Yes, do come round. I'll meet you at the station.' She met me at East Putney Station. She had a white V-neck sweater on and black ski pants, I remember; and I had a red skirt and a black cardigan. And off we went to her place. Her husband Frank was there, and one of her nephews. She had a bar in the lounge. We all sat and had drinks and chatted, and she got sloshed; and at half past seven, she said to them to go off to bed. She wanted them out of the way. I can remember putting my hand down her V-neck white sweater, yeah... So, a couple of hours later *we* went off to bed.

And that was it. From that day on. 28 December 1963. I was nineteen, and just coming away for a year's working holiday; but by the March, I'd cancelled my return ticket home. And I took out citizenship in 1973 to make sure I could stay.

We've been together more than fifty years, now. Mara is older than me by twenty-four years. She'd had a very, very interesting life before I met her. She'd married a chap who'd been a racing car driver at Brooklands back in the 30s, a very handsome man. They divorced because the marriage was never consummated; he was a masochist. Mara started nursing training the week after war broke out in 1939. She was bombed out several times, but escaped injury. During the war she met Vivien, and lived with her for many years in Putney. And then she met Frank. Mara's into spiritualism and he was too, healing and so on. She married him, but Vivien was still on the scene and lived in the house with them. Then Vivien got pregnant!

So that was the end of that: she went off and married the chap.

Mara had bought a house in Stockwell; the whole street was due for demolition and she bought this big four-storey place for a pittance and did it all up. She had let it out into bedsits, the whole lot, so they were doing quite well there. Well, she was in a pub chatting to a lady and said she needed some work done, and the lady said, 'Oh, my daughter will give you a hand, she's very good.' So that was how Mara met Wyn: around the same age, very butch, and a real cockney. Wyn was painting the place for her and doing it up; she was handy that way, and ended up living there in the house. Then Mara left Frank, and she and Wyn went down to Bexhill. Mara bought a restaurant there, and spent a couple of years running that. From there she went to Mumbles and had a B&B, again with Wyn. And then Frank said he wanted to get back with her. So she went back to London in 1960, and bought the house in Putney in '60 or '61.

It was a nice Edwardian house. Upstairs she had a couple of bedsits, one in the front and one in the back, and there was a spare bedroom for me. She and Frank had the big downstairs bedroom, a very large room with two single beds in it. From our first night together, Mara never went back to that bed. And he must have known what was going on. I didn't realise it at the time, because I'd never lived in a house before, always a bungalow; but when Frank finally moved out, about six years later, we came down to that bedroom. There were people upstairs, then, and it was 'twang, twang, twang'! I'd been quite unaware that you could hear, downstairs, what was going on in the bedrooms upstairs. Mara must have known. So it was, as I tell people, a *ménage à trois*, but he wasn't getting any *ménage*!

Mara and I fought like cat and bloody dog. For the first couple of years I was packing my bag every few months. I'd go down to the station. We were chalk and cheese. She's a far deeper person than me, far more intelligent and spiritual, and she says to me, 'It's just sex with you!' But she wasn't slow in those stakes. She had an elderly aunt living in Wales, and every few months she'd go down to look after her and do things for her in the house. And whenever she came back, after a week or a couple of weeks away, I'd take the day off work, and then we'd spend the day in bed.

When her aunt died, Mara suggested we take the cottage over, because London was expensive, especially Putney. So we moved down there, to a little cottage from a big house. She had to put in a bathroom before we got down there. Kitchen, bathroom and two tiny bedrooms upstairs, a nice little lounge, just cosy. So it was fine for us, though it was cold, because there was no central heating: a Rayburn in the lounge, that's all. Well, it was a huge change. It was a dump of a town. I thought it very backward. We were fourteen years in that cottage, until the landlord tried to raise our rent and it was time to get a place of our own. So we looked around and bought the bungalow a few miles away, where I still live.

Mara always had a lot of men friends. At nineteen years of age I'd never heard the word 'bisexual', but that's obviously what she was. More lesbian; but she'd be saying to me, 'So-and-so fancies me,' and all this, and that would really wind me up. She's been absolutely faithful to me, but I can't say the same. I got a bit involved with a girl at work once. And then in 1976 I went out to see my mum for six weeks, and had a one-night (plus one day) fling, with a girl I met in a gay bar. I was bloody besotted. Stupid, stupid!

I came back home in the September, and after that fabulous, fabulous summer there was six weeks of rain, every day. Coming up through the Welsh Valleys, it was foul, awful. Mara picked me up and it was a nightmare being in the house with her, the guilt was absolutely overwhelming me. I was so off with her! I said, 'I'm leaving.' Well, she was shattered. I moved out, and I even made enquiries about leaving Wales and going back to Australia. The only time I've seen Mara cry was when I left her. She's not a lady for tears at all; it was the only time. Finally, after about three weeks, I thought, 'Right, I've got to come to my senses here,' and I went back to her. I never told her the reason I left. She asked why, and I said, well, because I was so unsettled, I'd had a lovely holiday, everybody was marvellous to me there, the weather was marvellous and I came back here and we didn't have a lot of social life down there. And I've stuck to that ever since, and never enlightened her.

In sickness as in health

Mara has dementia now. I suppose the first sign of it was about eight years ago – but I didn't know that, then. There was one day when she just *raged* at me for the whole day. I don't think it was anything I'd said, she just raged, on and on. I sat there thinking, 'What's going on? What is going on here? I can't tell the doctor, she's not going to believe me. And I can't tell her nephew and his wife, because they won't believe me either.' And the next day she was calm; not a thing. So, of course, I didn't bring it up... and then after a couple of years, things just developed.

She was deteriorating mentally. I was being accused of things, and she started getting on the phone and ringing here, there and everywhere. Just pressing numbers. She'd be trying to use the phone to work the television. She'd be ringing the police, and they'd say, 'What's wrong?' She'd say, 'She's not doing what I'm telling her to do.' Or she was on the phone to her nephew, who was living in Gloucester, saying, 'Come up and sort things out in the house. You sort her out.' Then an hour later I'd apologise for what I hadn't said, and 'Oh that's fine,' and she'd ring him and say, 'No need, it's all right.' She'd do the same to the solicitor. 'I want to change my will, come over.' Then an hour later, 'Well, if you really mean that apology...' So she'd have to get back on the phone to him. And this was done a dozen times over a couple of years.

By this time she was nearing ninety and had several physical illnesses, too. She'd had bowel cancer some years before and got through that with radiology; but, as a result, she had bowel trouble and got very scared of going out anywhere. In 1997, she said to me, 'I want you to retire next year and look after me.' So I said, 'All right.' I had a good job by then, working for a land drainage civil engineering company; I'd been with them twenty-two years. The job suited me down to the ground, because I could dress in trousers. We would have these lorries coming in and I'd be leaping up on the lorries with the fellas, helping them unload, and that was great. So it was a very good job. But, as I say, in '97 Mara said, 'Would you leave?' so I left the following May. They gave me a terrific send-off.

A couple of months later, Mara developed polymyalgia rheumatica. She was on steroids for about eighteen months, but we got past that, too. And over the years her legs stopped working; she hasn't walked for about nine years now. By the time she was ninety, she'd spent practically the whole previous two years in bed. She was finding it too much effort to get up. She was having falls, too. She'd fall out of bed and I'd spend maybe four or five hours trying to get her off the floor. She was unable to get on her knees, because they were so painful with arthritis, and I'd have pouffes or whatever, trying to get under her bum and build it up, or push the mattress right across to get her onto the base of the bed. From one o'clock to five o'clock in the morning I could be doing that – not knowing that if anybody fell, you could ring the ambulance and they'd come and pick them up. When I found *that* out, I had them ten times in two years.

Hard, hard work

For a couple of years, I'd been saying to her, 'I think we need some care for you, you know, carers coming in?' She was in a wheelchair by then, so that I could push her around the house. And I'd say to her, 'I think a bit of care would be helpful.'

'Yes, all right then.' I'd get on and make arrangements, then an hour later, 'No,' she'd say, 'I don't really want anybody, give them a ring back and say no.'

So I'd do that. And this would happen every few months. Then, finally, I said, 'No, you really, really do.'

She was drinking – she's always been a drinker – and she was getting aggressive. She'd be chucking things at me, or if I came too close I had to dodge her walking stick. And so I got the carers in, and they were coming three times a day, because she couldn't get out of bed, and she couldn't get to the loo any more. We didn't have a washing machine. I used to do the washing all by hand in a bucket, soak it in a bucket, or in the bath. And that was hard, hard work. I was eating as normal, but the weight was dropping off me. My doctor gave me a thorough examination, thinking something awful was going on.

So I got the carers in. They'd come in three times a day, morning, afternoon and evening. They'd use a hoist, which she didn't like. Of course, being a nurse, she thought they were bloody awful, and the training they'd had was pathetic. One day, we were all in the room and she suddenly said, 'Sandra's a lesbian! But I'm not.' Now except for telling her nephew and his wife, about six months before this, Mara had *never, ever* told anyone about our relationship. Then she said, 'We had a short fling, but that was it.' Well, I wanted the ground to swallow me up. The girls just stood there stunned for a second and then got on with what they were doing.

For a couple of months, I got somebody in to sit with her while I went shopping for a few hours, because I came home one day from shopping and found her on the floor and she didn't know how long she'd been there. So I got these people in – a couple of ladies – and they told me she was very demanding.

Three weeks before Christmas 2012, Mara went into a local care home for respite care; and then on Christmas Eve she came home. The whole week was like living on the edge of a volcano, I had to be so careful what I said or did.

A few days after Christmas, she said, 'Hasn't there been any mail for me?'

I said, 'Yes. But I'm just dishing up dinner, so we'll have a look afterwards.'

She said, 'No, I'd like it now!'

I said, 'Well, I'm literally dishing dinner.'

'I want it now.'

So I gave her the mail, we had dinner, and an hour later she rang the police: 'My carer has been withholding my mail from me.'

Ten minutes later there was a ring at the front door: a

community support officer. I explained the situation to him, but he couldn't take my word for it, so I gave him the social services number and he rang them.

He then went into the bedroom and said to Mara, 'I've rung social services, and they think it's best you go back into the home.'

'No, I'm not. I'm staying here, this is my home and I'm staying here!' He was very good with her, he spoke to her a long time, but, 'No, no, I'm not.'

Then he said, 'How about if you go in on Monday, then?'

'Yes,' she said. 'Right, I'll have the weekend at home. I'll go in on Monday.'

So, on New Year's Eve, the ambulance came and took her back for two weeks' R & R, while a permanent placing was found elsewhere. By then I weighed eight and a half stone – not a good look at five foot ten! Only three weeks later, a friend remarked, 'You look a lot better, Sandra.'

On my own now

It's a lovely place. Not posh, but very homely. I wouldn't want her anywhere else. The first few weeks weren't too bad. I kept popping in often, every day – because I'm only four and a half miles away, thank God. And then she was getting worse. For instance, she had a lot of money in her handbag – *hundreds of pounds* (she used to keep a lot of money in the house, as much as a thousand quid). I thought well, there's no point in asking her for it, so I just tried to grab it out of her bag. It ended up in a big wrestling match in the room with everybody watching. Nobody took a blind bit of notice, not the carers, not the residents, nobody. And things just got worse. The solicitor would be going down often, because she'd be demanding that he go, and of course, they're charging every time. Although he was my solicitor too, he wouldn't tell me bugger all, because she was his client, you know. We had never had a civil partnership or anything like that, so I couldn't get a thing out of him. I was so frustrated. And Mara's nephew couldn't get anything out of him, either. Until, finally, they got the psychiatrist there to do a capacity test, which showed that she does not have mental capacity. So after that was settled, then he was fine with me. She'd been trying to get the will torn up and kick me out of the house.

She has dementia, Alzheimer's, paranoia... You can have a conversation with her, yes, but you soon realise that things are not right. And every time they come to see her, after four or five months, she's gone down, they say. Sometimes she won't let me see her. I saw her on her ninety-fifth birthday, in April 2015, and again three days later; I did not see her then until the end of September. I thought I'd never see her again, quite honestly. On my birthday that year, I rang the home and said, 'Can you ask Mara if she'll see me, as it's my birthday? I'll leave work to have afternoon tea with her.' And she wouldn't see me. Fortunately, her increasing dementia has now taken a different course, and she is happy to see me when I visit.

Although I'm on my own in our home now, and I was desperately lonely at first, life is good and I have a wide circle of friends. But I remember how, after we'd had a row, Mara used to sing to me, 'Oh, you'll miss me when I'm gone.' And I do! I love her so very deeply. I've found that out in these past three years, more than I ever realised before. Yes, I do miss the sex, I have to be honest – but I don't want another partner. I wouldn't want to live with anyone, because there's no room inside me for anybody else.

~

Mara died in April 2018, just as this book was going to press. Sandra was supported with great kindness by the staff at the care home and was with Mara when she died.

JT

JACKIE

My father was killed in 1945, right at the end of the Second World War. I was about nine. He was a dispatch rider and he was killed in a bombing in Glasgow. So of course, that was a huge thing, but I didn't really think it was anything to do with me. Somehow it seemed to be all to do with our mum, who just sat in the chair and shook for what seemed like weeks. My eldest sister left school when this happened and went out to work, and our mum started working, too. So my other sister, Ann, and I were sent to board at the Catholic school we were already at. I screamed and shouted when I knew I had to go to boarding school – I can remember screaming and screaming about it. But actually, in the end, I was quite happy there, I think. I had crushes on the teachers – but that's very standard, isn't it? It happens a lot. We had little or no sex education there. I think the games mistress used to do it; yes, she told you about when you started your periods. But I wouldn't call it sex education, really. So when I did fall for a woman, I was just – well, blown away by it.

When I left school, I chose to train as a speech and language therapist. We had moved to London by then and I did my course in London, living at home, because I had been away for ages. Our mum was there, but out at work every day. I started training in 1954 and qualified in 1957. I had boyfriends during that time. There was one chap who I quite liked – but I certainly wasn't in love with him. He was a Catholic, too, and his mum thought this was going to be perfect, but no. And I had another boyfriend who came and stayed a few times, but nothing serious. I was certainly not in love. And there wasn't much sex – really nothing serious.

When I qualified, I got a job in Kent, in what was then the School Health Service. I worked in three clinics, in different places. I had a scooter – a Lambretta. I remember that at one time I did a clinic in Ashford; and on a Friday I sometimes used to drive up to London from Ashford, to go and see my mum. All that way on a Lambretta! Oh, my goodness! I thought nothing of it. I wouldn't do it now. So that was my first job. In one of the clinics, in Tonbridge, I met Clare. I suppose we just used to see each other around quite a lot in the clinic, and then at some point one of us said, 'Why don't we go out and do something?' or 'Why don't we have a meal together?'

We were blown away by it

It was then that it just went *pow!* Exploded, I'd call it – that kind of experience. It just took me by storm, really. I was overwhelmed by this... I think for both of us it was like that. We were blown away by it all. Clare was quite a bit older than me, perhaps ten years or so, fifteen years it may have been. She had worked in Africa for quite a long time and had done lots of very, very interesting things. She had been in some heterosexual relationships, but she'd never been in love with a woman before, and probably had not really been in love.

I was living in a horrible flat in Tunbridge Wells. It wasn't a self-contained flat, it was just the top floor of somebody's house. They were terribly frugal and it was always cold, it was cold air coming up the stairs all the time and lino everywhere – I can see it so clearly – and the bed, that was the crucial thing, the bed creaked. It was an iron bedstead. So that's a very clear memory. I don't think I told anybody. I certainly wouldn't have told my mum about the relationship. Though my middle sister had a gay relationship, so she understood. I told her because I felt I could. But I didn't tell anybody else. I used to spend a lot of time with Clare and her family and I don't know what they thought, but they very much accepted me, so that was comfortable. My mum was very *un*-accepting of Clare; she didn't want to know, really.

I then began to find out about some other people. There were teachers that I knew from my school visits and I found out that the two of them were living together, so I started putting two and two together. Clare and I became close friends with them.

A long relationship

Eventually Clare and I got a cottage together, near Tunbridge Wells. It was a long relationship. After about eight years in the School Health Service, I moved to a hospital group. I worked in a rehab unit; then ear, nose and throat; and then with plastic surgeons in relation to children with cleft palate. I fell for a physio I was working with and we did have a short affair. We did both tell our partners, and we got through that. Yes, we did get through it...

Then I decided that I was going to do a postgraduate year. There was a postgraduate diploma course at Reading University in teaching speech therapy. And during that time, Clare's sister and family had moved to just outside Reading, so I lived with them for the year that I was doing this course. Clare died a long time ago, now, but I'm still close to both of her nieces, very close, and go and stay with them. So I was close to the family, very involved with them; but I don't know what they thought about the relationship. So I finished that course in 1972 and got a job at Birmingham Polytechnic (now Birmingham City University). I was appointed to set up the degree course in speech therapy.

Although our relationship was changing, Clare and I moved together. We lived just outside Lichfield and we had a lovely house there, a large garden and, yes, it was okay. But our relationship had faded quite a bit, the sexual aspect of it had gone. It was all right for a while, but in about four years it was getting rocky. And that was when I met Val. She was a mature student, so obviously we had to be very careful. I did tell Clare. And as a result, we eventually separated. Clare went to work with women who had been abused and she managed the home they were in, which she was very good at. She had been a nurse and health visitor and she was compassionate. I think it was painful for Clare, because I had something positive going on but she hadn't. I kept in touch with her. I did still see her; I didn't abandon her. Eventually she moved down to Dorset because her sister and family had moved there, but I saw her regularly throughout the rest of her life.

An active retirement

Val and I didn't start living together for quite a time, because she had a flat before she qualified, quite near to where I was living, and she was going to work. I had a house in Sutton Coldfield; Val's flat was between there and Birmingham. My work life continued to be very interesting. I took early retirement from my job in Birmingham. Soon after, I had a phone call from Zimbabwe, from a professor of linguistics, who said, 'I hear you are leaving Birmingham, we wonder if you could come and run our degree in Zimbabwe?' And I said, 'Well I don't really think so, but I'd like to meet you.'

I did a lot of work in Zimbabwe, over quite a long period. I spent a lot of time with the speech therapists there. In the end, they didn't get a course off the ground, but we did take five Zimbabwean postgraduates and design a course for them with University College London, where they did their academic studies. Then they did their placements back in Zimbabwe, and I monitored their placements. So that was all good stuff.

After that, I worked for two years in Plymouth. I was still living in Sutton Coldfield, but I went each week down to Plymouth: they had a diploma course which had to be converted to a degree. So I was driving each week to and from Plymouth, and often used to go off to Dorset to see Clare. She died in 2003. I was phoned immediately she died, and Val and I went straight down. Val, who is an ordained minister in the United Reformed Church, led the service.

Val and I have been together for a very long time, now; we are in a good relationship. We've been in a civil partnership since 2008 and are committed to supporting each other in the long term, but we are not currently living together. That is partly because Val is a minister in the United Reformed Church and I've become a Buddhist, and those spiritual paths are a bit divergent. I gradually became more and more involved in Buddhism, and eventually, for a number of reasons, started to attend the Shrewsbury Sangha. And then I thought, where I need to be living is Shrewsbury. So Val and I talked about this, discussed it, and she accepted that. We had a very big house in Sutton, and we sold that and were able to buy two houses. Mine is tiny, but fine. So that's where we are up to.

A very wonderful time

And there is another relationship. In 1976, a woman came to stay with me, because she was an external examiner for our course. I knew she was gay because I knew who she lived with. I didn't see her for years, ages and ages, after that, and I then heard that her partner had died. I wrote to her and said I was very sorry. I didn't hear from her for ages, but I didn't necessarily expect to hear back. This was in 2000. I'd been living with Val for several years. Then, suddenly, a card came out of the blue, saying, 'I can remember staying with you and having a very nice meal, you're a good cook, perhaps would you like to come and see me?' She lived in Lincolnshire, which was quite a way, so obviously it wasn't just a day trip, so she said, 'Perhaps you'd like to come and stay, you could stay with me...' And it was, again, one of those things that just went, *bang!*

Well, we started seeing each other a lot. We fell deeply in love. We loved being together. She was a bit older than me: she was seventy-two when we began our relationship, I was sixty-five. I told Val about it; she was very generous and accepting. Miriam and I had a wonderful time. Val doesn't like travelling and things like that, and Miriam loved travelling. We were always going abroad and doing wonderful things. But it's a sad story, because after about five years, Miriam started getting quite depressed, and sort of removed from me a bit, and she was starting Alzheimer's. I supported her and used to visit her a lot, but eventually she needed to go into care.

Not her next of kin

Our relationship started seventeen years ago now. Miriam is in her late eighties. When the time came that she was going to have to go into care, I fought, I absolutely *fought* to have her near me, because, well, I'm the person closest to her in the world. She has no family – I think that's classic, isn't it? – but she has a 'nephew', Geoff. He isn't a real nephew, but the nephew of her late partner – with whom she wasn't in any civil partnership, because there weren't such things, then. So, no relation. He has Power of Attorney for finance and property, but there is none for her health and welfare. I had been the person to take Miriam to all her appointments (hospital visits, GP, chiropodist and so on). I took her to the appointment when her dementia was diagnosed. Anna, who is the wife of the nephew, knows that, but she didn't support me. I fought to have Miriam near me, but they overruled that to have her near them, which is an hour and three-quarters' drive from where I live. I visit every week.

I went to Age UK about it, and they arranged an appointment for me with a solicitor in relation to my rights, and to knowing about Miriam's health and welfare, because of course there was no Power of Attorney. Had I been clued up, I would have taken that out when she was well enough. It is very important that homosexual couples realise they need to take out health and welfare Powers of Attorney for each other.

But, actually, the solicitors fought for me. They suggested I should take further advice, so I've spent thousands on this, because I just think it was terribly important to fight it. I absolutely fought for one thing, which was that the care home would phone me at the same time as Anna and Geoff, if Miriam was ill or had an accident. I eventually won that, they agreed to that. It's not much to ask, is it? And when Miriam had a fall, smashed her face, I was the one that received the phone call; Anna was away for five weeks. So I got in the car, went to the hospital, and was with her when she had her face stitched up.

Then the care home changed hands, and now they *won't* agree that I'm phoned at the same time. No, Anna and Geoff have to be phoned, and then *they* can phone me. This leaves me with a basic underlying anxiety that I will be the last to know if something happens, and I am the furthest away.

There are ongoing problems at the care home. Recently I was there when Miriam was not at all well, and she had a really bad episode when I was present. At my next visit, when we were having lunch, a carer asked me to see that Miriam took her medication, which I did. At the next visit, this same carer opened the front door and I asked her how Miriam was. She said she couldn't tell me. I asked why not and she said because I was not the next of kin. I said, 'Miriam does not have a next of kin.'

Before that, at a meeting with the home manager, I had noticed that the notes said Anna was next of kin. I objected, but it still remains. It's the doctor, actually, the GP, who remains in touch with me. She has been excellent and is willing to tell me everything about Miriam's health. Some time ago she tried to arrange a meeting for these matters to be discussed by all concerned. This included the care home manager, and Geoff and Anna. The solicitor I was using was also invited to attend. No one would agree to meet, so the meeting never happened. But I know I can get in touch with the GP if I have concerns. I have recently been in touch with her to say that I wish to be with Miriam when she dies. She says that Anna and I will be seen equally in this; and that is fine.

Val is very generous. I'm not sure about heterosexual couples, what they do, but Val has accepted Miriam. Miriam used to come and stay and Val knew all about the relationship. Miriam and I used to sleep together in our house. Val has always supported me in relation to Miriam, and accepts absolutely that I visit her.

I go and see Miriam every week. Or I did, until I broke my leg in 2016, and then couldn't see her for several weeks. The very worst thing about breaking my leg was not seeing Miriam. After a few weeks I had a phone call and it was Anna, saying she was there visiting Miriam, and would I like to speak to her? (Would I like to speak to her!) Miriam talks a lot of rubbish now, but Anna said it was the first time she had spoken that afternoon, so I'm sure she knew me. And Anna said, 'Oh, I'm terribly sorry! I don't know why I haven't thought before to phone you.' She knew about my leg and she said she would phone again. She never did so. But I am glad to say that, even after that long gap in visiting, Miriam still remembered me. I feel this might be because I go so regularly and because I spend five or six hours with her at each visit. I am currently feeling very anxious, as Miriam is not at all well, and I think her death might be approaching. How I wish I was near her! It takes me an hour and three-quarters to get to her. When I go now, I usually stay over so that I can see her on two days. She now needs to be fed, so I am able to do this.

The experience of watching someone you love become less and less able with dementia is so painful. I am fortunate in knowing a close schoolfriend of Miriam's, who I can phone and talk to about Miriam and about my pain.

It's important to change attitudes

So, there are important issues in relation to LGBT people and Alzheimer's. It's important to change attitudes towards LGBT clients in services for older people. I think that being old is different for many gay people, because by and large they haven't got any family. That must be one of the major things. And if they haven't come out either, they're very isolated. I was horrified when I was told that there had been this survey of something like 150 care homes in Wales, and they said they hadn't got any LGBT residents. Complete rubbish! Some of them even ticked 'not applicable'. Well, what does that mean?

I'm a volunteer with a set-up here called Friendly Neighbours. They do befriending – visit-befriending – and taking people to appointments and so on. I happen to do dog-walking with them. So, through SAND (Safe Ageing, No Discrimination), I suggested that I should speak to Friendly Neighbours, and ask if they had gay and lesbian people on their books, for visiting. And they said they don't have any. LGBT older people are much more isolated, and I think they lack friends. They lack family, they lack friends. And they keep themselves hidden.

I'm saying 'they' because I don't see myself in that way, because I am very out. I think I've now become much more out, because I feel it's really important for other people, people who know me and I'm friendly with – and they may love me, and they accept me – I think it's really important that they know. Because they may think gay people are weird. Queer. And for other gay people, it's really important to be open, because it helps them, too, if they are gay and not out, it helps them to be out. And of course, Buddhism has helped me to be more honest, because they're completely accepting in the Western Buddhist Order, which is the one I'm involved with, called Triratna. I can't answer for other places, because there are other places in the world which are completely different, but there are quite a lot of same-sex couples in Triratna and that's known – they're out, there isn't any cover-up. We're encouraged to be open in every way. When I visit Miriam I'm absolutely open, and she's absolutely open. She would not have been so open before... But you know, I don't care what other people say, or think.

Although Val and I are currently not living together, we see and support each other a lot. It is most likely that, as we are getting older (I'm eighty-one and Val is eighty this year) we will, in the not-too-distant future, live together again. Neither of us have close family near: Val has a sister and nephews in Australia, and I have nieces in South Africa and cousins here. This lack of family is perhaps not unusual in older lesbians.

I know quite a few lesbian and gay couples here in Shrewsbury. I belong to SAND, which won a 2017 Age UK 'Spirit of Age' Award for Equality and Diversity. There is an annual Rainbow Film Festival, and for the last two years Shrewsbury has been one of the hubs for the National Festival of LGBT History. I feel very fortunate to be living here.

~

Since Jackie completed this account, Miriam has sadly died. However, the management of the home had changed and the new manager was far more supportive. This meant Jackie was able to stay with Miriam in her last few days and to be with her when she died.

JT

8

AND FINALLY...

It is an enormous privilege to share other people's lives in the way that an oral historian does. My gratitude to all my research contributors and collaborators (and not just to those in this book) is unbounded. What's more, the process is full of surprises. Unexpectedly, I have witnessed a journey travelled by many of my collaborators over the handful of years we have been in touch. Women who were secretive and frightened when I met them have slowly pushed the closet door open – sometimes just a crack, sometimes further. While I do not mean to claim that taking part in my research was the cause of all these changes, occasionally our work together has been part of the journey.

This last story is one such. When I first met Pauline and Hilary, some twenty years ago, they were still very cautious about disclosing their relationship. That was because for many years – as you will see from their story – they had every cause to be discreet. When I started out on my research, they did not feel able to take part, even under pseudonyms.

So what changed? Well, no spoilers, but when they did come out, it was in the most public way imaginable: with the wedding of their dreams, surrounded by their loving families. Shortly after that, we recorded the conversation of which the following story is a part. Because, 'finally', they want the world to know. They even agreed to have a picture of themselves on the front cover of this book. It shows them as teenagers in 1955, soon after they first met.

Theirs is an inspiring story, of a love that has survived trials and tribulations for sixty years. Only now, approaching their eightieth birthdays, can they say at last, 'We feel safe.'

JT

~

Pauline (left) and Hilary, the evening before their wedding, 2017
(photograph: Sean Oakes)

PAULINE AND HILARY

Pauline: I can remember very clearly the first time I saw Hilary. It was in Penrhyn Bay, in North Wales. I was seventeen and she was sixteen, and we were both on holiday. One day I was taking some time off from family, strolling by myself down to the beach. It was just a small, quiet part of the beach, where there were rocks; and this person was sat on the rocks, pen in hand. There were very few people on the beach at that point, and we got into conversation. Well, I suppose I started it! And then she stopped her writing, I went over, and we sat on the rocks and chatted away.

Hilary: I'd been there a week, just with my parents. It wasn't really the most joyous thing to go on holiday with your parents at sixteen, as an only child, and be doing what they were doing, and Mum saying, 'Well, we could sit on this seat and do a bit of sewing, if you like. I've brought a couple of tablecloths, and all the threads...' We were meant to be on holiday! I was trailing round like a lost sheep after them. My father and I would have the odd pitch-and-putt, and he'd say, 'Come on, put a smile on it! You're enjoying it! I don't suppose there'll be many more holidays where we'll all come together.' And I'm thinking 'I do hope not!'

So I was off to the beach, writing a letter to the boy I was supposed to be engaged to at the time, who was doing National Service, trying to think what I could put, because we weren't doing a lot to write about. Then suddenly, this person was strolling along the beach, smiling away; and she came and sat on the rocks, next to me, and I was just so *comfortable*...

Pauline: Then we walked along the beach, and then we walked back together, and then back to the boarding houses where we were staying.

235

Hilary: I was very late in for tea, and that wasn't a good start to proceedings at home, but we'd made arrangements for the evening, and there was the promise of the theatre in Llandudno, and a cinema we could possibly go to… We were going to do something every day for the rest of the week. It was going to be great; and we never were apart in that week.

Pauline: We went on Little Orme, and we went on Great Orme…

Hilary: … and walked, and walked, and walked.

Pauline: I'd had boyfriends, too, and one in particular of fairly long standing; but once I'd had the feelings I had about Hilary, in those first few days of knowing her, I was very much aware of the difference. Everything about it was different.

Hilary: It was so nice. You touched hands as you were walking, or you even held hands in the cinema. You couldn't do that in the theatre, because there was a bit more light. You couldn't go and sit on the back row, either, that looked a bit too obvious. And I thought, 'If life goes on like this, it's going to be a ball!' But how could it? We had to go home. And we lived so far apart: Pauline in Cardiff and me in Yorkshire. But Pauline seemed to think that, not to worry, there'd be a way, she'd make it happen. She made everything happen, she was a real goer – I loved that spark. Anyhow, we exchanged addresses, and after that we came home.

Pauline: We wrote to each other. I imagine I initiated that, too, but the replies were coming back – flowing back, fast and furious.

Hilary: Her letters came with plans and arrangements: if I could get a train to Manchester, she'd find the times of the trains, and she would meet me at the station. 'Catch the earliest train that you could possibly get on, and be sure you get on it, and I'll tell you which station…' She was on a mission! And I was so excited. I couldn't get through the week. I was singing away at work, all the modern songs which I'd never really joined in – everything meant something – and everyone knew I was happy, but I couldn't tell anyone why. We would meet up in Manchester, and we'd go out to Cheadle, where Pauline's aunt lived, have a meal there, then go for a walk. The aunt would say, 'It's a bit silly going out when it's raining.' And we'd say, 'Oh, it's all right, we'll take the umbrella.'

Well, we couldn't get out quick enough! We'd both hold the umbrella, and our hands would be touching. It wouldn't really matter whether a little finger was over one of the other's thumbs, or whatever... Oh, the feeling in your tummy, the butterflies, the excitement! Then you'd look round and the sun's shining, and we were still huddled under the umbrella!

Pauline: The first time we slept together was at my aunt and uncle's in Cheadle. My other aunt, who was single and lived with them, insisted on taking the small bedroom, and we had the double bedroom...

Hilary: My engagement had long been over – I'd had to just say it had burnt itself out, that we were too young. Pauline and I knew by then that we wanted to spend our lives together. We wanted that desperately – we couldn't wait. But how? We were trying to scheme how we could do that, and maybe get a flat together. So when it happened that our relationship had to stop, it was devastating. Awful.

Torn apart

Hilary: One day I walked into the house, as you do, after work, and my mother's face was like thunder. I didn't know why. Had I done something to upset her? I walked in, went to where the letter was always stood (the familiar handwriting, the buzz in my tummy, and I couldn't wait to take it upstairs) and I thought, 'That letter's been opened.' I picked it up.

And she said, 'Yes, you'd better read it.'

I said, 'It looks as though you've already read it.'

'I have. And wait until your father comes home!'

I was destroyed. I read the letter, and it was wonderful, but everything was smashed. In pieces. We had phones by then, and it was a matter of 'You get on the phone...'

I said 'No, I'll write.'

'You won't write!'

Well, I was glad in some ways, because I needed to talk to Pauline – but my mother was going to stand there and make sure that I'd said it was over, that it had to be. And it was really blackmail: Pauline's father was in politics, and my mother was going to threaten to bring him down if I didn't do as she said. I didn't want that for Pauline; I would rather take the pain myself. So it had to end. That was it.

Over a couple of years, our letter-writing, and those visits to Pauline's aunt, had got more frequent; and the letters had got very much more... personal. What you couldn't do, or what you couldn't talk about, you could write about, and wish for and hope for. So the letters were very loving, very emotional. There were endearments: 'to my loving, hoped-for wife of the future' or however we worded it at that time; 'and hopefully as a husband I'll look after you and love you forever' and all those sort of things. To have that in writing was absolutely beautiful. And my mother made me destroy all of them. It felt like betraying Pauline. It still makes me cry to think about it.

Pauline: I was affected in a very similar way, although probably it wasn't obvious to anyone. But in those next few weeks, I did become physically ill. So much so, that my dad had to say to Mum that he thought I would have to see a doctor, because they couldn't get to the bottom of what it was about. In the end they did get me to see a consultant. I had to say, in sort of roundabout terms, not exactly what it was about, but why: that it was to do with a relationship, and it was having this effect on me because it was unfortunately not going to be possible any more. I had to be under that consultant for quite a while, actually. I couldn't say point blank what it was about, but I think that Mum and Dad realised. They knew we'd met up at my aunt and uncle's, and they didn't question any of it, in that sense; they knew I was happy. But now this had happened, and I was so ill, they were being advised to try and help me to get over it. Oh yes, it was a very traumatic time.

The years between

Hilary: So, for a couple of years, we didn't see each other at all. I married during that time, and I didn't encounter Pauline again until after I was married.

There was a friend of my family who had been in the RAF. She had loved it, because she could be whoever she was, there. And when I first began to understand my feelings for Pauline, I realised that this friend was in some sort of relationship with another woman. I couldn't yet talk to them about it – they were a lot older than I was – but she was always very nice and kind with me. I always admired her strength and I think she knew I always respected that, but she could never voice it, or guide me, or anything like that. It wasn't a thing that was ever spoken of. In later years, I think she felt she could perhaps have helped me more, and that she'd let me down, but what could she have done? I wouldn't have wanted to cause family problems for her. So you had to deal with it and work it out for yourself.

She used to go to a club where ex-servicemen and women could go and you could take friends. I think she must have known, deep down, the trouble I was in, and she was trying to help. So I went with her to the club, and the person helping behind the bar was a certain gentleman who, in the end, became my husband. He worked for the electricity board, like my father, and he was an up-and-coming trainee engineer. (In the end he would become my father's boss.) Well, my mother jumped on that bandwagon – she was almost joining the band and leading from the front! She couldn't speed it up quick enough. So, because of the pressure she put on us, we married in a very short time. We had our honeymoon; and I knew it wasn't going to be a success, even then, really.

We had to live with my parents, at first, which was very difficult because my mother allowed us so little privacy. And then later, when the children came, that was wonderful. When I was a child, people used to call me Tommy, because I was such a tomboy, though I wasn't aware then that that was my leaning. I used to like to have a penknife, a pea shooter, and all those things. I didn't think about it, I was just me. But I always hoped to have children; so when I got to the stage of life where I did have a child, people used to say, 'I wonder what kind of a mother she'll be, when she's such a –' But I was always very maternal, actually. My husband wasn't a particularly hands-on parent, because he worked a lot and was involved in things at work. But he soon realised that things weren't quite right...

Once I'd got married, I thought it was a chance to write and tell Pauline this, and to ask her if she was all right, because I had been thinking of her. I wasn't putting too much in a letter, but I really wanted her to know she was often in my thoughts. I wasn't able to say a lot more than that. She must have written back and said it would be lovely to meet up, just to see what the other looked like now, and how they were coping with life. She was still coming to her aunt's, with whatever boyfriend she was carrying it off with at the time to make things respectable, and we decided there was a chance that we could all four get together – just to catch up, just to see that the other was all right.

I think by the time we met I might have been in the early stages of my first pregnancy. So everything looked as though it was going well, as life should be. Anyhow, Pauline and her boyfriend came over, and we went out for a meal. Both menfolk were engineers and got on really well. Pauline and I, as ladies do, left the table to go to the ladies' room, where you can have a natter. Well, we walked through the door into the ladies' room and, wow! You only had to both open the door at the same time, and your hands touch on the door, and you just knew. It was still there. More than ever. And even though we were in a public place, we just held one another, and we *bled* from head to toe with the pain of it. It was still there. And here we were...

Pauline: You wonder how you survive those things, thinking about them now.

Hilary: But we had to go back in there and carry that off. Not a word was said, because words were not needed. We just both knew. It was there. I think we might have met up a couple of times after that, but you couldn't say anything. It was too dangerous. We had to keep it very balanced, but we did know.

Things had to change

Pauline: Some time before that, I had made the decision that I was going to study food technology at a college at Bolton. I suppose the thought in my mind was, I would at least be in the north of England, near to Hilary, and who knows what life might bring? God knows how your mind really works. So, I went on a week's training course in connection with that, and in the course of that, I met Cynthia. She lived in Bridgend, which was outside Cardiff, and we did start to meet each other. She got to know my family, and I did hers. We holidayed together. Things like that.

But then I made the decision, suddenly, that I wasn't going on with that training. There must have been reasons – perhaps it was because I'd seen Hilary – I couldn't deal with it, really; even seeing her, or meeting up, in those situations. So I made the decision to go into social work. It was just a feeling that, somehow, things had got to change. I suppose I thought that there was no future in anything else. Eventually I made the decision that I would go back to Cardiff, to a social work post, so I could be seconded for training at the university. I did that and got my qualifications. That was what I was doing – and seeing Cynthia – when my brother got married. And Hilary and her husband were invited. They came to the wedding with their little girl, and their second child was on the way.

Hilary: We were coming down for the weekend, but I stayed on.

Pauline: Yes, her husband went home, and Hilary and her daughter stayed. Then I took them back to Yorkshire –

Hilary: – about a fortnight later. I didn't want to go back. It was idyllic. Pauline's mum and dad were marvellous. The warmth and the love! And we knew, by the time that I stayed on, that was how we wanted to be. But I went home, and I had my son. A handful of years went by like that – seeing Pauline and still living with my husband – until it was decided that we just couldn't go on like this any more, and Pauline said we ought to talk about it.

My husband knew that it was definitely Pauline I wanted, and he tried to understand it. We talked to him and he thought he could find answers that would work for all of us. But I couldn't do that to Pauline – it was putting her through hell, anyway. So he had to accept that we were going to separate and I was going to be with her. One minute he would be for it and the next minute he wouldn't, and I wouldn't know where I stood. Then we all three sat and talked about it. Now, *that* was difficult. The children were in bed, we were talking about it, and I had to voice that Pauline was the person I wanted, when he was sat there and he was the father of the two children. He said to Pauline, 'Are you prepared to be able to bring them up?' She said yes, and of course it didn't mean to say he wasn't going to see them. And he said, well, he would want to see them, every weekend; so we had to say that, yes, we would do that.

A memorable journey

Hilary: We decided to do it at Easter, because it was the end of term. I packed the car, got as much as I could in, and off we trundled. I think the children thought we were only going for the school holidays. It was no good telling them we were leaving Daddy, at that point. And they were excited to be going to Auntie Pauline's. Well, after about three-quarters of an hour, before you go over the Pennines, we got to a very major crossroads and the brakes suddenly went on the car. No brakes, no nothing, and it's a busy time, after school, and traffic is going from Huddersfield to Barnsley. What do I do?

Fortunately, there was nothing coming across the road at that crossing and I thought, I've just got to get onto the forecourt of that garage. I just had to throw the car into bottom gear and hope no other car was coming and it would stop. I tried to keep calm, so the children weren't even aware that I wasn't going in for petrol. The car stank, because of putting the handbrake on at speed and pulling it up like that on the forecourt. There were no mobile phones then, so I went into the garage and asked if I could make a phone call. Pauline asked where I was and said, 'I can't come all that way, because I'm on call.'

Pauline: It was the weekend and I was the senior person on the team, and at certain times you've got to be available.

Hilary: So she said, 'I can come as far as Stalybridge. See if you can get a bus into Huddersfield and catch a train, and I'll meet you there.' The children were asking why we were catching a bus. I said, 'Well, because the car won't go any more.' Then they asked, 'What are we going to do once we've gone on the bus?' and I said, 'Well we're going on a train,' and that was really exciting! So, we got the bus to Huddersfield and then a train into Stalybridge and Pauline met us. This was on 7th April 1971. I've still got those train tickets. Then the next morning, we had to arrange for the car being picked up, and first we had to go over and empty it. Then we had to start thinking about school, and things like that.

Pauline: My feelings were very mixed at that time, because, although we were getting what we had always wanted, in every way, I had to take account of everyone in the situation, and that was very difficult. We particularly had to take account of the children. I had the responsibility of being the breadwinner: and by that time, I was in a very senior position in the local authority, which was a lot of responsibility too. That could always have been a problem, if people had known our circumstances, because of how things were then. But that was the situation we were faced with, so that's what we accepted, and we rose to the occasion.

My mother and father were always very supportive, particularly my father: because of his political experience, he was very aware of my situation. He was supportive, but equally he talked to us about how difficult a position we could be in. When we exchanged rings in 1970, making a commitment to each other, he had been very concerned, because he felt that we were advertising the fact of what we were and there might be implications, particularly to do with my work.

Hilary: And you did lead two lives, really, between work and home.

Pauline: In some respects, I had to do that, yes. They were difficult times in that way, and one had to face the facts and get on with it. In that day and age there were very few women in the top management of the local authority; but I think, because of the way I operated, it wasn't questioned.

Trials and tribulations

Hilary: It wasn't a good time for the children, they were backwards and forwards like pawns. I would take them to their father's with their clothes for the weekend and then he would send them back. As it turned out, that was only for two years, because he died; but we still took them over every week to see his parents, sometimes twice a week. And they weren't nice with me at all.

They carried it off in front of the children, but my son would say, 'I was going through Grandma's bureau and there were some photographs, and you're there, but you're not there, because they've cut your head off, or blacked you out with felt pen.'

I said, 'Well that's very unfortunate, and I'm sorry you've seen that,' and then we had to have discussions about it. I said, 'Because of what's happened, Grandma's upset and can't cope with it, but I'm sorry those photographs are where you found them, and you've not been told why, but thank you for telling us. We can only explain it to you, and hope that when you're older you'll understand.' And that's how we always tried to be.

My mother had been fine again once I was married and had the children. I think she thought I'd got over that 'phase', that I'd moved on and everything was fine. Now, I hadn't told my parents that I had left my husband and gone to live with Pauline. But one day when I was taking the children to their other grandparents, my father was cycling back from seeing his mother and he recognised my car. We stopped. The children were pleased to see him, because they were actually seeing more of their other grandparents than my parents.

My father said, 'Where are you going now?' and I said, 'We're going home.' But we were on a main road that was obviously going eventually to Manchester, not to where I used to live, so I had to tell him. He cried – he was heartbroken – and it upset him to cry in front of the children. He knew he had to go home and tell my mother that he'd seen us, that I was now living in Cheshire, and that, what's more, the children were quite accepting of us. Well, my mother would have nothing to do with me after that, for months.

Then, eventually, she sent me some Post Office savings stamps. It was only a few pounds, but I thought, she's trying hard here, and she really wants to see the children. We discussed it, and Pauline said, 'How about if you just take them over? At least you will have made the move.' My dad was pleased that we'd gone, and slowly but surely they came round to visiting us. But then – I don't know what went wrong with Mum again – there was a dreadful incident. I was in a car with Mum and Dad, and by coincidence we met Pauline and her mum, coming in the opposite direction. We pulled up –

Pauline: And my mum got out and tried to be friendly, tried to talk to Hilary's mother.

Hilary: She did, in soaking, soaking rain; but there was no way Mum was going to talk to her, or get out or anything. In the end Pauline's mum had to get back into the car. We were both devastated, and my father, again, was really upset. He said, 'I'm here once again, between my wife and my daughter.' And Mum said, 'Well don't blame me, I'm not excusing any of this.' So that was terrible, and I threatened I wouldn't see her again, at that point.

Pauline: But two years after we moved into our own house, they moved house to be near us.

Hilary: They said it was because they didn't want me making that long journey over the Pennines; but that was rubbish, because I was still taking the children over there at that point to go and see their other grandparents. It was because Mum felt she was losing control. So, we only had that two years; after that, it was hell. Because Mum thought, as she was on the bus route, she could just pop in any time. In the end, I had to say, 'I'm sorry, Mum, but no. Just suppose you decide to pop up and see us, and it's a nice surprise,' and she said 'It would be,' and I said, 'Yes, but not if you come up the stairs, and we're sat on the settee holding hands. And I'm not having that. I want to feel safe in my house, not that you're going to come and walk in on something you don't want to see, accept or understand.' So, the ground rules had to be made straight away, and she didn't like that.

It wouldn't have mattered if Pauline's mum and dad had arrived like that, they would just accept it, and I thought that was lovely. But I think they were more understanding, because they'd had to fight for acceptance for themselves, coming from two families with different religions. It had given them some understanding, though in a different way. If you experience something, you can help somebody else through that.

My dad died in 1992. Before he died he begged me to make sure I looked after Mum, which was a big thing for him to ask me to do. So those following years were really difficult, because she did think that she should have me all the time. As she was getting older, I was going there two or three times a week. She wouldn't have a phone, so I couldn't contact her that way. She said, 'They have phones here, and if I need you I'll ring, and if you don't want me ringing you when I need your help, you'd better come down and see me more often.' I just couldn't do that. I was already going a couple of times a week, and I'd got the children and our life. I couldn't do more.

In the end, as she was getting older and couldn't do all the housework herself, we organised for someone to come in to do things for her. But she wouldn't let them through the door.

She said, 'I have a daughter.'

They were saying, 'Oh yes, but you can't expect Hilary to do everything for you.'

And she said, 'Why not?'

I didn't have a choice. Our life was totally on hold in that time. For years. There were times when we wouldn't know how it would be after she'd gone. Or whether we were even going to *have* time together after she was gone, because there was such a strain on both of us. Pauline had had a stroke in 1995, and although she had made a full recovery with the help of an excellent consultant, it was all a terrible strain. One of us could easily have gone before Mum did.

It was a relief when she died. I had done everything I possibly could for both of them, and when they'd gone, I could close the gate. Literally – because once Mum had gone, and I came back from the undertaker's, I put the car in the garage, put the lock on the gate, and it all fell away from my shoulders. The responsibility had gone. I walked in the door and Pauline knew from my face. She just held me. And there was a difference in us, afterwards, because we were free. That's the word: we were *free*. My son said he was glad we'd got time together at last, and we should make the most of it, not have a care in the world and not think of anybody else but ourselves. I thought that was very mature and generous of him to say that, and not, 'We've got our mother back.'

Pauline: I thought, and I was prepared for it, that there would perhaps be quite a big reaction, afterwards. There would be a big void, because Hilary loved and cared for her mum right the way through it all, but her mum made it so difficult for her. I felt that there might be difficulties, afterwards, though I was sure we would deal with them somehow. But it wasn't like that. It was immediately a togetherness. That's always been there: it's been one of the factors that's been so strong, always.

Finally

Hilary: From when we were seventeen, eighteen, all we ever wanted was to be married. Why couldn't we be married like everybody else? We had the same love for each other, respect, care and consideration for others, that people had who *were* married. Why couldn't we have that? One day, hopefully, we would. We'd always talked as though we were husband and wife. That sounds ridiculous, like playing a game, but it was real. In 2005 there was civil partnership, and that was a kind of progress, but there were a lot of gaps in it: it wasn't marriage. I wanted Pauline to be my wife, and me to be her wife, and she wanted that too.

Then in 2014, we haven't got Mum to cope with any more, and same-sex marriage is made legal; and blow me, we couldn't do it! We'd just finally found a house we wanted (we'd been looking for about ten years) and at that time Pauline couldn't cope with anything but moving. Although she was now in better health, the upheaval of moving put a lot of strain on her. Then, just as we were settling in, my son was taken very seriously ill, and that was another upheaval. I thought, 'Well, it's just never going to happen; it's a dream. But keep going. You've waited for it for forty-odd years, you can wait a little bit longer.'

Pauline: Then at Christmas 2016, I said to Hilary, 'I want us to think about something that I've just noticed, which might make us decide it's time to do it. You know how it was that we moved in together on 7th April '71? Well, next year it will be 7th April '17, you see...' And Hilary thought about it, oh, only for a second or two, and said, 'Oh my God, that's perfect!' So I said, 'Is that a yes, then?'

Hilary: And I said, 'It's a yes.' So it was a proposal, in a way.

Once we stopped crying and I cleared my eyes enough to look at the calendar, I said, 'Golly, it's a Friday. I've always thought a Friday would be rather nice.' And Pauline said, 'So, have I got all my Brownie points, then?'

All the family were absolutely delighted when we told them And they all came to the wedding; even the ones in Tasmania attended via Skype. The wedding was everything we could have hoped for and more. It really was a dream come true – it was magical.

Pauline: And the wedding music was a song called 'Finally'. It talks about being together and being stronger than we ever dreamed we could be; and about taking our vows, 'finally'. At the end of the song it tells how we've waited for the day when our love could be set free. So you can see why we felt it was written just for us.

Hilary: So appropriate, after all those years! I was delighted when I found it. We had to listen to it quite a few times to stop crying every time we heard it, so that we would be able to use it. The wedding was forty-six years to the day since we'd moved in together. The registrar got quite emotional when she realised, and she said afterwards that she would never, ever forget it, it was the most wonderful day, and she was glad she had had the privilege of taking the ceremony. It's everything we ever wanted. We've been lucky enough to have lived to the age we are, because not everybody goes on and are still together at seventy-eight.

Pauline: I'm nearly seventy-nine.

Hilary: Yes, but you were only seventy-eight when we got married, so I haven't married an old lady! I feel there's still a romance there. It's richer than ever now because it is complete, and that feeling is safe, it's warm, it's comfortable. It's everything that I could've possibly dreamed of. I know I've always been looked after, cared for and respected by Pauline, and I'm fortunate in that. But now, it's just complete, and it's wonderful and safe.

Pauline: Yes. Life is complete. How we are together is more complete and, again, I would say safe, in the sense that we know those formal aspects of marriage are there now. The rest, really, is what is between us, which has always been there. Right from day one.

Hilary (left) and Pauline, Penrhyn Bay, 1955

FURTHER READING

Stories of lesbian life and history do not come along very often, especially in the UK – which is one reason for this book. Some of the titles listed below (in order of publication date) are quite old and no longer in print, but second-hand copies can usually be found online.

Threads: Stories of Lesbian Life in Northern Ireland in the 1970s and 1980s (Threads, 1980). Collected by a woman called Jayne, with a foreword by playwright Brenda Murphy, these tales capture memories from the beginning of a lesbian community.

Look Me in the Eye by Barbara Macdonald and Cynthia Rich (Sisters Ink, 1983; Women's Press, 1991). Still relevant more than three decades later, these wonderful rants by two feisty old feminist lesbians address ageing, invisibility and ageism.

Long Time Passing: Lives of Older Lesbians by Marcy Adelman (Alyson, 1986). An early inspiration for *Now You See Me.*

Lesbians Over 60 Speak for Themselves by Monika Kehoe (Haworth, 1988). Kehoe was an older lesbian who was tired of being invisible, so she set up the first-ever study of older lesbian life in the US, then wrote about it. A hero!

Inventing Ourselves: Lesbian Life Stories from the Lesbian Oral History Group (Hall Carpenter Archives, 1989). Fifteen stories from women of all ages, distilled from interviews which are still in the Hall Carpenter Archives.

Daring Hearts (Brighton Ourstory Project, 1992). Subtitled *Lesbian and Gay Lives of 50s and 60s Brighton,* this collection of seaside memories is an atmospheric trip down memory lane.

Women Like Us by Suzanne Neild & Rosalind Pearson (Women's Press, 1992). This book came out of two wonderful British films (*Women Like Us* and *Women Like That*) shown on Channel 4's *Out on Tuesday* series. Older lesbians tell their stories.

Boots of Leather, Slippers of Gold: The History of a Lesbian Community by Elizabeth L. Kennedy and Madeline Davis (Routledge, 1993). Classic study of the working-class community in Buffalo, New York, from the mid 1930s up to the early 1960s.

From the Closet to the Screen: Women at the Gateways Club 1945-85 by Jill Gardiner (Pandora, 2003). This thoroughly researched history of London's iconic lesbian bar includes many reminiscences from women who frequented it.

Lives of Lesbian Elders: Looking Back, Looking Forward by D. Merilee Clunis *et al.* (Haworth, 2005). A lively collection of stories from an American oral history project conducted in the 1990s.

Whistling Women: A Study of the Lives of Older Lesbians by Cheryl Claassen (Haworth, 2005). Interesting account of a group of older lesbians living in North Carolina.

Tomboys and Bachelor Girls: A Lesbian History of Post-War Britain 1945-71 by Rebecca Jennings (Manchester University Press, 2007). Scholarly (but very readable) overview.

A Gift of Age: Old Lesbian Life Stories by Arden Eversmeyer and Margaret Purcell (Old Lesbian Herstory Project, 2009). Based on interviews with American lesbians.

Gateway to Heaven: Fifty Years of Lesbian and Gay Oral History by Clare Summerskill (Tollington, 2012). Lesbians and gay men reflect on their lives from the 1940s to the turn of the century, with perceptive commentary from the author.

NOTES

Introduction

1   *The Lives of Older Lesbians: Sexuality, Identity and the Life Course* by Jane Traies (Palgrave Macmillan, 2016).

Chapter 1: Nobody Saw Us

1   'Hard work' is published in *The Losing Game* (Mariscat, 2010) and reproduced with the permission of the author, RV Bailey.
2   Maureen Duffy's first openly gay novel, *The Microcosm* (1966) was groundbreaking for its time. It tells the stories of a range of women of different ages, classes and ethnicities in twentieth-century London.
3   *The Well of Loneliness*, Radclyffe Hall's novel about a masculine-identified lesbian 'invert', Stephen Gordon, caused a scandal when first published in 1928, and was banned for obscenity. It was not published again in the UK until 1949. For many of Leo's generation, it was the only fictional representation of lesbian life available.
4   This poem, 'Words, Words, Words', is published in *A Scrappy Little Harvest* (IDP, 2016) and reproduced by permission of the author, RV Bailey.

Chapter 2: Innocence and Ignorance

1   The UK's longest-running social organisation for lesbians, Kenric was started in London in 1965 and has since spread through much of England and Wales. Web: kenriclesbians.org.uk
2   The Gateways, an iconic lesbian club in Chelsea, London, is described in Monica's story in Chapter 1. For a full history, see Jill Gardiner's book, *From the Closet to the Screen*, listed in Further Reading.
3   The Campaign for Homosexual Equality or CHE (originally known as the Committee for Homosexual Equality) was formed in 1969. Web: www.c-h-e.org.uk
4   *The Silver Rembrandt* by Kate Foley was published by Shoestring Press in 2008. Her latest full collection, *A Gift of Rivers*, came out from

Arachne in 2017. Other works include *Electric Psalms* (Shoestring, 2016); and *The Don't Touch Garden* (Arachne, 2015), a poem incorporating part of this life story.

Chapter 3: Always Like That

1   CHE: See Chapter 2, Note 3, above.
2   Sue Sharpe's classic study *Just Like A Girl* (1994) is based on her research in London schools. By comparing the attitudes of girls from working-class backgrounds in the 1970s and then the 1990s, Sharpe shows how society continues to constrain women.
3   Although lesbians were usually welcome in gay male pubs and clubs, there were a few lesbian venues in bigger cities. The Robin Hood and the Raven in West London were popular lesbian haunts in the 1950s and 60s.
4   Kenric: see Chapter 2, Note 1, above.

Chapter 4: Wives and Mothers

1   London Lesbian and Gay Switchboard: an information and support service, founded in 1974, now called Switchboard LGBT+ Helpline. Phone: 0300 330 0630. Web: switchboard.lgbt

Chapter 5: Wearing the Trousers

1   *The Killing of Sister George* is a 1968 film, directed by Robert Aldrich, adapted from a play by Frank Marcus. From the viewpoint of the twenty-first century, the film is a strange hybrid, mixing the worst kind of negative stereotyping of lesbians with a rare moment of cultural visibility. It was a mixed blessing for the lesbian community; but a scene shot at the Gateways, using club regulars as extras, was of special interest.
2   *The Well of Loneliness*: see Chapter 1, Note 3, above.
3   The Minorities Research Group, founded in 1963, was the first organisation in the UK to promote the interests of lesbians. Based in London, it reached out to women all over the country through its newsletter, *Arena Three*, which appeared monthly from 1964 to 1971.
4   Kenric: see Chapter 2, Note 1, above.

Chapter 6: Identity and Politics

1   *The Killing of Sister George*: see Chapter 5, Note 1, above.
2   The Robin Hood: see Chapter 3, Note 3, above.
3   The Gateways: see Chapter 2, Note 2, above.

Chapter 7: Not Her Next of Kin

1   Lasting Power of Attorney is available to anyone (straight or gay, single or in a relationship), but must be put in place while the individual still has mental capacity. It nominates one or more people to take decisions, if necessary, in the future. There are two types of power: 'health and welfare' and 'property and financial affairs'. Web: www.gov.uk/power-of-attorney

2   SAND works for a better future for old LGBT people. Website: lgbtsand.wordpress.com

3   *The Well of Loneliness*: see Chapter 1, Note 3, above.

ABOUT THE AUTHOR

Jane Traies is the author of *The Lives of Older Lesbians* (Palgrave Macmillan, 2016) and a number of other publications in the field of ageing and sexuality. As Jay Taverner, she was also joint author of the lesbian historical novels *Rebellion*, *Hearts and Minds* and *Something Wicked*.